Gendered Paradoxes

Educating Jordanian Women in Nation, Faith, and Progress

FIDA J. ADELY

D1008935

The University of Chicago Press
Chicago and London

Fida J. Adely is assistant professor and Clovis and Hala Salaam Maksoud
Chair in Arab Studies at the Center for Contemporary Arab Studies and the
School of Foreign Service at Georgetown University.

The University of Chicago Press, Chicago 60637
The University of Chicago Press, Ltd., London
© 2012 by The University of Chicago
All rights reserved. Published 2012.
Printed in the United States of America

21 20 19 18 17 16 15 14 13 12   1 2 3 4 5

ISBN-13: 978-0-226-00690-1 (cloth)
ISBN-13: 978-0-226-00691-8 (paper)
ISBN-10: 0-226-00690-5 (cloth)
ISBN-10: 0-226-00691-3 (paper)

Library of Congress Cataloging-in-Publication Data

Adely, Fida J., 1971– author.
    Gendered paradoxes : educating Jordanian women in nation, faith, and
progress / Fida J. Adely.
        pages cm
    Includes bibliographical references and index.
    ISBN: 978-0-226-00690-1 (cloth : alkaline paper)
    ISBN: 0-226-00690-5 (cloth : alkaline paper)
    ISBN: 978-0-226-00691-8 (paperback : alkaline paper)
    ISBN: 0-226-00691-3 (paperback : alkaline paper)   1. Women—
Education—Jordan. 2. Young women—Jordan—Social conditions. 3. Girls'
schools—Jordan.   I. Title.
    LC2410.J6A34 2012
    371.822095695—dc23
                                                        2012004808

♾ This paper meets the requirements of ANSI/NISO Z39.48-1992
(Permanence of Paper).

CONTENTS

ACKNOWLEDGMENTS

I begin by extending heartfelt gratitude to all those in Jordan who welcomed me and trusted me enough to talk about their lives, schooling, and experiences as Jordanians today. Thanks to the staff of al-Khatwa School, especially the principal who gave me full access to the school and its people. Her life's work as an educator was impressive, and I shall always hold her efforts and her humility in great esteem. I also extend my gratitude to the teachers who allowed me to come into the privacy of their classrooms and learn about Jordan there. There were many students at al-Khatwa who welcomed me into their circle of friends and into their families, sharing their convictions, worries, and dreams. I thank them for their openness, which was critical for my research and for my education about Jordan. Finally, I will always be touched by the perseverance of the families I met to make a better life for their children under difficult circumstances. I only hope that I have represented their struggles fairly.

The field research for this project was generously funded by a Fulbright Fellowship for 2004–5, a Council of American Overseas Research predoctoral fellowship from the American Center for Oriental Research (Jordan) in 2002, and an Oman Faculty grant from the Center for Contemporary Arab Studies at Georgetown University in 2009. The completion of this manuscript was also made possible by generous support from the Graduate School of Arts and Sciences at Georgetown in the form of a Junior Faculty Research Fellowship in fall 2009 and a Summer Academic Grant in 2009.

Along the way many of my teachers, colleagues, and friends have supported me both intellectually and professionally. Lila Abu-Lughod has been an inspiring mentor and model. Her work on women in the region has been invaluable in helping me to make sense of many of my own interactions and experiences with women in Jordan and has pushed my own thinking in these areas. She has provided critical feedback and direction for this project from its conception, and I have benefited tremendously from her comments, questions, and support.

At Columbia University (Teachers College), I also benefited immensely from the advice and friendship of Lesley Bartlett. She has been a constant source of encouragement as well as a careful reader of my writing, and she has always been generous with her time. I feel lucky to have had the opportunity to work with her and other colleagues at Teachers College, especially Hervé Varenne, who has served as both an intellectual and a professional mentor. Earlier versions of this book benefited from the careful reading of Lou Abdellatif Cristillo, Mat Carlin, and Todd Nicewonger.

At Georgetown, Rochelle Davis and Melissa Fisher provided me with intellectual and emotional support as I completed the first draft of the book manuscript. Our writer's group was critical to getting the book completed. As my colleague at the Center for Contemporary Arab Studies (CCAS), Rochelle has also been a wonderful mentor and friend. I also extend my thanks to CCAS for financial support at critical conjunctures of this project, and to the staff and faculty for being supportive colleagues and friends.

Perhaps no one else has had to read so many rough drafts of this book as my friend and colleague Betty Anderson. Betty has given me lots of feedback, pep talks, and advice. She has been an invaluable friend and colleague throughout this process, and I am indebted to her for many hours of reading my work. I would also like to thank Louise Cainkar and Kim Shively for careful reading of particular chapters. This book has also benefited greatly from the careful reading and editing of Sam Dolbee, whose speed and efficiency are unmatched. The comments and questions of two anonymous readers commissioned by the University of Chicago Press have considerably improved this text. I thank them for their careful reading and advice. At the press, I would also like to thank Elizabeth Branch Dyson and her team of dedicated editors, especially Renaldo Migaldi, for their dedicated efforts and professionalism.

My interest in Jordan has in many respects been a personal journey to learn about the home of my parents and countless family members. When I first came to "study" Jordan, I also began a process of coming to know my grandparents—Shaikha, Wadea'a, and Adeeb. Their lives were a testament to the great changes that Jordan has evidenced in the past few decades. I only wish I had had the opportunity to learn more from them before they left.

This book is in many respects a book about the critical role played by family in the lives of young women in Jordan. When I began my PhD program with a full-time job and an eight-month-old baby girl (followed less than four years later by her sister), everyone kept asking me how it was I was able to do it. Of course I never did it alone. In New York, I was aided by my family, without whom this would have been completely impossible. The limitless support and availability of my siblings, particularly as aunts and uncle, were essential to making this possible. Thanks to Kathy, Suzanne, Hannan, Amy, Lena, and Tariq.

In Jordan, my parents-in-law, Dia and Hanna, provided critical support during my visits to Jordan. My father-in-law's long and respected career as an educator in Jordan was critical in opening up many doors to me and in gaining people's trust. My mother-in-law, in addition to sharing interesting insights about her experiences as a woman, has over the years fed me, taken care of my daughters, and made me feel at home always in Jordan.

I met my partner, Aiman, on my first long journey to Jordan, and he has remained with me throughout, doing more than his share as a parent and providing a critical lens through which I have come to know Jordan. Aiman is my greatest supporter. He has also served as my personal anecdote against the sweeping generalizations about Arab men that I continually encounter. I could not ask for a better spouse, father of my children, and partner in life. Our vibrant and inquisitive daughters Laila and Samar have throughout been patient as they anxiously awaited the arrival of this book. They have helped to keep me grounded, reminding me of the other important things in life.

Finally, I must dedicate this work to my parents, Issa and Ibtisam. Shortly before I was born they left Jordan and came to the United States with the intention of returning. They never returned, leaving behind many of the dreams they had for their own newly independent country and their entire social network. They decided to stay in the United States, not without regrets, in part because of the education they believed this country could offer their six daughters. They struggled with the politics and the cultural differences that often made our lives turbulent. I have learned so much about Jordan through these struggles. The more I learn about Jordan, the more I appreciate the paths both of my parents have traveled and their unending sacrifices. I hope that in some small way my efforts to learn and write about Jordan can pay them back. To them I extend my love, deepest respect, and gratitude.

A Day in the Life of Nada

The al-Khatwa Secondary School for Girls is located in Bawadi al-Naseem, a city of about fifty thousand that stands sixty-five kilometers northeast of Amman, Jordan.[1] It is one of three high schools in the city and enrolls about six hundred students in grades 10 through 12. Most high school girls in Bawadi al-Naseem spend their days between home and school. School is an important space in their lives. Nada is one such student—an eleventh grader, she has lived in Bawadi al-Naseem all of her life and has been at al-Khatwa since tenth grade. Despite occasional conflicts with teachers or classmates, Nada enjoys school and especially the camaraderie of her friends. She is known among her friends as the peacemaker as she is always resolving disputes between friends. Nada also likes to tell jokes and has been known to pull a few practical jokes at school, like the time she hid her friend Rula's shoes when Rula went into the prayer room and left her shoes at the door. Nada studies hard and hopes to go to college, although it is unclear whether she can achieve this goal since her grades are not very strong.

Nada rises each day around 6:30 a.m. to get ready for school. In the winter months it can be quite difficult to get up as there is no heat and the water is freezing cold. The first thing she does in the cold months is light the small kerosene heater in the main room, the room in which the family gathers to eat and watch TV, and where the girls in the family sleep. Today is a relatively warm day, however, so she washes first, dresses, makes her father some coffee before he heads to work, and has some tea and bread with yoghurt. For school she wears pants with the green school uniform—a long shirt that comes to mid thigh. She also covers her hair with a headscarf. When she first started wearing the headscarf in ninth grade, she was excited to be like the older girls. Now she sometimes wishes she did not have to wear it, but on most days she is relieved that she does not have to deal with her hair, which is unwieldy. Some of Nada's friends rise earlier to do their dawn prayers, but Nada does not pray regularly. Her friend Samar has been encouraging her to do so. And during the previous Ramadan, Nada had begun to give some thought to becoming more committed (*multazimah*) by doing her regular prayers, but still she does not feel ready. Her younger siblings walk together to the local elementary school, while she walks the short distance to her own school. Her oldest sister, Shereen, is a teacher in town. Another sister is at the university studying chemistry. Amaney, who is three years older than Nada, is at home studying to retake her high school completion exams (*tawjihi*) so that she can get a grade high enough for a place in the public university. Her oldest brother, Muhammad, is in the army, and her brother Jamil, who did not pass tawjihi but refused to repeat it, is looking for work.

This has been a challenging year for the family. Nada's father's health has been failing, and there have been a lot of unexpected medical expenses. Her father has missed many days at work and does not get sick pay. Her mother used to do some babysitting to help supplement their income; however, she has been caring for Nada's grandmother for several months now so has been unable to earn the extra income. Muhammad has been in the army for two years, but because of his modest salary and the cost of transportation and his cigarettes, he usually does not save enough to help out the family. Shereen, the schoolteacher, has been helping the family stay afloat financially. Jamil is frustrated with being unemployed; he is paying the price for not passing the tawjihi. He knew that he was not a good enough student to get the necessary grades on tawjihi, and that is why he refused to retake the exam even though his mother begged him. Nada is hoping she will do well enough on the same test to go to a public university and eventually work to help support her family.

On her way to school she sometimes runs into her neighbor Nisreen who is Christian. Although there are not many Christians in Bawadi al-Naseem, several Christian families live in Nada's neighborhood, and she and Nisreen have been friends since first grade. The walk is pleasant on most days although when it rains the street can get quite muddy. Although most of Nada's classmates walk to school, not all do. Some are driven by family members, while others come from distant parts of the city or surrounding villages and travel by bus to attend high school in Bawadi al-Naseem. For the most part, Nada's teachers, who are all female, live relatively close to the school. Most are driven to work by their husbands, while a few have their own cars. Nada needs to be in the schoolyard by 7:45 for the morning assembly. She tries not to be late as recently the principal has begun shutting the gate so as not to allow girls who are late to slip in undetected. Once Nada was late (having stayed up too late with relatives who were visiting from Amman the night before) and was made to stand outside the gate with several other unlucky girls until the morning assembly was over. Then the principal let them in and gave them a severe scolding and ordered them to clean up the schoolyard as punishment. Most days however, Nada gets to school on time and lines up in formation with the other eleventh-grade girls.

For the morning assembly, the nearly six hundred girls at al-Khatwa line up in rows by class and section and every morning follow the same routine. The tenth graders are the largest contingent as they have over fifty students in each section. After tenth grade, a proportion of these students will go to the vocational school because of their poor grades; those with strong grades go on to the humanities or the scientific track, both of which are offered at al-Khatwa. Thus the class sizes in eleventh and twelfth grades, the secondary phase of high school, are smaller. Nada has gone through the motions of this morning ritual every day of her school life since first grade. Line up, recite the *fatiha* (the opening verse of the Qur'an), and sing "Long Live the King." Usually, at least one patriotic song follows this, and then the girls are made to do a brief set of calisthenics. At Nada's high school, the girls barely feign effort, and none of the teachers or administrators really push them to perform the exercises vigorously. Nada remembers how excited she used to be about this morning assembly when she was younger; she and her friends competed to see which grade could sing and recite the loudest and with the greatest enthusiasm. Now the assembly feels limp after the repetition of so many years. However, from time to time school administrators try to enforce some enthusiasm, yelling at the girls to stand straight, pay attention, or raise their voices.

The school staff also regularly conducts uniform inspections during the morning assembly. Nada's friend Sawsan is usually in violation of the dress code—most frequently by wearing nail polish, but occasionally with high heels or even makeup—and she tries to hide behind Nada during morning inspections. Nada does not understand the point of getting all dolled up for school, but she knows there are many girls who are trying to make themselves look prettier, older, whiter, thinner, and the like. Nada has no such preoccupations, and anyway her mother would never let her go to school with makeup on. After some announcements, the girls go to their classrooms. They are supposed to march in line quietly, but the girls are usually quite rowdy in the halls. The day begins with their chatter and laughs, unless of course it gets too loud and then the school secretary's screams for quiet can be heard throughout the halls.

Nada's class, "first secondary humanities b" or *awal thanawi ba*, takes the stairwell up to the second floor. On their way they pass pictures of the king and his father and grandfather, as well as "Jordan First"[2] signs that have been distributed by the government. Once they get to the classroom there is less in the way of decoration. The walls are white and badly in need of paint. Some handmade signs made by students from previous years adorn the classroom walls, some patriotic and others directing students to keep their classroom clean and their appearance neat. Students had also clipped some pictures and newspaper articles about the Palestinian intifada and posted them on the walls. This year, some of Nada's classmates worked with the history teacher, Dia, to make patriotic signs in keeping with the "Jordan First" campaign for their classroom as well. The room is sunny, as it is upstairs and has big windows that let in the light but also the cold in the winter months. In the winter the girls wear jackets and sweaters in the classroom to stay warm, and some students even wear gloves. Luckily, none of the windows in *awal thanawi ba* are broken.

Nada has seven periods a day and a half-hour lunch break; every day she takes Arabic, English, Islamic studies, math, and social studies. She also studies computers three days a week. On the other days she is supposed to take physical education (PE) and art, or a special activities session. However, of these, PE is the only elective that is offered and even then not all of the time. The girls dislike PE anyway and prefer to just sit in the schoolyard during that period, especially as the weather warms up. Each group of students is assigned a classroom, and they remain in their classrooms throughout the day, with the teachers coming to them for different subjects. Nada has seen schools in America on television and wonders what it would be like to have lockers and switch classes. She finds it tiring to be in the same classroom the whole day, save for the half-hour break. Some of her friends are constantly looking for ways to get out of the classroom; when teachers come late or do not show up at all, girls take advantage and leave the classroom.

One time, the Arabic teacher did not turn up in her classroom as expected because she had to leave school early to take her sick child to the doctor. One of the girls went to the teachers' room to inquire about her and returned claiming that another teacher had told them to just go home. About ten girls promptly left, while the remaining thirty-five students stayed in the classroom or in the schoolyard. When the administrators found out that the ten girls had left the school early, the principal, assistant principal, and secretary called them all to the office the next day and scolded them.

Furthermore, the principal said they would all be publicly reprimanded at the school assembly the next day. The girls were very upset and begged the principal not to publicly name them. Nada's good friend Ibtisam had been one of the ten, and she came back to class crying. She was mortified at the prospect that she would be publicly scolded. Nada knew why Ibtisam and some of the others were upset. They feared that a public scolding would hurt their reputations, especially since the staff had implied that they left school early so that they could wander around town unsupervised. Ibtisam was particularly worried as she had some cousins in the school with whom she was not on good terms and she feared they would exploit this incident to speak ill of her. In the end, the principal never acted on her threat. Nada guessed she just wanted to teach the girls a lesson by scaring them.

This school year the teachers and staff have become increasingly frustrated with the girls in Nada's class. They have been misbehaving quite a bit since the winter break, and the teachers are losing their patience. Nada is frustrated as she feels the teachers generalize when it is only a handful of the girls who make the most trouble. At the same time, the behavior of a few, and their disrespect for the teachers, were making it increasingly difficult for anyone to learn anything.

Nada's favorite subjects are English and Arabic. She thinks she would like to study languages and become a translator or journalist, but her teachers tell her that teaching is the only realistic possibility for a girl from Bawadi al-Naseem with a degree in languages. She is not sure if she would like teaching, but she really admires her English teacher so she might consider it. Of course she knows of many young women who have graduated college and applied for teaching jobs who sit around waiting for a teaching post for years, making this career path problematic as well. Her friend Layla also wants to study languages, and she already writes for the main newspaper in Jordan in the youth section. Nada likes the idea of being a journalist too, but in Bawadi al-Naseem there are not any journalism jobs. She would have to go to Amman and she is not sure if that would be possible, although her brother may move to Amman and so she might be able to live with him. She has also heard that some girls take jobs in Amman and live in dormitories, but these girls are still a minority. Of course, it is too early to think about these issues. First, she needs to do well and get into the university.

Besides English, Nada is also looking forward to religion class today as she finds her religion teacher, Miss Suheil, to be dynamic and fun. This is the first time that Nada has found this subject to be so engaging; in the past she always thought of it as her most boring subject. Teachers can really make a difference, thinks Nada; a teacher can really lead a girl to love a subject or to hate it. On this day, Nada is sitting with her classmates waiting for Miss Suheil to arrive. Jumana, who always sits near the front, is discussing her favorite television program, *Star Academy*, a reality TV program produced in Lebanon that many of the girls have been obsessed with lately. In this program a group of young people from around the Arab world are chosen to live together, train together, and compete as performers (singing and dancing). It is like the American program *American Idol*. Nada's teachers frequently criticize this program as immoral, but she ignores the criticism, as do many of her peers, because she and her sisters love watching this program. Her friend Nadine's mother is obsessed with *Star Academy* more than any of the schoolgirls, but some of her friends' parents have forbidden them from watching such programs or have refused to have satellite television for fear of such programs. These parents are particularly offended by the way in which participants, males and females, live in the same house.

Amina is seated in the opposite corner of the classroom. She certainly did not watch *Star Academy* the night before. Amina, the president of the student prayer room committee, is very religious and finds such programming offensive. She prefers to watch al-Manar, the Hizbullah channel, as well as channels devoted to teaching about Islam. In class this day, she is again talking to her classmates about the importance of being good Muslims. Some of Nada's classmates listen to her attentively, while others ignore her. Nada has mixed feelings about Amina. On some level she admires Amina's degree of religious commitment, but Nada also finds Amina to be too pushy and at times judgmental, so she keeps her distance.

Fadia is talking about the latest news from Palestine and Iraq. Fadia likes to talk about current events, as does Amina. Although many of Nada's classmates are well-versed in the details of regional politics, most are more interested in lighter talk—about friends, superstars, and boys—and on this day some complain that their fathers monopolize televisions at home with the nightly news. Nada sometimes feels guilty for not paying more attention to what is happening in her part of the world; her social studies teacher, Tamara, is always complaining that her generation no longer reads newspapers or follows the news. But Nada finds it all too depressing and prefers to watch programs that are entertaining.

Nada turns to Fedwa who is in her usual spot in the back of the room showing her friends the new treasure she has acquired from her brother. He always brings her perfumes, lotions, and makeup. Sometimes Fedwa also brings in photographs of American or Arab pop stars. Nada and her classmates love looking at these pictures, especially pictures of the Backstreet Boys. This morning, Nada sees Fedwa pull out her mirror, adjust her headscarf, and apply some makeup even though it is forbidden. The mirror is then secretly passed around during class to various friends. "Who is she fixing herself up for?" wonders Nada. As if reading Nada's mind, Ibtisam leans over and says, "Did you hear that Fedwa likes this guy who works in a mobile phone shop on Queen Noor Street? She walks by his shop every day." Ibtisam goes on to clarify that Fedwa has never spoken with this person, but she wants to look her best when she walks by.

Miss Suheil finally arrives, and after making some small talk with the girls, she begins the lesson. "Islam and Work." She discusses the need for people to be "respectable" in the workplace and refers to taxi drivers as an example of workers who have "bad habits." Nada knows that some of her classmates have male relatives who are cab drivers, and she wonders if they are offended by the teacher's comments. Miss Suheil also talks about the bias Jordanians have against "working with their hands." She says, "We all want our children to be doctors and engineers."

Nada and her classmates know exactly what Miss Suheil is talking about. Nada's cousin Ahmed wanted to marry a girl he met in another city where he worked as a medical technician, but the girl's parents would not even consider him as a suitor because he had only gone to a two-year college. Miss Suheil's lesson also leads to a discussion about the number of Jordanians with degrees in fields like engineering who do not have jobs despite their education. Amina says she has a relative with a college degree selling falafel on the street. Other girls talk about difficulties their male relatives are having getting married with or without college degrees because of the cost of living.

Samar interjects, "And all the men want to marry a civil servant, a working woman with a government job. They come and ask after a girl and they say, 'Is she a *mawadhafa* (employee in the public sector)?'" Miss Suheil adds, "The other day a mother of a potential groom was in the teachers' room inquiring after single teachers." Fadia wonders aloud, "But how are we to find work if men can't even find jobs?" Lorees argues that her work will be caring for her children. Miss Suheil, responding to Lorees's comment, emphasizes that women can do both. Fedwa, who is one of thirteen children, asserts that the problem with today's society is that when women work they neglect their children. As for Nada, she hopes she will have a well-paying job someday so that she can help her family, although she is not sure how she will feel once she has a family. She also knows that some of these things are out of one's hands, nothing but fate.

Time is nearly up and the math teacher will be here soon. Nada really likes math, but since she was placed in the humanities track, it is not likely she will be able to pursue a major in math or science in the university. Just before Miss Suheil leaves, Indira, an eleventh grader from another class, comes in to make an announcement. She informs the girls that the Ministry of Education wants students to attend an Independence Day celebration at a nearby university and that they should plan to be there on time the next day to board the buses. Many of the girls groan and a few say they will not go. Others are happy to miss class. A couple of Nada's friends will be performing at the Independence Day event—one will sing and the other will recite poetry. Nada used to participate in such events but decided that being in the music group at school was taking too much time away from her studies, since the group practiced during class.

After a couple more classes, Nada and the girls of *awal thanawi ba* join the rest of the school for the midday break. It is not really a lunch break, as the main meal of the day is a late lunch around three with one's family. Some of the girls bring a sandwich to school, but most buy potato chips or cookies from the school canteen if they eat anything at all. The canteen sometimes has small sandwiches as well. Some of Nada's classmates do not have money to buy anything from the canteen, and if Nada has some extra money, from time to time she will treat them. She is, however, often without money, and her friend Kareen, whose father is a successful doctor, treats her sometimes. Jenine, a girl who has come to the school only recently, is very poor. Her mother is divorced and living on a farm in a nearby village. Jenine often does not have enough money for bus fare home from school, and some of the teachers try to help her. In this respect, Nada feels that the school is a nice community.

During this break the girls wander around the yard and chat. On this day, Nada's friend Ibtisam, whom she usually talks to at the break, is sitting on the stone steps sulking. She will not even talk to Nada. Nada keeps asking her what's wrong, but Ibtisam ignores her. After a while, though, Ibtisam reveals that she had a major argument with her mother the night before. Ibtisam feels that her parents favor her older sisters and brother. She complains about having to wear hand-me-down clothing, and she says her father regularly insinuates that she is not smart enough to get into college. Nada knows that Ibtisam often feels this way. Her sisters were very successful and were the top students in their departments at the university. Her father recently suggested that she switch into the vocational track since she is not getting good grades. Her two older sisters both excelled in the scientific track, the most prestigious of the academic tracks and the most difficult to get into. Nada tries to cheer Ibtisam up. She tells her that parents always compare siblings so they can push them to do her best. As for the hand-me-downs, Nada has little sympathy, as she has worn only hand-me-downs herself and life is expensive in Jordan. Not all parents can afford to buy new clothes for every child.

After the break, Nada completes her classes and then prepares to go home. She lingers a bit in the yard with some friends. It's a beautiful day, sunny but cool in the shade. Nada thinks her school—at least the outdoor grounds—is the most attractive one in the whole city. The school building and the classrooms are nothing special, but the schoolyard is lined with trees on one side, and it has a small olive grove adjacent to the yard. Nada and her friends are outside enjoying this scenery when one of the teachers comes out and tells them it is time to go home. The students are never allowed to linger for long. Nada catches up with Nisreen and they walk home together. When Nada arrives home, she helps her older sister prepare lunch. The girls share the housework, dividing up the tasks from week to week. Nada usually does the dishes or the sweeping and the mopping. Her brothers are not responsible for the housework, although her brother Jamil helps from time to time. Jamil also runs most of the errands for the family. Her mother has been helping to take care of Nada's grandmother in the mornings, and so Nada's sister has been doing most of the lunch preparation. Her father usually takes a nap after lunch. Nada sometimes naps after lunch and then completes her chores. Then, if she has homework, she will do it. The remainder of the evening she watches television with her family. Currently they are following a Turkish soap opera, and sometimes they stay up late to watch an American movie. Nada loves this time with her family, when the work is done and they can all sit back and watch television.

Nada lies in bed trying to sleep. She thinks she will attend the next day's Independence Day rally. It will be a nice break from school, and she can see her friend Hanan play the *tabla* (drum) for the first time. She also can't stop thinking about her favorite Turkish soap opera and the intense romance between the two main characters that seems doomed to fail. She wonders if women anywhere lead such lives—lives of intense romantic love, intrigue, and family defiance. Although she sometimes daydreams about boys and future romance, she could never imagine going against the wishes of her family for love. She knows she will not marry as her mother did—at the age of sixteen to a complete stranger—but still there are limits and one's family is one's support. With these thoughts in her head, Nada finally falls asleep.

ONE

Ambiguous Times and Spaces

Gendered Paradoxes

In the summer of 2005, a local teacher and friend, Amaney, invited me to come speak to a group of girls ranging in age from twelve to eighteen at an Islamic center in Bawadi al-Naseem, Jordan. At the time, the World Bank had just released what it termed a gender assessment of Jordan, and I decided to discuss the findings of this assessment with the young women (World Bank 2005). A central message of the World Bank report, one I conveyed to these young women, is that Jordan's development presents a paradox—a "gender paradox" (World Bank 2005: 61)[1]—for despite equal access to education for women at all levels, high rates of fertility persist,[2] and female labor force participation is relatively low. When I opened the floor for discussion, one young woman raised her hand and asked, "Why doesn't the World Bank consider it a good thing that we can have high levels of education with high fertility?" Given the centrality of kin relations in accomplishing almost any task in Jordan, official or otherwise, and the status accorded to the family and mothers in Jordan, this comment was not surprising, though it is rarely represented in development talk about the region. And yet this perspective was not uniform across this group of young women. A debate ensued about what was good for women, men, families, and the overall well-being of the community, with some of the young women drawing upon religious references to support their different viewpoints. Much of the debate at the youth group that day focused on the purpose of education and the issue of the desirability of women's work outside the home. That which appeared as a self-evident paradox in a development document was far more nuanced in the eyes of my interlocutors. Underlying this discussion, and similar ones I participated in during fifteen months of ethnographic research in Jordan (as well as several follow-up visits), are key questions about education: What is education for? What does it mean to be an educated woman in Jordan today? What is required to be a successful citizen, as well as a good Muslim, mother, and wife? What are the desirable pathways to womanhood and success?

The representation of women's educational attainment as a development paradox in Jordan, and the Middle East more broadly, is in keeping with a larger industry of defining Arab Muslim women in terms of development problems to be addressed through the expertise of development institutions (Abu-Lughod 2005, 2009; Hasso 2009).[3] It is also clearly linked to a persistent and historical discourse about the Middle East, which characterizes its women as oppressed and powerless victims and its culture as retrograde. The global preoccupation with education in the region has figured strongly into such representations, with the state of education being linked to extremism, cultural backwardness, and even violence.

Despite the important contributions of scholars studying women in the region over the past few decades, the popular image of Arab Muslim women continues to be that they are oppressed, weak, and passive victims.[4] Recent political events have served only to solidify if not deepen such images (Abu-Lughod 2002; Hirschkind and Mahmood 2002).[5] The rhetoric about Arab Muslim women at times seems little changed from the discourse of European colonizers around the turn of the twentieth century—a discourse that framed colonialism as in part a project to save oppressed women in the region (Ahmed 1992; Lazreg 1994; Pollard 2005; Shakry 1998). Central to this discourse then and now has been the belief in the transformative potential of education.[6]

Since the turn of the century, when European colonizers, local reformers, and statesmen in the Middle East raised a call for women's education, modernization and development have been inextricably linked to this project (Ahmed 1992). Initially, the discourse about the need to educate women was tied up with new conceptualizations of the family, childrearing, and household management in a modern society (Najmabadi 1998a; Shakry 1998). With time, the education of women came to be viewed as a panacea, with education being linked to a host of development outcomes in health, economic development, and eventually women's empowerment (Vavrus 2003). Frances Vavrus discusses this perspective:

> An empowered woman is one who takes an active role in controlling her fertility, practicing safe sex, and protecting the environment, and schooling is supposed to help her achieve these goals. Despite the desirability of such a scenario, however, women's choices about childbearing, reproductive health,

and environmental conservation are shaped by social and political considerations that the independent figure of the feminist modern does not take into account. (41)

Here, Vavrus emphasizes that assumptions about the links between empowerment and education fail to account for the sociopolitical considerations that affect women's choices. This holds true in much of the development literature about women in the Middle East, where the discourse of women's education for empowerment continually reifies Arab Muslim women as a homogenous category without attention to class, geography, and other forms of distinction or difference. Furthermore, Arab women are constructed as always in opposition to their families and communities. Their empowerment requires separation from their social networks; indeed these networks are typically framed as the primary obstacle to their progress (Adely 2009a).

This framing of gender, education, and development does not escape young women in Jordan. As they progress through their education, they become increasingly enmeshed in this narrative of education for success and for empowerment. Many young women are conscious of how the world beyond Jordan views them; their teachers are even more attuned to the ways in which they are viewed and represented by Western experts, non-Muslims, and the elite of their own country.[7] Women are both produced by and partake in the making of contemporary Jordan, during an era in which mass public education has transformed popular notions of knowledge and progress, respectability and faith, and marriage and family, albeit not always in predictable ways. The representation of Arab Muslim women's development as paradoxical by the World Bank, the United Nations Development Program (UNDP), and other development agencies—the prevailing assumption that education will make women "like us" or at least like the ideal of the autonomous Western woman that is regularly held up as the goal for all women (Abu-Lughod 2002; Fernea 2000; Mahmood 2005)— makes it difficult for us to recognize alternative goals and behaviors as important and powerful. This book complicates such assumptions, pointing to the possibility that different women might have different needs, desires, values, and expectations. It also highlights how forms of distinction such as class and geography shape and constrain possibilities for women in Jordan as they do for women anywhere. All the Jordanians I met were interested in progress for themselves, their families, and their country; however, the overwhelming majority defined progress within familiar discourses about family, respectability, and morality rather than in opposition to them.

Despite the preoccupation with women's education, surprisingly little of the scholarship in the region has paid attention to schools as important institutions in the lives of girls and/or the meaning of education for young women *and* their families. A great deal of discursive space and resources have been devoted to understanding "what is wrong with education in the Middle East" in policy and development circles. This book argues that the questions we should ask are more fundamental. How do young women and their families define development and progress? How do adolescent girls educate each other everyday about what is good, pious, or desirable? Does the "inter/national"[8] ideal of education for global citizens encompass all that is worth knowing? Does "development" for women as it is defined by dominant global institutions exhaust the possibilities for a secure and respectable life?

Drawing on ethnographic evidence that examines education through everyday social and cultural practices and as a contemporary promissory project that is deeply gendered, I argue that the characterization of women's development through education in Jordan (and the Middle East more broadly) as *paradoxical* continues to rest on an assumption that progress and development for women unfold along a single, universal path—that of delaying and reducing family obligations in order to enter the paid workforce. Through an engagement with the experiences and narratives of a group of adolescent girls and the adults in their lives, I show the limits of such a conceptual framework for making sense of education and its effects in the lives of these Jordanian schoolgirls. I also demonstrate that despite the reality of patriarchal structures that delimit the worldview and opportunities available to females (and males), young women are nevertheless actively engaged in shaping their life trajectories—trajectories that are characterized by strong connections to family and kin (Joseph 1993).

Throughout my fifteen months of ethnographic research with adolescent girls in Bawadi al-Naseem, Jordan, I learned much that was predictable—the girls wanted to have fun, to spend time with friends, to love, to marry, and to be respected. This book opened with the story of Nada and "a day in her life." Although hers is a "fictionalized" account—a conglomeration of many different experiences that I observed and heard about in the course of my research—her story illuminates some of the most significant issues a young woman (and a high school student) faces today in Jordan and particularly in Bawadi al-Naseem. It also encapsulates the major themes that are the subject of this book—nation, faith, development, and the meaning of progress.

Girls like Nada struggle with what it means to be mature and successful women. For most, higher education is clearly part of what they imagine is necessary for success. But higher education is not necessarily tied up with dreams about successful careers—although it may be. From the perspective of the families of these young women, education is an important strategy in ensuring that their daughters will be secure, happy, and respected members of the community. However, the means of achieving happiness and security are strongly shaped by socioeconomic circumstances of particular families, and the terms of respectability are in flux. Success, respectability, and even security could be defined in contradictory terms linked to values and realities not fully encompassed within paradigms of women's empowerment. Andre Mazawi (2010) has argued that the battle to define the purpose of knowledge and education in the Arab world today is a battle to "name the imaginary" (203). The imaginings of a group of young women and their families are the subject of this book.

The world that young women face today in Jordan, and the region more broadly, is an ambiguous one, in which the gendered expectations and norms are openly debated by politicians, religious leaders, media pundits, representatives of nongovernmental groups, and the like. They are also negotiated in the day-to-day practices of women, young and old, as the women in Nada's family show. Education—the spread of mass schooling, near-universal secondary enrollment, increasing access to higher education, and the dominance of a global narrative about education's purpose—is a contemporary force that figures strongly in the making of both gendered ambiguity and gender transformations. Schools—both local and state institutions—are critical arenas in which young women negotiate these dynamics and search for clarity and meaning. In this sense, schools are important spaces for girls as they navigate through a range of images, messages, and mandates and construct a vision of what is possible and desirable. It is not only the official curriculum and formal lessons that make this place significant; the girls themselves are actors in this process of negotiation.

Education here is also an idea, a discursive project of global development organizations, a nation-building endeavor, and a local bureaucratic institution. As a contemporary modernizing project with significant force in young women's lives, it creates new possibilities and desires, just as it creates new forms of hierarchy (Ahearn 2001; Levinson and Holland 1996).[9] It is also the institution in which the state, its ideology, and its bureaucrats interact most directly with young women; in schools, the regime's representatives work to cultivate the loyalty of young people and to articulate a vision of Jordan as developed and enlightened. Teachers, as well as the pedagogical content they are prescribed, also have a role in shaping the experience of young women. These actors, as well as state representatives and development experts who make education reform policies and establish educational goals, are all engaged in the construction of competing visions of progress for women. However, the most significant actors here are the young women themselves. This is not to say that they act alone; they are embedded in family and community networks that shape their life trajectories. Family is central in the decisions about a girl's future. However, adolescent girls do partake in the construction of these future possibilities, especially in school. At the al-Khatwa School, evidence of this gendered work was apparent in the day-to-day lessons, peer interactions, and debates (Ortner 1996).

The efforts of the secondary school students to make sense of education and their status as educated females—daughters, sisters, community members, citizens—were clearly reflected in their engagement and entanglement with four themes central to contemporary politics of authenticity: *nationalism* and the terms of national identity; *faith*, the role of religion and the requisites for pious living; morality and the terms of gendered *respectability*; and *progress*, particularly the promises of contemporary education for development. I analyze each of these themes in the chapters to come, providing an ethnographic depiction of how each emerged at al–Khatwa and in the lives of its students, arguing that it is both *in* schools and *through* schooling that such struggles manifest themselves.[10] The complexity of these struggles, and the desires and constraints that structure the possibilities for these young women, make it essential to begin with their stories. The introduction with which this book began gives a glimpse of some of their narratives, and throughout the book the reader will be introduced to several young women. It is through their experiences and their efforts to negotiate the tensions that emerge in deeply gendered political and cultural contests that I relay the central place of schooling in constructing their encounters with the uncertain world they face today.

This book revolves around the lives and experiences of a group of high school girls, their school, teachers, and families. Primarily, it draws on ethnographic research in and around the al-Khatwa Secondary School for Girls, one of three public high schools for girls in Bawadi al-Naseem, in eight months in 2005 and in three follow-up visits in 2008, 2009, and 2011.[11] I also conducted research in a high school in the nearby town of Tel Yahya in 2002 for three months. My initial research in Tel Yahya provided much of the foundation for my early thinking about the cultural significance of educational spaces for young women. Perhaps no other group of citizens in Jordan faces the tumultuousness of the contemporary era more than teenage girls do in their day-to-day lives, as they go to school, befriend one another, fall in love, and work to construct a path and an image of a life desirable and secure. The available and desirable paths are not entirely clear and are characterized by contradictory forces and moral projects—local and beyond. Persistent debates and conflicts surrounding the image of acceptable womanhood, the terms of proper public faith, and the status and role of an educated woman in Jordan today remain central to larger debates surrounding cultural authenticity and progress. The girls at al-Khatwa Secondary School contended with such struggles in very personal and everyday ways, even as forces global, regional, and national in turn shaped these experiences. The efforts of the girls at al-Khatwa to negotiate these contexts are the central "data" of this book. Girls were both shaped and limited by these contexts, and responded to them in the course of their daily lives.

Competing Visions of Desirable Womanhood

When I first began my research on education, development, and gender in Jordan, I was regularly directed by Jordanians with whom I spoke about my project to meet women considered successful by the community. "You should speak to Dr. Sumaya, she was the first doctor from her village," I was told. Or, "Fida, you should speak to Dr. Hala at the university, she was one of the first female professors." And, "You should speak to so-and-so's wife, she is a prominent lawyer." Some of the people I met also spoke proudly about the successful women in their own families. I heard about the sister-in-law of a teacher who had a Ph.D. in genetics and who was so accomplished that she had been invited to present her research in England. Mothers and fathers spoke proudly of their daughters. Ibtisam's mother told me that her oldest daughter was the top student in the physics department at the university. Another student expressed pride in her sister who was studying medicine at Jordan University.

Perhaps these were models that my interlocutors felt were particularly important to share with me, a Jordanian American researcher interested in women and education. Yet the status accorded to highly educated women (and men) was consistent with all that I heard from those I came to know over the course of my ethnographic research in and around schools in Jordan. Being educated—and specifically being an educated woman—was consistently framed by parents, educators, and girls themselves as something positive. Furthermore, the image of educated women was in keeping with the image that the regime has emphasized for Jordan of a moderate, forward-looking, and developed nation. Women and their development are central to this narrative, even if the terms of their development are at times openly contested in Jordan today. Young women face myriad images of desirable and successful womanhood. Many of these images are contradictory in what they demand and in the ideals to which they urge young women to aspire.

The most prominent images of women are perhaps those of the women of the royal family. These women, in particular Queen Rania, the wife of the current King Abdullah II, and Princess Basma, his aunt, and their public good works are regularly front-page news in Jordan. Female cabinet ministers can also be found in the media from time to time. Elite and powerful, they present an image of women as publicly engaged and politically savvy. They are the fulfillment of the international development ideal for empowered women, although their elite status limits their reach as models to be emulated by young women such as those at the al-Khatwa School. Images of glamorous pop singers and movie stars that appear around the clock on satellite television are problematic in a different way. In these depictions, women's typically scantily clad bodies are proffered as models of beauty, female liberation, and wealth and opulence. Often images of modern romance with its attendant forms of consumption pervade such television programming as well, like the Turkish soap opera that captured Nada's attention as she lay in bed trying to sleep (Illouz 1997). Each of these models, however, is somewhat removed from the realities of the life of young women today, although their presence is not inconsequential because they present an idealized beauty that is largely unattainable but increasingly desired. More immediately, in the day-to-day, girls encounter adults in their lives—mothers, teachers, doctors, saleswomen, civil servants—each of whom reflects a variety of ways of being a woman in Jordan today.

Alongside such images and personal encounters, many segments of Jordanian society are also engaged in debates about acceptable pathways for a *pious* woman. In an era in which new forms of religiosity demand new ways of enacting piety, the emphasis on public forms of piety has had particular implications for women (Deeb 2006). The basic modes by which women demonstrate their commitment to religion—such as prayer and fasting—maintain their importance. However, other ways of performing piety have emerged in response to modern realities, institutions, and organization of space, including the pursuit of education. Those who actively seek a more pious life must assess and evaluate how one should act Islamically in the variety of situations one encounters in daily life, with consequences for all the women who are members of the broader community. For many of the participants in the contemporary religious movements, education is key to such assessments, as decisions about pious living should be based on knowledge of religious teachings and texts (Deeb 2006; Limbert 2005; Mahmood 2005; Shively 2008). One result has been new forms of Islamic dress that offer different standards for modesty. But living piously is not exclusively about dress, which Nada's companions demonstrated as they debated how often to pray and whether television shows violated Islamic norms. From the need to renegotiate female-male interactions, to demands for public service or volunteer work, to the mandate to teach others about true Islam, young women are presented with a variety of images of what it means to live piously in Jordan today, and these also present different ways of being a woman. Thus what piety demands of women in a contemporary era is regularly negotiated by women seeking to cultivate their religious selves and/or seeking to make others more pious by example, by the acquisition of knowledge, and by teaching.

Conceptualizing Schools and Schooling

Hervé Varenne (2007) argues that those interested in the anthropology of education must move beyond schooling and focus on the social processes of educating each other that human beings engage in through social interactions of all kinds. Varenne conceptualizes this educative activity as deliberation, "the joint activity of people talking about something that happened outside their immediate setting, making practical decisions about what is to happen next, and then publicly reflecting on what just happened" (1569). I argue that schools in fact provide a critical arena for such deliberation for young women in Jordan. Given the limited access that adolescent girls have to public spaces in which such deliberation may occur, schools are all the more important.[12] The interactions and experiences I draw on here are very much the stuff of "difficult deliberations" in school (Varenne 2007: 1562).

Understanding the significance of schools and schooling in the lives of adolescent girls in Bawadi al-Naseem and the region more broadly requires examining school at three levels. Schools function simultaneously as local spaces for girls (spaces of significant deliberations), as state socializing institutions, and as contemporary discursive projects of modernization and international development. Building from this framework and my ethnographic evidence, I argue that the effects of schooling for young women have been mixed. The spread of public education in Jordan—which began as early as the 1920s and proceeded with full force after independence in 1946—may not have produced all of the outcomes that development narratives assume, but it has not left Jordan unchanged. Schooling in Jordan as elsewhere produces new struggles by generating new expectations and presenting new possibilities. By virtue of their institutional form and pedagogical methods, schools also model new ways of conceiving of the world and acting on it, setting in motion forces and principles outside the control of these state authorities (Kaplan 2006; Stambach 2000; Starrett 1998). Understanding education's effects requires a multilevel analysis of contemporary educational institutions that takes seriously the mutually constitutive nature of schooling in its ideological and material dimensions.

Schools such as al-Khatwa are decidedly local institutions, staffed by sons and daughters of the community, reflecting local norms, hierarchies, and conflicts. For young women, the significance of these spaces and experiences cannot be underestimated. Nationally, schools are the main conduits for state efforts to socialize young people as loyal citizens, as well as workers prepared to partake in the nation's development.[13] Since Jordan was created by the British in 1921, schools have been central to the project of making Jordan and cementing a link between the Hashemite monarchy and the people who populate this colonial creation (Anderson 2005). The struggle to maintain this link continues today as the nature of Jordan's national identity and the legitimacy of the regime are challenged by demographic realities, economic crises, and regional conflicts as well as some of the very transformations that education has facilitated, as I discuss more extensively in chapter 2. States are rarely totally successful in their efforts to control the production of knowledge through public education, as they must contend with other forces in and around school and because the young people who are the subject of their efforts are never completely determined by them (Anderson 2005; Coe 2005; Luykx 1999; Starrett 1998). These historical and contemporary challenges are in turn shaped by Jordan's dependency on the West and by the extensive development industry that has a hand in shaping the policies and the discourses surrounding educational reform, women's development, economic strategies, and a range of other spheres of policy and action meant to facilitate Jordan's development and political acquiescence and ensure regime stability.[14]

The socializing function of schools then is not hegemonic—the actors in school do not speak with one voice, and the state itself is represented by different actors and produces its own contradictions. A student's peers and teachers can have influence over her, and for adolescent girls in Bawadi al-Naseem, schools are the primary space for interaction with peers—for building friendships beyond those with siblings and other family members.

Even how young women come to "read" television programming and other forms of media is partly shaped by discussions with friends, debates in classrooms, and the advice of teachers. Analyzing schools in this light illuminates the unexpected consequences of schooling, and it forces us to take seriously the role of adolescent girls themselves in negotiating and defining acceptable and desirable pathways for an educated Jordanian woman.

A State of "Always Becoming"

In many respects the stories of the al-Khatwa students are stories of youth or adolescence. Nancy Lesko (2001), writing about the historical treatment of adolescents by researchers and social practitioners in the United States, argues that adolescence is particularly fraught because of the characterization of adolescence by adults as "always becoming" (89) or unfinished. Because of the assumed malleability of young people, youth and adolescence have often been viewed by adults as a phase of great potential and risk. Young people are the targets of much monitoring, intervention, and control; competing disciplinary projects work to shape them and contend for their loyalties (Lesko 1996b). Since Margaret Mead first addressed the issue of adolescence in varied cultural contexts in her 1928 book *Coming of Age in Samoa*, the experience of adolescence as a life phase across cultures has been the regular subject of analysis in the social sciences (Bucholtz 2002; Mead 2001; Schlegal and Barry 1991). Much evidence points to the culturally constructed nature of all life phases, as Mead herself argued when she contrasted the adolescent angst of American teenagers with what she viewed as a less conflict-ridden adolescent experience in Samoa (2001). Although Mead's findings have been the subject of much debate and controversy (Levy 1984; Shankman 1996), the basic premise of the cultural contingency of categories such as adulthood, motherhood, childhood, and adolescence is now widely accepted especially in the anthropological literature.

Even within particular societies, the ways in which life phases are categorized or individuals are labeled is context specific, classed, and gendered. The way in which the concept of youth or *shabab* is employed in contemporary Jordan conveys the fluidity and contingency of this life phase somewhere between childhood and adulthood. Adolescence or *murahaqa* marks a set of more determined physical milestones as indicated by the onset of puberty. Youth, on the other hand, captures a process of "two-part maturity" whereby coming of age is about both physical maturity or *bulugh* and intellectual maturity or *rushd* (Messick 1996: 78–79). Thus, one might be considered fully mature in physical terms but still a youth and still in need of direction. Contemporary social transformations, such as extended formal education, the later age of marriage, and the shift to more nuclear-based family living arrangements, have further changed contemporary notions of youth. In a context where marriage is still the marker of adulthood, many have argued that the delay in marriage works to prolong "youth" and create an extended period of "waithood" (Singerman 2007).

Due in part to the demographic shifts witnessed throughout the region, namely, the extreme youthfulness of the population (and here "youth" is more specifically age-marked typically to the ages of 15–24 or close to this range),[15] "youth" as a category in Jordan and in the Middle East more broadly has garnered much public attention. The academic scholarship on youth in the region has generally fallen into two spheres. The first has been concerned with the "youth bulge" as a development challenge. The work of economists and other affiliated scholars at the Middle East Youth Initiative at the Brookings Institution is a good example of this approach, and scholars working with this initiative have produced several working papers pointing to the economic challenges faced by youth, such as finding a job and starting a family.[16] The second major approach to youth is concerned with what I would characterize as youth counterculture, or the popular culture of select youth in the region. Some of this work has been criticized for focusing too much on youth cultures that are elite and/or similar to the West and hence more easily discernible as "youth culture" (Swedenburg 2007). Very little of this work examines youth in educational spaces (Adely 2009b).

Youth in Jordan are the subject of much discourse and programming as well. The Ministry of Youth and Sport and its local offices throughout the county, as well as other national and international agencies, regularly sponsor events and campaigns for youth to encourage a range of habits and beliefs. State institutions are preoccupied primarily with promoting patriotism and good citizenship. For example, the youth initiative spawned from the "We are all Jordan" campaign of 2006 lists as one of its primary objectives "To promote volunteerism and foster love of serving the country and society and strengthening the sentiment of belonging and loyalty to the nation and its leaders."[17] In addition to the nationalistic bent of youth programs, Arab Muslim youth have also come under the lens of development agencies and policymakers and have increasingly become the subject of development efforts. In Jordan some of the youth development issues that have taken center stage range from environmental awareness and conservation to entrepreneurship, tourism, and traffic safety.[18]

Efforts aimed at fashioning youth around the globe are deeply gendered, particularly in the ways they seek to define, categorize, and control adolescent sexuality (Bettie 2002; Holland and Eisenhart 1990; Lesko 1988). For most girls in Bawadi al-Naseem, adolescence brings with it constraints as well as possibilities. As they reach this age, many girls face new restrictions on their mobility and expectations for greater modesty in dress and comportment in public (although, as emerges throughout this text, what actual practices and behavior this entails is regularly debated and negotiated). School authorities are central to monitoring and controlling the behavior of girls; teachers, staff, and even students at al-Khatwa worked to impart lessons about appropriate behaviors for girls. The state curriculum also contributes to these lessons through the content and activities it mandates for school. In Jordanian schoolbooks one finds an array of at times contradictory lessons on topics ranging from women and work, to appropriate dress for men and women, to the responsibilities of wives and husbands in an Islamic family, as I mention throughout this book (see also Anderson 2007). The state, and the education officials who are its representatives, also call on girls to take center stage in patriotic performances, to read speeches and poetry on the king's birthday, or to take the lead in youth workshops organized by UNICEF or UNESCO. At the same time, for many young women in high school new opportunities abound as they mature, continue their education, work, and consider marriage.

Nevertheless, young people are not merely subjects of disciplinary projects. Indeed, al-Khatwa students are actively engaged in defining authenticity and possibility. Given recent social and economic transformations, these young women make their way into adulthood on an at times ambiguous path. The life of a youth in Bawadi al-Naseem is not that of the reified conflict-ridden American teenager, nor is it the romanticized ideal of conflict-free youth in "simple" societies. One main difference in Jordan, however, is that family members are among the most significant others in an adolescent's life. Although school affords students such as those at al-Khatwa a space in which to build new bonds and attachment to nonkin, families continue to play a central role in these women's lives. Young people are deeply embedded and invested in their kin relations, and kin-based allegiances and support systems continue to be the primary source of protection, resources, political access, and identification in Jordan today, even as they also continue to be the primary institution of social control in a girl's life.[19] Thus, youth cultural projects are very much communal and familial ones.

The cultural projects that compete for sway with young people emerge out of a particular historical and political context that shapes the politics of culture and authenticity in Jordan today. Because women and their bodies continue to be central markers of legitimacy and progress in Jordan and the Middle East more broadly, this context is also vital for understanding young women's constraints and opportunities and how they may negotiate them (Kandiyoti 1991). I delve into this context more extensively in chapter 2. Suffice it to say here that various dynamics all have a hand in structuring young women's lives and visions of progress: contemporary legitimacy struggles that pit national allegiance against kin-based ones, the promises of development against persistent economic struggles, the regime's religious authority against competing beliefs about proper forms of religiosity, and state and global visions of progress for women against the realities that constrain women's lives. Because efforts to shape and monitor the socialization of youth are deemed so critical for winning local and global battles for hearts and minds, schools are at the center of debates on authority and authenticity (Kaplan 2006; Mazawi 1999, 2002; Starrett 1998, 2006).

Contents of the Book

The emergence of state-sponsored schooling has been central to state-building around the world; in Jordan this has been no less the case. Chapter 2 charts the history and events that have shaped contemporary Jordan, highlighting the gendered dimensions of these processes. Tracing the efforts of the Hashemite regime to expand state control, I explore the emergence of state-sponsored schooling as central not only to state-building efforts but also to the emergence of state opposition. These historical struggles provide a basis from which to examine the interplay of gender, class, religion, ethnicity, and kin-based allegiances in shaping the prospects for development through education. An analysis of regional and global politics, as well as the power wielded by foreign aid in Jordan, provides further depth to this historical contextualization.

In chapter 3, I engage specifically with the state's project of socializing students as patriotic and loyal citizens, pointing to the conflicts that are brought into play through nationalistic educational projects and discourses. Through an analysis of the daily assembly, musical performances at patriotic events, and the interpretation of such events by participants and critics alike, I demonstrate how such events put women at the center of Jordan's national narrative of progress while simultaneously challenging the legitimacy of the state in some people's eyes. Most significant here are the ways in which patriotic rituals with girls at their center serve to challenge the moral authority of the regime while simultaneously emboldening its power.

Questions of moral authority are also closely linked to the power to interpret religious knowledge and define the terms of religious propriety. Much of the national and regional debate about the place of Islam in public life has focused on the status of women; women's issues have been hotly contested in conflicts over the power to define religious orthodoxy. Yet other than the analysis of curricular content, very little scholarly attention has been focused on the role of schools in such contests. In chapter 4, I demonstrate that outside the formal and intended curriculum, there are myriad ways and spaces—in the classroom, in the prayer room, in the schoolyard, in the teachers' room—where actors in school are engaged in efforts to teach each other about religion, religious practices, and living as pious Muslim women. In addition, struggles over religious authority are enmeshed with similar struggles outside of school, specifically with a local piety movement. Competing interpretations of Islamic orthodoxy come to the fore in schools in unique ways, and schools provide a space and new tools for negotiating these tensions.

Nevertheless, moral authority is not solely expressed in religious terms; morality also draws on local norms and is closely tied to the family, kin, or tribe and broader notions of tradition. It is shaped by contemporary notions of progress and success. The global narrative of education for development and female empowerment neglects the unexpected ways in which education has transformed basic conceptualizations of successful personhood, morality, and progress. Chapter 5 examines conceptualizations of "respectability" and the ways in which gendered norms and educational performance intersect in the construction of who is a good girl. Here, I illustrate how efforts to monitor and discipline the behavior of girls in and outside of school are entangled with new forms of respectability generated by schooling, as well as tensions between the prohibitions on relationships between boys and girls and the parallel preoccupations with getting married in the era of a "marriage crisis." I shed light on the multiple discourses that circulate about love, romance, and relationships and demonstrate how they complicate ideals of womanhood with which young women grapple and some of the most apparently hegemonic gendered expectations.

Building on my analysis of education and its association with moral authority, contemporary religiosity, and respectability, chapter 6 examines the links between education and women's development. Education for women has been considered a critical component of modernization and development since the turn of the twentieth century in the Arab world. In recent decades women's waged labor has become synonymous with progress for women. I discuss mainstream assumptions about the benefits of education, and I examine the ways in which the Arab world has failed to fit the seemingly predictable patterns related to educating girls espoused by international agencies as well as national officials. Drawing on ethnographic data, I explore expectations created by schooling through the experiences and stories of young women at the al-Khatwa School and their families, and I discuss how the state, teachers, and families try to shape the expectations of the girls at al-Khatwa in both predictable and unpredictable ways. This ethnographic exploration serves to problematize the education-for-empowerment equation that so often undergirds discussion of women's development in the Arab world by considering the ways in which people—students, parents, teachers, and school officials—construct their own conceptions of what is good and desirable.

Each of these issues—national identity, religious authenticity, respectability, and progress through development—is central to debates about authenticity and authority in Jordan today. In everyday life, the polemics of authenticity may come down to questions about what is proper dress; which academic track in high school is valuable and/or respectable; who can succeed on the high school completion exam; what constitutes beauty, or who is pretty; and what makes an attractive marriage partner. Such matters may appear to be the quotidian substance of adolescent life for girls in a city in Jordan. However, they are equally the stuff of national, regional, and global politics and institutions, part of the "webs of significance" (Geertz 1973) in which their live are entangled.

Conducting Research at al-Khatwa as a Jordanian American

In 2002, I commenced research with observations in schools and with informal conversations with secondary school students (females), their teachers, and their families in Tel Yahya, a town near Bawadi al-Naseem. With the knowledge that the majority of girls went to high school in Jordan, I was interested in the experience of schooling itself—both as a daily educative and cultural process and as a development project imbued with notions of success and progress. In 2005, I focused my research on the al-Khatwa Secondary School for Girls in Bawadi al-Naseem and the families of students there. My approach to learning about the experience of schooling for adolescent girls and for the adults who helped to shape this experience was ethnographic. It consisted of observation, interviews, and some participation, primarily as an English teacher, but also in a number of other roles I was asked to take on while at al-Khatwa.[20] At al-Khatwa, I interviewed seventy students, twenty-four teachers, and two staff members.[21] All interviews were conducted in Arabic, and the large majority were tape-recorded. In addition to individuals connected to al-Khatwa, I interviewed a number of young women from other high schools, a few alumnae of al-Khatwa, and several teachers from other schools.

I attended school daily for seven months, observing classes, special events, and a range of other social interactions that emerged in the day-to-day life of the school.[22] In all I observed about ninety classes. Observation meant that I took a seat in the back of the classroom and listened to the day's lesson as presented by the teacher and student conversations.[23] At first, when I was still something of a novelty, teachers introduced me, sometimes referred to me during class, and reserved some time at the end of class for me to talk with the girls. However, as I became a regular sight at the school, I would usually slide into my seat and observe quietly. During these observations, I took fieldnotes. Initially, I observed all subjects and every teacher, save for one who was uncomfortable with my observing her class. Eventually I focused my attention on classes where there was more likely to be dialogue (religion, history, social studies, and civic education). I also spent the day with particular groups of students on some occasions.

I talked with students during their free periods and in the schoolyard and over time came to know certain students very well. Both the students and their teachers found it odd that I should want to be with the girls during recess. At first the young women were not sure what to make of me. The more outgoing of them approached me and asked questions about America; the majority kept a curious distance. However, once I started attending their classes, introducing myself, and discussing my research interests, the students seemed more at ease with me. Although I was an adult, I was external to the school hierarchy and worked hard to make this clear to the students. The students started to seek me out when they had issues to discuss or just when they were bored. Many felt comfortable confiding in me about a number of issues, from school-based grievances to personal affairs. I also spent a considerable amount of time talking with teachers in the teachers' room, the assistant principal's office, and the school canteen, where some congregated during their free periods. I also observed special events of various types and sat in on school meetings.

In addition to the school-based research, I visited the families of fourteen students, with the express purpose of interviewing family members about their daughters' schooling as well as their own experiences with school. I met with family members, primarily mothers and older sisters of al-Khatwa students. Typically, my visits consisted of much more than an interview and went on for several hours during which I answered questions about life in America, became acquainted with younger siblings, and passed the time with several family members exchanging small talk about life in Jordan. I met some fathers and an occasional older brother. Although I did not speak to many of the al-Khatwa girls' adolescent brothers, mothers I met frequently spoke at length about their sons, primarily because many of their sons were struggling academically and/or giving their parents a hard time about school.[24] I visited several of the families multiple times, and after first meetings, subsequent visits became more social.[25]

In my first weeks at the school, much of the conversations centered on the temperature because the schools were not heated and it could get bitterly cold in the classrooms. Soon began the persistent questions about America and America's education system and requests for me to compare the two systems and to come to some conclusion as to which was better. Eventually, however, students and teachers alike came to understand that I was interested in the school as a social space (*al-madrasa ka-makan ijtima'i*) and its influence on young women, rather than educational quality or outcomes per se. The questions about America were consistent throughout my time there and expanded from queries about the U.S. school system to curiosity about teenagers, dating, religion, and parent-child relationships in the United States.

In many respects, my research was facilitated by my own background as a Jordanian American. My parents are Jordanian Christians who immigrated to the United States in 1970. Although they intended to return to Jordan, they never did. In fact for almost ten years, my mother, my siblings, and I did not see Jordan. Since my undergraduate years, however, I have regularly returned and, indeed, have built my academic career around the study of the Middle East and Jordan in particular. For me as an anthropologist, this has been a particularly intriguing process of cultural exploration and construction. The Jordan I knew before the age of eighteen was constructed by my parents and the Jordanian immigrant community (largely Christian) we were connected to in New York. It was colored by my parents' rural roots and by a Jordan they had frozen in time, and to a degree romanticized, in their memories. For me as a young person, being Jordanian was shaped very much by my experiences coming of age in the United States in a largely working-class immigrant community.

With time, study, and research, I came to know Jordan as a place much more vibrant and in flux than I had envisioned it in my youth. When I began to study anthropology, I began to understand this shift in my own thinking as related to the broader reconceptualization and theorizing of culture that the discipline had pursued over the last few decades. But even before I discovered anthropology, living and working in Jordan (and traveling throughout the region) laid the empirical groundwork for this (re)thinking. This evolution has provided me with critical insights about Jordan that would not have been available to me otherwise. My research at al-Khatwa Secondary School was also greatly facilitated by my father-in-law's long and esteemed career as an educator in and around Bawadi al-Naseem. It was through his contacts that I gained my first entry into schools in 2002, an experience that sparked my interest in continuing my research in this area of Jordan. In this way, I also came to know many educators and future research interlocutors. Being linked to him meant that in addition to being an American researcher, I was also a Jordanian with ties to a local family that was well-known and respected. This introduction eased my entry and increased people's willingness to speak with me.

As people came to know me, my familial roots, and current connections to Jordan, they began to think of me as a Jordanian, or daughter of Jordanians, who lived in America. The fact that I was from a Christian family was not unusual, given the presence of a Christian minority in the community, many of whom were educators. It did serve as an entry point for discussion with some students who asked me about the celebration of Christian holidays, the pope, prayer, and fasting. Some of the al-Khatwa students had attended a local Catholic elementary school and so were more familiar with these traditions. I recall only one occasion when my religious status was raised as an issue. I was informed by one student that some of her peers questioned whether I should be allowed to go into the prayer room given that I was not a Muslim. The issue was never raised again, and I came to know the girls active in the prayer room quite well with time. In general, students and teachers alike were much more interested in America—American schools, family life, and teenagers—as well as my own perspectives on U.S. foreign policy and its cultural norms and values.

In writing about these lives, I have grappled with my uneasiness about the process of representing people and events—shaping them to fit into chapters and categories that are more conducive to analysis and to academic publishing. These concerns bring me back to al-Khatwa and the frequent jesting from one teacher in particular: "Be careful. Fida has got her pen and notebook out again." On one occasion, after I had joined a group of teachers for a coffee break under the shade of a tree, this same teacher said to me: "We are going inside, Fida; you know we do have work to do. We don't just sun ourselves and drink coffee." She then turned to her colleagues and said for my benefit, "She probably will tell them in America that all we do is sit and drink coffee and that this is why *we do not develop.*" All was said in jest. I had grown quite close to this group of teachers, going on visits with them and inviting them to my home on occasion. But underneath the humor was a reminder that most Jordanians were cognizant of the representations of their own lives that were produced and circulated elsewhere. These female professionals knew that they were generally thought to be oppressed and underdeveloped by outsiders and that even many of their fellow citizens in the capital shared such sentiments. My presence was a reminder of the power of this discourse to shape their lives in multiple ways.

Throughout this book, I work to be explicit about how I was positioned in various situations. For in addition to triggering many conversations about life in America, my own position as researcher/observer led to particular conversations and prompted particular types of reflection on tensions or conflict that the young women at al-Khatwa faced. In presenting my data, I have striven for breadth by reporting the experiences, histories, and perspectives of a variety of girls and their families, while also working to provide a "thick description" (Geertz 1973: 6) for a smaller number of actors in order to convey the complexity and contingency of particular lives (Abu-Lughod 1991). Wherever possible, I also integrate what I heard and saw at al-Khatwa and in Bawadi al-Naseem within a national and global context that has played a part in shaping the local schooling experience and the subsequent meaning with which this schooling is imbued. In this sense, I consider this to be a "strategically situated ethnography," a form of multi-sited ethnography that is physically centered on a "local" place but works to understand larger systems and peoples' articulated awareness of these other forces in their lives (Marcus 1995: 110–11). Understanding the historical trajectories and shifts in Jordan and in the region is critical for understanding the significance of current debates and conflicts. Finally, I have sought to convey the complex web of influences and factors that shape the choices of the young women at al-Khatwa each day, in the hope that ethnographies of particular lives can make these women and their families more real, speaking back to the often dehumanizing narratives about oppressed and passive Arab Muslim women.

TWO

Jordan and the al-Khatwa Secondary School for Girls: People, Place, and Time

Transjordan was created as a British mandate in 1921 as part of Europe's parceling of the Levant after World War I. Amir Abdullah of the Hashemite family, the great-grandfather of the current king, was given nominal leadership over the newly created mandate and with British support put down tribal rebellions that sought to challenge this British arrangement. Prior to these British designs, there was no country of Jordan of which to speak. Rather, people organized themselves according to kin-based loyalties both politically and economically. What became Transjordan had been part of the Ottoman Empire, and particularly during the late Ottoman period, Ottoman officials and institutions were also present (Rogan 1999). The story of the making of Jordan, then, is a story of a British-imposed state and Hashemite efforts to create a nation and a national narrative that had the Hashemites at their center. An independent state was declared in 1946, but full independence from the British, who continued to control the military, did not come until 1956. According to Andrew Shryock (1997), it was after 1956 that the project of creating a national identity began in earnest; but even before then, the expansion of state bureaucracy and military control laid the groundwork for the ideological work to come (Amadouny 1994; Anderson 2005; Massad 2001). Thus, the making of Jordan was a multipronged process of exerting physical control over the land; constructing the state as the "supratribe" that would provide security and services through the extension of state institutions; and creating a national history and tradition through the ideological work of these institutions, central among them schools.

Since their arrival in Jordan,[1] the Hashemites have been tasked with establishing a state, creating a national identity where none had existed, and establishing themselves as the legitimate rulers of this nation. This has involved a process of "moving forward," extending the arm of the state, developing, and modernizing, while simultaneously looking back to create a link to the past that would support the royal family's claims to legitimacy as rulers of Jordan (Anderson 2001; Layne 1994). To this end the regime has worked to construct a uniquely Jordanian identity by the creation of a "tradition," shared history, culture, and values—Arab, tribal, and Islamic—and linking this history closely to the Hashemites (Anderson 2001; Layne 1994; Shryock 1997).[2] Education has been at the heart of this process of creating and sustaining a Jordanian tradition and a shared history, as I discuss more extensively in chapter 3 (see also Anderson 2001 and 2005). The ideal of the Jordanian woman and the state policies that shape women's lives have also been central to both of these processes—the process of modernizing and moving forward, as well as the efforts of the regime, and its critics, to claim authenticity through shared history and traditions. In Jordan, as in much of the region, women have been a focal point of these competing imperatives (Clark 2006; Kandiyoti 1991).

This process of nation building has not gone unchallenged. The persistence of strong kin-based allegiances,[3] as evinced for example, in conflicts between young men from different families or towns on university campuses, is a regular and immediate challenge to these efforts (Shryock 1997).[4] Historically much of the monarchy's support base has relied on tribal configurations; the regime has long emboldened and at times reified tribes and tribal categories and continues to favor kin-based affiliation in its gerrymandered election laws. Yet the persistence of kin-based loyalties may prove to be a double-edged sword. At the very least it has been the source of violent conflict among citizens in recent years.

Another major challenge to the construction of a national identity is demographic. Jordan has had a large influx of Palestinian refugees at critical conjunctures in its history. In 1948 between seventy and a hundred thousand Palestinians fled or were expelled from their homes with the creation of the state of Israel and the Palestinian catastrophe or *al-Nakba* (Brand 1995; Massad 2001). In 1950, Jordan formally annexed the West Bank, and over 750,000 West Bank Palestinians became de facto Jordanian citizens. In 1967, when Israel occupied the West Bank and Gaza, another 400,000 Palestinians arrived in Jordan, over half of them made refugees for a second time (Farah 2005; Massad 2001). Jordan also faced other major population influxes: after the Gulf War in 1991, many Jordanians (most of them of Palestinian origin) were forced to leave the Gulf, and in recent years many Iraqis have fled to Jordan. I will discuss each of these in greater detail later in this chapter; for the time being suffice it to say that beyond the major resource issues posed by the swelling of the Jordanian population almost overnight several times in its short history, the fact that a majority of the Jordanian population is of Palestinian origin continues to pose a major challenge to the construction of a Jordanian national narrative and shared identity with the Hashemites at its center. Furthermore, the persistence of the conflict in Palestine, as well as the war in Iraq, continues to have a profound impact on Jordan's stability.

Today Jordanian citizens of Palestinian origin make up a majority of Jordan's population.[5] Throughout its history the regime has been engaged in efforts to delineate a uniquely Jordanian national identity with a demographic majority that may not always share this identity.[6] In its early years this was further complicated by Jordan's annexation of the West Bank and claims to guardianship over Jerusalem (Katz 2005). When the Jordanians lost control of the West Bank and East Jerusalem, the Palestinian conflict erupted within Jordan's borders, as Jordan became a base for Palestinian resistance to Israel. In 1970, the Jordanian regime launched a war (known as Black September) against Palestinian armed groups based in Jordan[7] (and their Jordanian supporters), who were viewed as having gone too far in challenging the regime's authority. This war killed somewhere between seven and twenty thousand people, among them Palestinian civilians (Massad 2001: 245).[8] After the war, the regime pursued policies emphasizing a uniquely Jordanian identity, building in part on constructed and romanticized Bedouin and tribal motifs, and preferential policies in the hiring of Jordanians in the public sector (Layne 1994; Massad 2001; Shryock 1997). Over the past four decades, the issue of national identity and the place of Palestinians in Jordan has emerged with regularity—sometimes implicitly and other times in explicit nationalist rhetoric meant to exclude citizens. The persistent conflict in Palestine and the regular assertions by some Israeli officials that Jordan should become the "alternative Palestinian homeland" continue to fuel such tensions today. Indeed, in a speech on June 8, 2010, on the eleventh anniversary of his ascension to the throne, King Abdullah II referenced the "so-called alternative homeland" and its threat to Jordanian national unity and stated emphatically, "[B]e sure that we will not accept, under any condition or in any form, any solution to the Palestinian question at Jordan's expense" (*Ad-Dustour*, June 9, 2010).[9]

The increased role of religion, religious institutions, and religious sentiment in the region has also posed particular challenges for the Hashemites, who have built their legitimacy in part on their religious credentials. Like much of the region, Jordan has been transformed by the emergence of new religious movements and public conceptualization of what religion demands in the contemporary era. This has entailed both contending with Islamic political groups, most significantly the Islamic Action Front (IAF), the official political party of the Muslim Brotherhood, as well as popular demands for a larger role for religion in public life. Jordan has been characterized by political analysts as the nation in the region that has best managed its relationship with political Islam (Brand 1998; Schwedler 2006; Tal 1995; Wiktorowicz 2001). The Muslim Brotherhood has historically viewed support for and cooperation with the regime as in its own interests, and they have benefited from this cooperation by, for example, receiving important cabinet positions such as the minister of education (Brand 1998). The Hashemite regime has similarly benefited from this history of cooperation and sought to placate Islamists through policies that did not threaten its own interests, most notably inaction with respect to the dependent legal status of women, particularly in the personal status laws, as I discuss later in this chapter. This relationship has been more conflict ridden with the current king, and in recent years the Muslim Brotherhood has been dealing with its own internal struggle for power between moderates and hawks.

Concerns about religious extremism in the region have also guided many of the regime's recent policies vis-à-vis religious discourse and education in Jordan. Struggles surrounding religious authority are intertwined with notions of identity and authenticity. A narrative about a crisis of authenticity is regularly voiced by political opposition forces, religious leaders, and media pundits. This narrative manifests itself in political debates, objections to foreign policy, concerns about educational reforms, and, perhaps most significantly, debates about women's legal status and the role of Jordanian women in society today (Clark 2006). In everyday life, new forms of religiosity also accentuate a disconnect between the regime and some of its citizens, and many Jordanians perceive the onslaught of Western media and foreign-aid-funded projects as a challenge to their culture and values. It is this context of political, cultural, and economic uncertainty that frames the educational experience of young women in Jordan today.

Education for Development

Throughout this book, the lives of young women at al-Khatwa and their experiences in school in Bawadi al-Naseem provide insight into the ways the confluence of major events and personal circumstance frame and limit the possibilities of education. From its earliest days, Jordan (the monarchy, state officials, and citizens) has placed much of its hopes in education. For the regime, the very foundations of the nation rest heavily on the hope of making loyal and productive citizens. Schools have also been part of the promise of security and prosperity that the Hashemites have offered. For many Jordanians, education has provided mobility; however, for Jordan's poor, the promise of education is illusory. The growth of a private sector of education that is superior in quality to the public schools while being financially inaccessible to the large majority contributes to the reproduction of inequality through education (Saif and Tabbaa 2008).[10] Not only do the best private schools provide better-quality education, they also enable the elite to develop the contacts and social capital needed to secure their privilege, as such schools do everywhere (Bourdieu and Passeron 1977). With unemployment for Jordanians under the age of twenty-five over 60 percent in 2003, the returns on education are not guaranteed (European Training Foundation 2005).[11] Nevertheless, most families continue to hold onto the hopes that their children will be educated and that this will provide them with the means to a better quality of life. They also seek the status education confers on their children as well as the family. For girls in particular, people hope that education will be a source of security and good marriage prospects (Jansen 2006). Yet education has also complicated the terrain for young women, for debates about what they can and should do with their education are intertwined with debates about what Jordan is and should become.

Women have figured prominently in the state's public discourse about modernization and tradition, and the state's efforts to propel "modernization" or development have had particular consequences for women, among them increased access to education, new patterns of consumption, and, as a result, new economic demands and household configurations. The role that women should have in Jordan today continues to be a matter of public contention, and as discussed in the previous chapter, competing narratives circulate about desirable womanhood (Brand 1998; Clark 2006). These debates are not new to Jordan, although their terms have changed in some respects with other developments in the country. For example, a cursory review of Al-Rai in 1975 reveals that debates about women's participation in parliament and in coeducational higher education were covered in a recurring opinion column entitled al-bab al maftuh (the open door). Women in Jordan continue to be recognized by many Jordanians as representing that which is Islamic, authentic, and legitimate, as they do throughout the region. At the same time, their "uplift" is consistently underlined as central to progress or development; their bodies continue to serve as markers of authenticity and progress (Abu-Lughod 1998; Kandiyoti 1991).

Given this context, young people in Jordan today (who constitute over a third of the population)[12] face a great deal of uncertainty about future prospects and possibilities; young women face even greater ambiguity as the image of proper womanhood is continually negotiated. Youth in turn has been constructed as a central trope in the public soul-searching about development, crisis, and possibility; the "youth bulge" is simultaneously framed as an obstacle, a source of instability, and the hope for a future Jordan (R. Farah 2005). Jordanians, like many other people, still have hope that education and schools will prevent crises big and small (Kaplan 2006; Starrett 2006). Regardless of how one assesses this optimism, schools are clearly an important venue through which to comprehend the difficult issues with which Jordanians grapple. Schooling—as a central element of the state modernization project, with all the concomitant popular expectations it has generated in the last few decades—is critical to understanding this place and time in Jordan. It is in this context that we can begin to understand the experience of schooling in Bawadi al-Naseem.

Bawadi al-Naseem

Mere mention of Bawadi al-Naseem to Ammanites evokes images of the desert and poverty. In reality, Bawadi al-Naseem, the provincial capital of one of the largest governorates, is a city of about fifty thousand. In the 1940s, Bawadi al-Naseem was just a village with a population of around five hundred (Reimer 2005). However, even before 1940 it was the site of important political and economic developments. In the first decade of the twentieth century, the Ottomans built the Hejaz Railway system with a station in Bawadi al-Naseem. In the 1930s, the extension of an oil pipeline through the area as well as subsequent oil operations demanded new infrastructure and labor, attracting both temporary laborers and merchants (Jordanian and Syrian) to the area in search of economic opportunities (Reimer 2005). After Jordan's independence, local residents were joined by members of the military, who populated bases in the area, and the civil servants, who came to service the new institutions of the government that cropped up as the city grew, among them schools. Today most people in town work for the government—in the military, the police force, the school system, or the civil service—or as small merchants and service providers.[13] As a result of this history, the population is composed of a mix of Bedouin from the area, clans affiliated with one of Jordan's major tribal confederations, as well as citizens from other parts of the country who have settled in pursuit of economic opportunities.

With these stirrings of economic development in and migration to Bawadi al-Naseem, the demand for state services also emerged (Reimer 2005); formal state education soon followed with the first public school in 1947. It was preceded by the establishment of a Roman Catholic school in 1942. Both of these developments mirror the expansion of education in Jordan. Prior to the establishment of the mandate of Transjordan in 1921, schools existed in limited numbers and in select population centers.[14] By 1946, the end of the mandate period, seventy-three public schools existed in Jordan with close to ten thousand pupils enrolled, about 10 percent of them females. Nongovernmental schools continued to outnumber public ones—one hundred were operating at this time—although private schools enrolled fewer pupils, with a total of 6,472 pupils, 2,640 of them girls (Matthews and Akrawi 1949).[15] In the 1950s, the number of government schools began to increase steadily, although slowly at first, with more significant progress in spreading public education in the 1960s and 1970s (al-Tall 1978). By 2008, Jordan had achieved nearly universal enrollment at the primary level with gross enrollment rates at 97 percent for boys and girls. At the secondary level, gross enrollment is 87 percent for boys and 90 percent for girls (UNESCO Institute for Statistics).[16]

By 2005, Bawadi al-Naseem had three girls' high schools—two "academic" ones, including the al-Khatwa Secondary School for Girls and one vocational high school.[17] Jordanian students, male and female, are placed in one of two tracks after the tenth grade (the last year of compulsory schooling), an academic track and a vocational track based on their academic record. The academic track in turn consists of four different streams: scientific, humanities, shari a (Islamic jurisprudence), and information management.[18] At al-Khatwa only two streams—the scientific and the humanities—were offered. The staff informed me that the top third (in terms of grader ranking) of all tenth graders were placed in science, the middle third in humanities, and the bottom third had to go to the vocational high school. Students in the scientific track could switch "down" to humanities; however, students in humanities technically could not switch up. Similarly, girls placed in vocational education had no flexibility, but I was told by teachers and staff that parents would use their contacts to try to get their children out of the vocational track or to move up into the science track. I discuss the implications of this tracking system further in chapter 5.

Another important dimension of the Jordanian educational system is the *tawjihi* exam (actually a series of exams), which determines whether a twelfth grader can attend a public university and which university and which major she may choose. There is a great deal of anxiety around this exam, given its role in deciding one's future and given that only about half of twelfth graders pass. Furthermore, passing *tawjihi* does not guarantee admittance to a public university. For example, in 2006, of the 54,000 students who passed the exam, only 28,000 gained admittance to public universities (*Jordan Times*, July 30, 2006). Today there are many private options for higher education, but their cost is too prohibitive for the majority, and public universities are still considered to be of higher quality. Those with greater financial resources have other alternatives as well. For example, in the public universities, through a system called *mawazi* students can pay a higher rate of tuition to get into a field of study even if they initially scored too low on the *tawjihi* to be admitted.[19] Finally, the wealthiest Jordanians have opted out of the *tawjihi* system altogether, by enrolling in elite schools that prepare students for study abroad. Absent such elite alternatives, the weight of *tawjihi* in determining one's future emerged as an important factor in the expectations of young women at al-Khatwa.

During the 2004–5 academic year, al-Khatwa enrolled approximately 580 students. Of these students, about 25 percent came from surrounding villages, either because their village did not have a high school or because their families felt they would get a better education in Bawadi al-Naseem's schools. About 3 percent of the enrolled students were Christians, while the remaining 97 percent were Sunni Muslims.[20] The large majority of the teachers at al-Khatwa were from Bawadi al-Naseem or neighboring villages; thus, they were products of the local school system themselves.

On the first day of my extended stay at the al-Khatwa School, I saw the school guidance counselor, Rashida. She remembered me from my first visit to the school in 2002. When I explained to her that I would be spending the rest of the school year at al-Khatwa to conduct research, she told me I would be better off going elsewhere. "Go to Amman," she said. "It would be better for you. Nothing happens here for girls." In part, her reaction was a response to the type of questions I had asked in 2002, questions she clearly remembered. When I visited then, I sought to understand the relationship of the experience of school-going to the mobility of adolescent girls and their access to other spaces such as youth groups, Qur'anic centers, and even the market. Recalling my earlier questions, Rashida pointed me elsewhere. "Here," she said, "the girls don't go anywhere." I explained that I was interested in what girls did in school—the social and cultural significance of their time there, the expectations these young women and their families tied to this experience, and the broader national and global narratives about education, women, and development. Over time, I would have to explain myself again and again to many of the Jordanians I met, many of whom were puzzled by my choice of field site and my departure from "traditional" research methods. I was frequently told by locals and others that I would be better off conducting my research in Amman.

I first conducted research in this part of Jordan as a doctoral student in 2002; I had three months between semesters in which I was supposed to wet my feet as an anthropologist. With limited time, I went where I had school-based connections for the ease of access. However, after this initial exploratory research, I decided to continue my work in Bawadi al-Naseem. In part, I chose to do so because as far as I knew, no one had ever conducted anthropological research there. Also, its population was an interesting mix of Jordan's populations (Bedouin, branches of some of the largest tribes, Palestinians, Christians, Syrians, *fallahin* or peasants). Finally, given its limited school options for high school (there were three girls' high schools), the differences in the experiences and effects of education had less to do with particular schools and more to do with the social and economic histories and particular actors.

As Rashida emphasized, life for young people in Bawadi al-Naseem was different from the lives led by youth in the nation's capital, just as any place is distinct. Many of the girls in Bawadi al-Naseem romanticized Amman and held it up as an example of what Bawadi al-Naseem was not. In addition to the greater opportunities for fun and leisure in Amman, several of the girls talked about the greater anonymity life in the capital would afford them. In Amman, they asserted, "No one knew you, or interfered in your personal business." The girls frequently complained that Bawadi al-Naseem was too small—they asserted that everyone was related to or knew everyone else—and that this fueled local gossip about adolescent girls. A group of tenth graders tried to explain this to me one day:

FIDA: I see that some of you stay after classes to talk with your friends on school grounds.

RAND: Yes, some of us do, but most of the times the teachers make you go straight home so you don't make too much noise in the schoolyard.

IBTISAM: The teachers get a bad idea about the girl who stays around after her classes are over. They think she is sticking around because she is waiting for someone [i.e., a boy].

RAND: This society, they see someone walking with a young man and they don't think maybe it's her brother or her uncle. They see you and they say, "Who is she talking to?"

At this statement, the girls got quite riled up. Ibtisam had clearly touched on a point that spoke to them. A bunch of girls jumped up out of their seats, yelling "Yes, it's true! They just want something to talk about." The conversation continued:

ZEYNA: And the mistake of one girl is put on all her friends. They say if one does something wrong, they are all no good.

RAND (trying to explain for my benefit): Our society has a lot to do with this. Bawadi al-Naseem is a conservative town, and we have certain customs and traditions related to women. If you study in Amman, it's different. Your neighbors don't pay attention to you. No one asks about the other. Here the neighbor comes and interferes in everything.

ZEYNA: It's also because of tribalism.[21] If a girl from one clan does something, then people talk about all of the girls from that clan—about the whole clan.

ALA': But tribalism has more benefits than negative aspects. For the boys, for example, if there is a fight with another tribe, they all back each other up.

Here the al-Khatwa students linked the preponderance of family ties in Bawadi al-Naseem to the prevalence of gossip and regular monitoring of their comings and goings. In their efforts to explain to me the constraints on their mobility and the links to gossip, these tenth graders made the link to family, kin, and clan and the ways in which one's actions could reflect on the larger kin group. Yet the girls also viewed kin-based links as important. Ala' specifically talked about the need for the support of kin for physical protection and defense. Given the prevalence of violence in boys' schools and frequent outbreaks of kin or regionally based violence among young men throughout the country, this was not an unrealistic assessment; it also harkens back to a not so distant past in which the need for the physical labor and protection was a matter of survival.[22]

The role of the family and larger kin groupings continues to be paramount in Jordan. The Hashemite regime has bolstered the significance of kin relations ideologically and materially by drawing on familial idioms to construct its own legitimacy (Amawi 2000; Anderson 2001) and by reinforcing tribal-based affiliations in its political maneuvering (Alon 2005; Anderson 1997; Brand 1998; Clark 2006). Andrew Shryock (2004) asserts that the function of tribes has shifted from providing for personal security and protection to providing other forms of security: "a need for 'jobs, money, places in the university, visas to the United States' and . . . the need for security has become a need for *wasta* (connections or an intermediary), for well-placed men who can intervene on your behalf" (54–55). These contacts are equally important for young women when they seek access to scholarships, places in the university, civil service jobs, job transfers, and a range of other favors.[23] In addition, a young woman's actions reflect upon her family, and her family's reputation is important for her future. Many young women in Jordan still expect that their brothers will be their protection for the future, should things go wrong in marriage or should they remain single. Even if in practice the terms of the "patriarchal bargain" in which women submit to the authority of male relatives in exchange for their protection are changing, this ideal and related expectations persist (Kandiyoti 1988; Olmsted 2005a). Thus, kin-based affiliations large and small are particularly relevant phenomena through which to understand contemporary Jordan and the lives of young women there.

Geography was also a significant force in the lives of these girls, and it figured into al-Khatwa students' conceptions of what was possible and even desirable. The ideal of Amman was in many respects just that—an ideal. Amman is made up of many worlds divided by class, geography, and social mores.[24] Although Bawadi al-Naseem is distinct from Amman (as is any other place), in many respects the experiences of young women in Bawadi al-Naseem are not unlike that of many young women around the country, even in Amman. I suggest not that their lives are representative of a majority, but rather that the experiences of the majority are not best captured by images of trendy and upscale restaurants found in parts of Amman that many Jordanians referenced as a point of comparison but that are best known to expats, foreign nationals working for international agencies, and Amman's elite.

When I visited some of these places in Amman in 2005, the contrasts with Bawadi al-Naseem were stark. A trip to Mecca Mall, a popular site for the upper class and some middle-class families,[25] reminded me how prohibitive such a visit could be purely in economic terms. The cost of a coffee in a small café in the mall was about 2 dinars ($2.86). The starting salary of a teacher at the time in Jordan was 180 dinars (about $257 per month). At this price, a cup of coffee would be out of reach to an average Jordanian family, let alone the indoor gym and play space to which I took my daughters, which charged 8 dinars ($11.44) per child. For most of the families I knew in Bawadi al-Naseem, the coffee would represent an unnecessary luxury, even for those who were better off financially, given college tuitions, private lessons, and examination fees to pay. Indeed, the large majority of Jordanian families, where the average annual income for the household was 5,589 dinars in 2003 (Department of Statistics), would find a 2 dinar cup of coffee to be excessively luxurious.[26]

Bawadi al-Naseem was characterized by much greater diversity than the stereotypical images of it that I often heard conveyed in Amman. Although many of the al-Khatwa students felt it was too small and too conservative, the expectations and opportunities for the al-Khatwa students could vary considerably. The different opportunities available to young women had as much to do with socioeconomic status and their parents' education and professional status as with gendered expectations. These realities could also converge with other factors such as national origin, number of children in the family, and the involvement of extended family in the day-to-day decisions that impacted a young woman. A brief look at the lives of five al-Khatwa students—Indira, Reem, Hiba, Haneen, and Yasmine—provides glimpses of the structures and circumstances that shaped their lives, and how they and their families responded to these configurations.

Indira

Indira was an eleventh grader from a well-known Jordanian clan with roots in Bawadi al-Naseem. Her father was a respected doctor with his own practice, and her mother was a school administrator. She was one of six siblings with one older sister in twelfth grade and four younger brothers. Her family had lived in the United Arab Emirates, where her father had migrated for work for several years prior to returning to Jordan, and Indira longed for what she saw as a freer life there. In part she wanted to be free of the gaze of her larger extended family and what she perceived to be the incessant gossip in Bawadi al-Naseem. Indira was a top student—a school star—and was frequently called upon to represent the school for special events and to participate in a variety of academic competitions on behalf of the school. She was charismatic, social, and well-liked. But when I spoke with her, the disenchantment she felt about education and what she viewed as the false promises of education for women became apparent. Indira believed that education was supposed to give girls greater equality with boys; however, according to her, education had not delivered: "I wish things hadn't changed. Long ago a girl knew she was a girl and that she would never become . . . she did not even dream to be like a boy. So they let girls be educated but they did this against girls' interests, because a girl now dreams." Indira had no concerns about going to college. She had the grades and was in the prestigious scientific track, and her family had the resources. However, Indira wanted more—greater mobility and autonomy. Education had not afforded her that.

Reem

Reem was part of a group of rambunctious tenth graders who were so close that they had all pledged to become police officers if they passed *tawjihi* so that they could stay together. Reem was one of seven siblings. Her father, who was deceased, was originally from Palestine; he came to Jordan in 1967 but never gained citizenship. As a result, although Reem's mother was a Jordanian citizen, Reem and her siblings were not.[27] They were deprived of many free public services, such as education, as well as access to certain jobs.[28] Her mother worked at a low-level civil service job. Her oldest brother dropped out of school in the sixth grade to work, and her oldest sister married after finishing high school and moved to Amman. According to Reem, her sister in Amman was quite unhappy. Another sister had passed the national high school exam but was at home trying to find work so that she could save money to go to the university; as a noncitizen she had to pay a higher rate of tuition. She was considering taking a job in a factory in one of the free-trade zones near Amman, but the hour-and-a-half commute discouraged her. Another sister, Layal, had left school in the tenth grade, according to her family because of a conflict with her principal.

Reem and her younger siblings were all in school, but Reem struggled with her schoolwork and was in danger of failing at least one class. Although she seemed to have fun with her friends, at times she felt "lonely" at school. She was very attached to her sisters and talked about the great times she had with them at home. She said they often listened to music and danced late into the night. However, her older sister had started attending religion classes at a local Islamic center and refused to partake in the music and dancing any longer because she now believed this was forbidden in Islam. For Reem it was hard to imagine what might come next in life. Although she talked about how important it was for a woman to complete her education and to work so "her husband would not boss her around," the possibility of her being able to do so was small. Her grandmother thought that she should marry, but Reem said she would not marry young. However, given her grades and her economic situation it was unlikely she would go on to college, if she even finished high school.

Hiba

Hiba was an eleventh grader considered to be a good student by her teachers. Her family was well off financially, and she enjoyed much support from home to complete her studies. When I asked, she said she wanted to be a journalist because this would enable her to travel and mix with other people. When we discussed this career choice with her mother one day, her mother said such work would be difficult for a girl because of the traveling involved. Hiba had two older sisters, one of whom was a teacher who was working on a master's degree in English linguistics and the other who completed her bachelor's degree in physics. Her older brother had failed the *tawjihi* and refused to repeat it. He was working in his father's business.

Hiba and her family lived in a newer part of town where large and sometimes lavish homes had been built, reflecting the good economic situation of her family. Her father was from a prominent local family and had taken over his father's business. Despite being obviously wealthy, Hiba's mother was embarrassed that neither she nor her husband had completed their education. Hiba's paternal uncle, her father's older brother, was studying to be an engineer in the United States, and as a result her father was needed to help with the family business. Hiba's mother stopped her education after *tawjihi* and married shortly thereafter. Of herself and her husband she said, "No one encouraged us to complete our education, but we encourage our daughters to finish and go on for higher degrees." Financially, they had the means to afford their daughters that opportunity.

Haneen

Haneen was a shy eleventh grader. Her father left school in the eighth grade to help support his family after his father died. He joined the military and retired after many years of service. After a brief stint working in the private sector, he returned to the military as a civil servant. When I met Haneen, her father was about to leave for the United States to try to improve their financial situation; however, he returned after a short time, having been unable to find a job and missing his family. Haneen's mother left school in the eleventh grade to marry, a decision she said she regretted. She worked as a volunteer for a local charity and also as a religion teacher at a local state-sponsored Islamic center. When I met her she was participating in a course to become an official Islamic education teacher.[29]

Haneen was one of five siblings. She had an older sister in the university and an older brother in a postsecondary training program for forensic science. Haneen was in the science track and said she wanted to be an engineer. Previously she had wanted to be a police investigator because her favorite TV program was about a private investigator, but she told me that she realized this was unrealistic. Haneen loved school and her mother joked that she would threaten to keep her home to keep her in line. Once, Haneen's father had seriously threatened to withdraw her from school because of a misunderstanding that led him to believe she was in a relationship with a boy. The misunderstanding was cleared up, and her mother made such threats only jokingly. Haneen's mother was adamant that she wanted her children and especially her daughters to be educated. On this topic she said to me, "Girls in Jordan face a lot of injustice, and their education will give them more independence. A woman who works does not have to ask for money. Work builds her character . . . gives her more strength." Although the economic situation of the family was difficult, because Haneen's father had been in the military she was guaranteed a scholarship should she get the grades to go to college. When I last spoke to Haneen's mother, she had opened a small shop with her husband to help supplement the family's income. However, Haneen was struggling at the university and had to repeat several classes that she had failed—repetition that her scholarship would not pay for. She was to graduate in 2011 but failed another class in her last semester. Nevertheless, her parents continued to pay her tuition in the hopes that she would graduate.

Yasmine

When I first met Yasmine in 2002, she was fifteen years old and all she wanted to do was talk about the World Cup games. She was an avid soccer fan, popular among her peers, and a less than enthusiastic student. She was one of the first girls to invite me to her home, and since that time I have come to know her family well. Her family struggled financially, and her mother, Um Waleed, was the primary breadwinner, working at several informal jobs as well as one low-level salaried job. Of her four sons, all older than Yasmine, only one had passed *tawjihi*; however, his grades did not afford him the chance to enter the public university, so he enrolled in a local community college, dropping out soon after. The other brothers worked in the military or public security services but, according to one of Yasmine's teachers, did very little to help support the family.

Yasmine's mother had very little schooling and married at a young age. Although she had hoped her sons would continue their education beyond high school, none had been able to for lack of grades or motivation. Given the family's poor economic situation and Yasmine's seeming lack of interest in school, I assumed that she would marry soon after high school if she even got that far in her education. When I returned to Jordan in 2005 I learned otherwise; Yasmine had passed *tawjihi* and was enrolled in her first year at the nearby public university. Indeed she came to see me at least twice seeking help with her English homework. Her mother continued to work hard to ensure that she could stay in school. At the same time she was diligently working her social networks to help secure a job for her son who had dropped out of community college.

These snapshots of students and their families at al-Khatwa give a small indication of the diversity in class, national origin, family background, and personal experiences of the young women who appear in these pages. They also illuminate some of the important developments that explain Jordan's current circumstances: Indira's family's wealth, enabled by migration to the Gulf; Indira's frustration with the lack of gendered equality; Reem's lack of citizenship, the dislocation of her family, the death of her father, and her sister's newfound religiosity; the economic challenges faced by Haneen's family and the security provided by military service; Hiba's mother's embarrassment about her and her husband's lack of education; Yasmine's mother's tireless labor to try to ensure that at least one of her children would get to college. Each provides part of the story about what it might mean to be an educated girl in Jordan today and what education can and cannot guarantee.

Bawadi al-Naseem has one of the highest poverty rates in the country.[30] The broader governorate in which Bawadi al-Naseem is located had a poverty rate of over 30 percent in 1997 (World Bank 2004). In 2003, the government estimated that the poverty rate had decreased to about 25 percent (Department of Statistics). However, several of the government-identified "poverty pockets," where the most extreme rates of poverty are found nationally, are located in rural areas in the vicinity of Bawadi al-Naseem (Ministry of Planning and International Cooperation). Although class distinctions were not as pronounced as they appeared to be in the capital, where conspicuous consumption could provide stark contrasts, they existed. The most obvious distinction was between the professional class and an "unskilled" working class that was typically poorer, although those with professional jobs were not always better off financially. The distinction between these two groups had as much to do with the social status that came with their professions and education as it did with income. Thus, for example, Hiba's mother was embarrassed about her lack of education and her husband's line of work—a "trader" as she put it—even though they were clearly quite wealthy by local standards. Indeed the status of being educated is one that Jordanians—ordinary citizens and state representatives—have embraced wholeheartedly both for the economic returns that citizens and the regime hope education will proffer (in the language of the state and its foreign funders this is typically framed as investment in human resources for a resource-poor country), and for the status it confers upon individuals, their families, communities, and the state (Jansen 2006).

Economic circumstances and opportunities could also be shaped by other factors such as dislocations and displacements, as in the case of Palestinians who were forced out of their homes and ended up in Jordan. Today, Jordan is home to the largest number of officially registered Palestinian refugees, who number 1.9 million.[31] However, not all Palestinians are refugees; they vary in class, place of residence, and experiences of dispossession. Most of those who are officially refugees also have Jordanian citizenship. However, some, like Reem's father, who fled from Gaza in 1967, were not granted citizenship, and as a result of the "Nationality Law," which decrees that citizenship can be passed on only by the father, Reem too was without citizenship (Amawi 2000). In the aftermath of the First Gulf War (1990–91), Jordan faced another major population influx; the "returnees," as they were referred to despite the fact that many of them had never lived in Jordan, numbered as many as three hundred thousand (van Hear 1995). Most of these Jordanian citizens who had been working in the Gulf at the time of the First Gulf War were of Palestinian origin. Some returned with significant financial resources that were invested in a real estate boom in Amman in the 1990s (van Hear 1995). However, for other families, like that of Jenine, an al-Khatwa student I discuss later in this book, expulsion was devastating in economic terms. Recently, Jordan has seen another major demographic shift with the influx of between four hundred thousand and five hundred thousand Iraqis since the U.S. invasion of Iraq in 2003 (Fafo Institute 2007; Sassoon 2009).[32] The long-term impact of such a dramatic influx has yet to be seen, although clearly for a country as small and resource poor as Jordan, this most recent population shift taxes the existing infrastructure. Although some of these Iraqis came with considerable resources, the majority today are poor, and most lack legal status in Jordan (Sassoon 2009). For young Palestinians like Reem and Jenine, life continues to be a struggle three generations after their families were dispossessed. As with the young Palestinian refugees near Amman that Randa Farah (2005) profiles in her research, education remains a goal, but the experiences of poverty and dispossession have tempered their expectations of its rewards. Reem's situation was compounded by the death of a parent. As anywhere, the death, illness, or disability of a parent leaves a family vulnerable, as does the rupture of traditional family structures—what the principal of the school, Um Nabeel, called "broken families" in a direct translation of the

English term. The principal spoke of the vulnerability of such families, and particularly female-headed households,[33] which resulted from death of the husband, divorce, abandonment, and in some cases polygamy. Yasmine's family was seemingly still intact, but her father was largely absent and did not contribute to the financial upkeep of the family.

Female-headed households could face financial difficulties and social stigma; however, not all female-headed households found themselves in such a situation. Some, like the family of Dunya, an eleventh grader whose father had died before she was born, were quite well off. Dunya's mother was a teacher, and her paternal uncles also ensured they were well taken care of. Furthermore, some divorced mothers worked outside the home and had the support of their own families. At the same time, divorced women and their children were often at the mercy of their extended family members and could face significant financial insecurity. The terms of divorce, women's rights to a divorce, and rights to alimony payment have been persistent sources of debate in Jordan among judges, women's rights advocates, and Islamists. For example, in 2001, the king pushed through a temporary law that allowed for *khul'*, the right for a woman to divorce without her husband's consent if she relinquishes her dowry and all financial claims upon her estranged spouse. In 2010, the law still had not been made permanent, and drafts for a new personal status law excluded *khul'*. The 2010 debates about *khul'* led to protests from some women's groups. Female Islamists, however, came out in support of the abolishment of *khul'*, arguing that this form of divorce jeopardized the family (*Jordan Times*, April 29, 2010). From the perspective of many in Jordan, threats to the family and Jordan's authenticity as an Arab and Muslim nation are numerous. The protection of the family, and women as the center of the family, continue to be pivotal to securing Jordan's identity. The concern with protecting family in Jordan has also been fueled by a discourse of "marriage crisis," namely, the inability or reluctance of young people to get married for economic reasons and as a result of social transformations (among them increased levels of education) that lead young people to delay marriage.[34] I discuss this more extensively in chapter 5.

On a different front, Reem's family had been touched by other developments in the region, namely, new forms of religiosity and new institutions of religious pedagogy in the form of piety movements and their related institutions. In Jordan, as throughout the region, religion has entered daily life in myriad new ways, from modern forms of Islamic dress, to media programming, to increased mosque attendance and new venues for Islamic education, to the way in which social relations are conducted. The presence of piety or *da'wa* organizations in Bawadi al-Naseem, such as the one Reem's sister had recently begun attending for religion classes when I met them, was evidence of such developments.[35] *Da'wa* literally means "call, invitation, or summons" and refers to the process of calling someone to Islam. Typically the work of these organizations, as I observed it, consisted of calling Jordanian Muslims to be more committed and pious through teaching about Islam in a variety of settings.[36] These groups were considered by many Jordanians to be more conservative in their interpretations of Islamic teachings on a range of issues from women's dress, to the mixing of the sexes, to music, to television watching. A number of students at al-Khatwa were involved in *da'wa* groups outside of school, and at least one student, Amina, viewed the school as an important space for her *da'wa* work. As I discuss in chapter 4, the school was also a primary space in the state's own efforts to control religious discourse and to protect youth from what the state considered religious extremism.

Developing Jordanian Women

Women in our society suffer from the underlying issues which extend from our past ages . . . the most important of them absolutely was the lack of education and culture. For now, Jordan has advanced a lot in this sector, and we only need to correct some of the issues. . . . Indeed women in the time of the Prophet participated in fighting and reciting Hadith. . . . Thus I do not find any objections to giving women all of their rights; and hence, I support her entrance into parliament.

The mother who shakes the bed with her right, shakes the world with her left, and with this starting point I say that the woman who tries to be far from the nature of her work and her natural position relinquishes her basic and holy duty, and it is to prepare and raise her children, raising them righteously and soundly and fostering in their souls a love of the homeland and its people and sacrifice on their behalf.

—*Al-bab al-maftuh* (the open door) column
(*Al-Rai*, January 19, 1975; January 20, 1975)

The situation of women in Jordan today cannot be understood outside the historical events and political and economic context I have just outlined. As in many parts of the region, gender roles and relations have witnessed significant change in the past few decades, and women, women's issues, and the role of women in Jordanian society continue to be integral to efforts to define progress, authenticity, and legitimacy. A key component of the state's modernizing project has been the expansion of state schooling and the education of girls. Over a century ago, throughout the Middle East, those who argued urgently for the schooling of girls—missionaries, colonizers, and local reformers—contended that girls' education was critical for modernization, as much of the discourse about modernizing, developing, and keeping up with the West focused on the backwardness of women or the oppression of women by men in Arab Muslim societies (Abu-Lughod 1998; Ahmed 1992; Amin [1899] 1992; Booth 1998; Najmabadi 1998a; Shakry 1998). These early educational efforts centered on the role of women as mothers of modern citizens, as well as household managers in the newly conceived private domestic sphere, with the "modern bourgeoisie family" upheld as the model to emulate (Abu-Lughod 1998: 256). The notion of the "couple" and companionate marriage emerged alongside these efforts to educate women, for a schooled woman was seen as the best companion for an educated man, as I discuss further in chapter 5 (Amin [1899] 1992). Access to school and literacy opened up new spheres of opportunity and potential, even if the "positive" effects of this schooling were not immediately apparent. However, like other modern bureaucracies, schools also served as a mechanism of control (Foucault 1977; Najmabadi 1998a). But even in this role educational efforts are paradoxical, as schools serve to control girls and protect perceived gendered norms while simultaneously complicating the terms of gendered respectability.

In many respects, the contexts for women's education today have changed dramatically in the past century as a result of urbanization, increased levels of education for men and women, and an increased role for women in public institutions and spaces. Yet efforts to examine the role of contemporary schooling in constructing new images of womanhood have been quite limited. The existing literature on schools in the Middle East is largely confined to an analysis of curriculum and/or public debates about education policy and content. Little scholarly attention has been focused on the ways in which educational policies are enabled or resisted at the local level. The research that addresses girls' education has tended to focus on gender bias in curricular content, enrollment of girls in particular fields, and school-to-work transitions.[37] Not enough attention has been paid to the day-to-day micropractices in schools that shape the gendered expectations and practices of young women and their relationship to the larger debates and power struggles within Jordan today (Heward and Bunwaree 1999). Schools are critical places for young women, and the meaning and status tied to schooling have far greater significance than existing research has conveyed.

Since the drive toward mass public schooling began in the late 1950s, Jordan has made major strides in enrolling girls and boys in school. Net enrollment rates at the secondary level and at the tertiary level are higher for girls and have been for over a decade now (UNESCO Institute for Statistics). In addition, dropout rates have been higher for boys in some areas, reflecting the pull of the labor market for males who are not doing well in school and/or whose families are in difficult economic circumstances (R. Farah 2005). Parents in Bawadi al-Naseem frequently complained to me about their sons who refused to study or to repeat their *tawjihi* exam. Thus, judged by girls' access to education, Jordan fares quite well, particularly in comparison to other countries in the region. The discourse surrounding the need to educate women is increasingly buttressed by a booming development industry that has been focused on empowering women and enjoys significant royal patronage. Indeed, many "local" NGOs are actually "royal" NGOs or RNGOs, most of them under the patronage of women in the royal family, most prominently Princess Basma, Queen Rania, and the former Queen Noor (Brand 1998; Wiktorowicz 2000). Today in Jordan, one finds weekly if not daily press coverage of workshops and conferences for women—to encourage their political development, to develop their entrepreneurial skills, to protect them against violence. These events are usually funded by foreign donors, organized under the tutelage of the royal family, and staffed by a new class of globalized Jordanian professionals. Indeed, a quick review of images of women in the official newspapers in Jordan in the first few months of 2005 found that the large majority of women that made front-page news were women of the royal family, some female ministers, or poor rural women in the process of receiving aid from the king or queen.

The actual impact of such development initiatives and of the very public displays of "developed" women on women's lives in Jordan is unclear. But the image that is being presented publicly, with women from the royal family front and center, is a clear one—the image of a modern and developed Jordanian woman. Alyce Abdalla (2000) in her study of one of the most well known aid projects for women, the Beni Hamida Women's Weaving Project for poor women, argues that the women who are meant to benefit from these projects might well be considered exploited labor rather than beneficiaries. She argues that the skills women are given are not marketable and that the women are given little power to make decisions about production, marketing, or even shades of color. According to Abdalla, the NGO sponsor of the project (initially the Queen Noor al-Hussein Foundation, which later became the Jordan River Foundation under the tutelage of Queen Rania) marketed their products to foreigners and employed designs and materials not indigenous to Jordan, leaving the project unsustainable. Andrew Shryock (2004) writes about the objections of local men to the exploitation of their female relatives in another such project in the Balqa region. He argues that "many people in nearby Balgawi villages suspect that their girls are being used as cheap labor or, worse, as bait to attract tourists and foreign aid" (46). As Shryock argues, in such development projects, women function to represent that which is authentic—village girls making handicrafts—so that NGOs can market Jordanian traditions for tourist consumption. In addition, as an example of the economic empowerment of poor women, they also stand for progress (48).

For the al-Khatwa students and teachers, direct exposure to and involvement in such development-inspired projects and workshops varied. A select few of the girls, among them Indira, were chosen to represent the school at development workshops held in town, such as the UNICEF workshop for youth leaders. The teachers and staff at al-Khatwa were regularly pulled into workshops and meetings related to the latest educational reform efforts and typically sponsored by some foreign or multilateral donor. Although they at times benefited from these workshops, picking up new skills, typically such workshops were viewed as impositions or an inconvenience, and not particularly useful in the classroom. One education administrator complained about the excessive amount of time she devoted to meeting delegation after delegation of education officials and donors who came through to visit schools. She felt it detracted from the proper functioning of her school.

Thus, in Jordan today, one finds a plethora of official public discourse in support of the development and empowerment of women as critical to Jordan's progress. But like the aid-supported projects and workshops that are meant to create a "democratic culture" in Jordan, high-profile workshops do not necessarily produce tangible change, even with the best of intentions and efforts on the part of the royal women. This not to say that the gendered dimensions of men and women's lives are stagnant—they are not. And, indeed the spread of education has been one key factor in the transformation of gender relations, the institution of marriage, and the expectations of young men and women and their families. The economic challenges of the current era, particularly after Jordan's implementation of structural adjustment and privatization, which began in the 1980s, and the decreases in remittances and migration in the aftermath of the First Gulf War in the early nineties, have also had their gendered implications.

Although the regime continues to pursue a policy of expanding educational opportunity for women and framing their "development" as key to national development in very public ways, the record of the regime in other arenas has been one of caution, particularly with regard to women's legal status. According to Laurie Brand (1998), under King Hussein, "placating, or at least not challenging the forces—tribal, Islamist, or simply socially conservative—upon which the legitimacy of the regime rests, has been the most constant feature of palace policy [toward women]" (149). Very few changes have been made in the personal status laws that continue to legislate women as dependents, or in the nationality law that does not allow a woman to pass on her nationality to her children, although there have been efforts by women's organizations and activists to change these laws (Brand 1998; Clark 2006). Personal status laws are particularly salient here, because in Jordan, and throughout the region, debates about these personal status laws or family law are the occasion for the most explicit and politicized debates about women. These laws govern a range of issues from marriage and divorce, to custody of children, to the rights of husband and wife and polygamy. In a postindependence era throughout the Middle East, attempts to change these laws have been the source of intense debates about Islam and what is religiously accepted, about authenticity and culture, and about human rights and the nature of the Jordanian polity.

When King Abdullah II initially took power, there were some indications that he was committed to taking a stronger stance on women's legal status in Jordan. In 1999, the government was directed by the king to review article 340 of the penal code, which allowed for reduced sentencing for crimes of "honor." Activists in Jordan had been lobbying for the abolition of this article for some time, and a renewed campaign against this code began in 1999. The king's cabinet approved such an amendment, but it was rejected by parliament. When the king disbanded parliament in 2001, the amendment was passed as a temporary law, one among many that the king pushed through during this period. Also during this period, an amendment to the personal status law, granting women the right to a divorce (*khul'*), was passed as a temporary law. Both temporary laws were rejected by parliament when it was reconvened in 2003 (Clark 2006).[38] According to Janine Clark, Princess Basma personally lobbied for the passage of *khul'*, meeting with parliamentarians and community and religious leaders (549). Despite these efforts, opposition to *khul'* persisted as late as the spring of 2010 (*Jordan Times*, February 21, 2008; April 28, 2010; April 29, 2010). Thus, the new monarch came into power making some efforts to change legislation and grant greater equality to women under the law; however, most of these efforts eventually failed. One significant change under Abdullah II has been to create a quota for women in parliament to ensure some female political representation. However, beyond this quota system, other changes in the legal status of women have not been legislated.

Some observers of these gender-related developments under the Hashemite monarchy, and particularly under Abdullah II, depict an enlightened monarch whose hands are tied. For example, the Programme on Governance in the Arab Region (POGAR), a UNDP agency, states:

> The Jordanian monarchy is being pulled in opposite directions by two competing political forces on issues concerning the status of women in the country. Since the mid-1980s, the nation's political liberalization has increased mobilization by both Islamic conservatives and women's rights groups. In recent years, the Jordanian government has achieved some gradual reforms despite Islamic opposition.

In some respects this is an apt assessment; however, this characterization is problematic in two respects. The first is to frame this conflict as one solely between the regime and Islamists, when opposition to such amendments has come from different corners, including the tribal leaders who have traditionally been viewed as the regime's allies. In addition, in the past, Christian lawmakers have supported legislation considered to be unfavorable to women in the area of inheritance rights (Brand 1998). Second, the assumption reflected here that the regime cannot afford to push these issues too far given the difficult political situation it faces is unconvincing. The regime has pushed forward many equally politically fraught programs, most recently normalization of relations with Israel and support for the U.S. invasion of Iraq, as well as economic policies such as increased taxation of goods and services, removal of subsidies, and privatization (Alyssa 2007; Greenwood 2003b; Ryan 2004; Schwedler 2002). In fact, Clark (2006) attributes the tenor of the political debates surrounding the legislative issues just discussed to a political climate engendered by opposition to Jordan's peace treaty with Israel, especially after the start of the Second Intifada. Opposition forces, Islamists, and leftists mobilized against the policy of normalizing relations with Israel and against increasing Western influence over Jordan's foreign policies and related pressure for reform of education.[39] As Clark (2006) points out, "The debate surrounding these three amendments soon became associated with Western interference, undemocratic practices, and declining morality" (551). Thus, gender politics emerged at the center of political contests in Jordan and at the "heart of the symbolic battleground over which issues of identity are being contested and constructed" (Clark 2006: 540). Gender issues, then, are indeed political and controversial, and the regime at times sacrifices its commitment to policies supporting equal rights for men and women to other political goals.

Conclusion

Faced with regional conflict and instability, growing religiosity of different political persuasions, as well as economic difficulties, the state has been engaged in an ongoing process of making and remaking itself—of exerting its hegemony over its citizens. Like many newly independent states, Jordan has sought to expand and consolidate state power through state-led development and the expansion of state institutions and apparatuses, among them schools. It has also constructed its legitimacy by asserting Islamic, tribal, and Arab credentials. However, this legitimacy has been challenged by increasing poverty and lack of economic opportunities for the majority, demographic realities, the continued escalation of regional conflicts, and the struggles to exert religious authority.

It is this history and these recent developments that shape the national and local contexts in which young Jordanian women enter adolescence and try to sort out their place and identity. School is the space in which they encounter the state most directly, even while sometimes encountering discourses that implicitly challenge the state. It is a public arena that plays a significant part in how they define themselves as Jordanians, Muslims, and young women—to their peers, teachers, families, and selves. Jordan, a resource-poor country, has placed many of its hopes in education. Most young women in Bawadi al-Naseem share these hopes—for a better life, a more secure economic situation, a good marriage, and the respect accorded to those who are educated. Nonetheless, many are discouraged, reading dismal prospects into the difficult economic situation and the limited job opportunities in Bawadi al-Naseem. Some girls like Indira are also frustrated by the seemingly slow-to-shift cultural barriers, while for others the obstacles are linked to individual family histories and challenges faced in their everyday lives. Some seek alternatives in Islam, others place all their hopes in marriage, and still others, despite their pessimism, see education as the only hope—"a weapon in the hands of a girl," as so many of the girls put it, in uncertain times. The political conflicts surrounding changes in women's legal status are intimately linked to the experiences of these young women. The political discourse surrounding these legislative changes both encapsulate local gendered struggles and contribute to shaping both the opportunities that education will provide and the obstacles that education cannot overcome.

The state is keenly aware of the importance of the educational arena, as states around the world are, for building loyal citizens and creating a shared vision for Jordan, and it tries to coopt new popular sentiments into this vision. Yet as a recent body of literature has shown, the state never has complete control over its local institutions. In fact, schools and the content of curriculum to be taught in schools are often among the most contested arenas in a society (Herrera 2000; Kaplan 2006; Mazawi 2002). In the chapter that follows, I will examine some of the state's efforts to construct loyal citizens at al-Khatwa through rituals, symbols, and performance. Like the very public debates about the rights and legal status of Jordanian women just outlined, these school-based patriotic projects reveal the ways in which women's status and their bodies are made to signify the nation, its progress, and its authenticity. This examination will reveal the contested terms of citizenship, faith, and respectability for women in Jordan today.

THREE

Performing Patriotism: Rituals and Moral Authority in a Jordanian High School

We are still singing and dancing

It was late February of 2005 and a staff person from the local Ministry of Education had come to the school.[1] He was sitting with some school administrators talking about upcoming patriotic celebrations that he was helping to organize. I hadn't been there when he first arrived so I asked about the nature of these celebrations.

FIDA: What is the occasion for these celebrations?

STAFF PERSON: The king's birthday.

FIDA: I thought the king's birthday was a few weeks ago.

STAFF PERSON: Yes, it was, but each governorate takes turns celebrating and it is our turn. We will have a parade and all the students will march.

BASHIRA (SCHOOL SECRETARY): All the girls? Can't we send some of them out? Not all of them will be willing to go anyway. They will say their parents won't allow it or their brothers will give them a hard time if they walk in the parade.

FIDA: So what do you do in this case?

BASHIRA: Well, we know which girls are telling the truth because we know their families. Some of them lie to try and get out of marching. We have marches frequently. Last spring we had a march in support of the king after a terrorist plot was uncovered in Jordan and the suspects were arrested. The king gave a speech after these events and the march was to show support for him.[2]

DIA (TEACHER): Families usually do not have a problem with their daughters participating. The school collaborates with the wider society; we work together.

FIDA: Who calls for such marches?

BASHIRA: The ministry in Amman.

At this point the staff person from the ministry office, who appeared uncomfortable with the conversation, rose and left the room. The others who remained continued the conversation.

TAMARA (TEACHER): There will be an event at the municipal hall to celebrate the king's birthday too. The Ministry of Education office here calls us up and requests that we send students to such events. Do you have similar celebrations and holidays in the U.S.?

FIDA: Yes, we do, but less than here, or maybe it's less overt.[3]

TAMARA: So you have progressed. You are past the phase of singing and dancing.

Upon first entering the al-Khatwa Secondary School for Girls in Bawadi al-Naseem in 2005, national symbols met my eye. The halls were decorated with pictures of the current king, Abdullah II, his father, the late King Hussein, and in some places Abdullah II's great-grandfather Abdullah I.[4] Pictures of Hussein, who ruled for over forty-five years before his death in 1999, were just as numerous as those of the current king. In the photos, the royal attire varied from Western business suits to military uniforms to more "traditional" dress, namely, the male head cover—the *hatta* and the *'iqal*. Each form of dress conveyed a particular image of leadership. The photos of the two kings—father and son—were often hung together, conveying an image of continuity between the two. Also prominent throughout the school were signs and symbols of King Abdullah's "Jordan First" campaign, an initiative launched in 2002 whose stated intention has been to put Jordan's priorities first in a time of escalating regional crises (Greenwood 2003a, 2003b; Ryan 2004).

The deployment of such national symbols is particularly pervasive in schools, as they are crucial sites for inculcating national loyalties. Indeed, the importance of modern educational institutions in the building of national cohesion has been a central tenet of the literature on schooling for nearly a century (Durkheim 1956, 1961). Yet national symbols are not without ambiguity. In Jordan, the terms of Jordanian national identity continue to be contested, a reality that leads to persistent efforts on the part of the regime and its representatives to solidify, constitute, and at times reconstitute what it means to be Jordanian through rituals and performances in schools—through "singing and dancing." Paradoxically, however, these efforts can serve to challenge the dominant national narrative of legitimacy. The ambiguity of the symbolic content of patriotic performances and rituals, as well as the need to reinforce, impose, and reconstitute the terms of a seemingly hegemonic national narrative by means of such rituals, can work to weaken their effect. In particular, at al-Khatwa, the regular and very public participation of young women in patriotic performances and the controversy that their participation elicited served to highlight competing moral projects and challenge a narrative of regime legitimacy that rests on moral authority and the ability to deliver on the promises of modernity.

Women have been at the center of the Jordanian regime's public discourse about development, with images of what the "modern" Jordanian woman could or should be proliferating in the official media and performances.[5] Among the venues for such displays are official speeches and platforms, television public service announcements, high-profile workshops sponsored by international development organizations, and the almost daily media coverage of the very public activities of women in the royal family. These images are meant to educate the Jordanian public about forms of citizenship and participation in the nation's development and the particular role women should play in these processes. Yet the role that women should have in Jordan today continues to be a source of much debate, and official policies vis-à-vis women have been inconsistent (Amawi 2000; Brand 1998). Gender roles and the status of women continue to be integral to constructions of national and religious authenticity, while simultaneously the development of women stands as a marker of the nation's progress (Abu-Lughod 1998; Ahmed 1992; Kandiyoti 1991).[6] The circulation of these competing gendered narratives, and the material and ideological constraints that shape their actualization, present strong contradictions for many young women. Women and their bodies serve as both symbols and actors in the struggles for moral legitimacy and the authority to define progress.

Drawing on ethnographic evidence, this chapter argues that the ambiguities of national symbols, particularly when read through a gendered analysis, function to challenge the regime's national narrative and its efforts to be authoritative. Schools are critical in this respect, both as a stage for regime-sponsored performances of its narrative and displays of state power and paradoxically, as a space for the diffusion and potential weakening of the terms of the state discourse. In the labor of implementing state-mandated patriotic performances and rituals, representatives of the state (local bureaucrats and state educators) at times highlight the tenuous nature of their symbolic content and open the door for resistance to the intended meanings. The opening vignette is indicative of such power struggles. The king, the epicenter of the Jordanian national narrative, was threatened by alleged terrorist plots, and students were made to march as a show of support for their leader. The king's birthday, a much less dramatic event, enjoined similar performances. However, these mandated displays of loyalty did not unfold without incident; not all of the girls agreed to march, some because they were uninterested and others because their male relatives objected to their marching through the streets on display, objections that were not necessarily religious in nature. Some found the mandate to march a sign of weakness rather than power. Indeed, such performances emboldened alternative narratives that also vied for the power to shape the symbolic content of the performances of young women.

At al-Khatwa these tensions were as evident in the quotidian rituals performed halfheartedly each day during the morning assembly as they were in extraordinary events such as the xenophobic speech of an eleventh-grade girl at a patriotic celebration. Although less spectacular, the daily ritual of the school morning assembly was rife with the national symbols upon which the regime has built its legitimacy (Arab nationalism, Islam, and loyalty to the king) for decades. In tandem with the fluctuations of state-building, such rituals are recrafted to reflect new realities and new challenges to state authority. In this chapter, I describe the efforts of local bureaucrats to "enforce" this daily assembly and the implications of their efforts. I also describe the ways in which the school staff employed this same morning assembly to exert their own moral authority. Finally, I highlight the academic and moral objections to the participation of young women in the singing and dancing for the nation, as well as the rationale given by those who fully embraced such participation. These seemingly innocuous patriotic musical events elicited the tensions embedded in such ritualistic displays of power.

Through ethnographic examples, I demonstrate that the patriotic rituals performed by students may indeed serve to rupture rather than reinforce the symbolic content they are intended to convey. As Aurolyn Luykx (1999) points out in her analysis of state rituals in Bolivian educational institutions: "Schools often operate under the implicit assumption that habituation to a ritual will lead to the absorption of its symbolic content. . . . Though the link between practice and ideology is rarely so direct as such rituals might imply, the *existence* of such a link is the basis of many disciplinary practices. . . . 'Docile bodies' are molded in the hopes that docile minds will follow" (101). In Jordan, the state is not the only one in the business of "molding bodies," nor do the representatives of the state always act in unison. We must consider then what happens when conflicting disciplinary projects come into play in the school arena. The students at al-Khatwa were participants in these struggles: some actively embraced or resisted particular disciplinary projects; others were indifferent to the efforts of various actors to mold them; and still others actively engaged in their own efforts to socialize their peers.

Creating and Recreating National Identity in Jordan

A critical aspect of building loyalty and identification with nations is performative, consisting of rituals, song, dance, and dramatizations designed both to instill patriotism and nationalist sentiments and to display official power. Such performances draw on key symbols and public representations of what comes to be defined by state elites as national culture and work to create a sense of national belonging with its attendant exclusions. These "invented traditions" do the work of connecting people in the present with a shared past, real or imagined (Hobsbawm 1983: 1); ritualization, or "imposed repetition" (4), does the work of establishing this link with the past.

For the Hashemites, a Hijazi family whom the British appointed rulers of Jordan, an important part of creating Jordan and making the Hashemites synonymous with Jordan has been the representation of such a shared past through ritual and patriotic performance, as well as the authoring of a Jordanian historical narrative with them at the center (Anderson 2001). According to Betty Anderson (2005), rituals and public celebrations in the early years of state-building served to "intermingle political ideas with traditional religious and historical celebrations and, by doing so . . . spread new political values" (89–90). She recounts the weekly processions of Amir Abdullah (who would later become King Abdullah I) to the mosque as one of the first ritual performances of the Transjordanian entity (i.e., before the mandate was granted statehood), giving the newly created citizens "a ritual to call their own" (90). King Hussein, Abdullah's grandson, engaged in processions on an even grander scale. Layne (1994) describes the ritual symbolism embedded in Hussein's trips around the country: "King Hussein also rules through movement. . . . [He] regularly engages in royal progresses (ziyara sha'biyya) throughout the country. In 1983 Hussein visited every region in the country, touching base with various constituencies and displaying to the entire country, thanks to national television coverage, the measure of his realm. . . . Hussein travels with bureaucrats and dispenses the fruits of economic development" (146). These national progresses functioned to establish the king as the ultimate provider or gift giver and to remind his subjects of their debt. Central to the Jordanian national narrative has been this construction of the Hashemites as rulers, fathers, and supreme sheikhs over the citizens of Jordan. The Hashemites' role as providers and protectors is continually reinscribed through the high-profile public giving that is meant to ensure loyalty. Customs, dress, music, and artifacts of an imagined tribal past have also been manipulated for this effort (Anderson 2001, 2005; Layne 1994; Massad 2001; Shryock 1997).[7]

Schools and school-related activities are a central stage for the performance of national culture and patriotic sentiment in Jordan as they are across the globe, from the daily Pledge of Allegiance in U.S. schools, to the legislation of patriotism in Japanese schools,[8] to drumming competitions in Ghanaian schools (Coe 2005). Throughout Jordan's short history, schools have served as important playing fields for the struggle between legitimate interpretations of what it means to be Jordanian. Jordanians are taught the Hashemite-centered narrative of their history throughout their formal schooling. They are also enlisted in the performances and rituals that are meant to impart shared national culture, commitments, and values. But the outcome of such state-led efforts in schools is unpredictable, for states and their representatives have no monopoly on the meaning people attach to cultural symbols (Coe 2005; Kaplan 2006; Luykx 1999; Starrett 1998). At al-Khatwa, girls were engaged in rituals and performances that were intended to instill patriotism and support for the regime. But these activities also served to highlight tensions embedded within patriotic images; at al-Khatwa these tensions were most apparent in the conflicts surrounding gendered morality.

"Jordan First": A Civic Education

Jenine and I were on our way out of her classroom when I noticed she was wearing a pendant. Jenine was among the minority of students at al-Khatwa who were of Palestinian origin, and I mistakenly thought the pendant was the map of Palestine. "It's Jordan," she told me. "Jordan First." As I took a closer look at her pendant I saw that the map had "Jordan First" written across it. I asked her if it was difficult for her as a Jordanian of Palestinian descent living in Bawadi al-Naseem (she had previously lived in Amman where the large majority of Jordanian citizens were of Palestinian descent). Fingering the pendant she said, "Yes, that's why I wear this." One of Jenine's classmates, overhearing our conversation, interrupted, "Why should she find it difficult? We make no distinctions." Jenine laughed awkwardly and we continued on our way outside.

Formal lessons about the nation and national loyalty are abundant in Jordanian schools as they have been since the 1950s (Anderson 2001; Dolbee 2008). In 2005, national and civic education was taught as a separate subject in grades 5 through 10 once a week in Jordanian schools. Twelfth graders also took a course called Al-Thaqafa al- Amma (The General Culture), which encompassed civic education lessons as well as Jordanian history and, in particular, the history of the Hashemite family.[9] In earlier grades, civic education was integrated into social studies courses. Lessons about Jordan—its establishment, history, and leaders—were also found in Arabic and English courses. However, some of the most explicit lessons in patriotism existed in the slogans, daily rituals, and patriotic performances that were the substance of everyday interactions and celebrations of the nation. One slogan that circulated widely and that was engraved on Jenine's pendant was "Jordan First."

King Abdullah's "Jordan First" campaign was officially launched by the regime in October 2002 to "deepen the sense of national identity among citizens where everyone acts as partners in building and developing the Kingdom" (Royal Hashemite Court 2008). The official "Jordan First" Document (Jordan First National Commission 2002) emphasizes what is evident from the slogan, that Jordan's interests must be primary and that they must be "in the forefront of all considerations of the State and the homeland, government and civil society." It is a call for Jordan's constituents to focus on Jordan's development and a warning to those who would place their priorities elsewhere. Within the document, the authors make references to Jordan's diversity and to Jordan as a "melting pot" that builds on "Jordanian pluralism as a source of strength." Despite this goal of national inclusion, the dominant message of the primary slogan is simpler: Jordan and Jordan's interests must be first and clearly this has not been the case in the past.

Most analysts link the emergence of the "Jordan First" campaign to regime concerns about domestic objections to policies related to the Palestinian-Israeli conflict and the intensified violence there in the aftermath of the Second Intifada, as well as U.S. plans to invade Iraq (Greenwood 2003a; Lynch 2004; Ryan 2004). King Abdullah, mindful of his late father's fall from favor with the United States during the Gulf War, was preparing to support the U.S. invasion of Iraq in March 2003.[10] Given the unpopularity of this war among Jordanians, the regime worked to draw attention away from it. "Jordan First" was intended to convey a clear message: citizens should unite, look inward, and focus on Jordan's development rather than on regional conflicts. The campaign was framed such that any criticism would be deemed unpatriotic in the hopes of quieting opposition (Schwedler 2002).

When the campaign was initially launched, signs and posters emblazoned with this message emerged throughout the country on billboards, across bridges, and in the offices of state bureaucrats. In schools, teachers told me that they were instructed through a professional development workshop sponsored by the Ministry for Political Development on ways to bring the campaign alive in their classrooms.[11] At the al-Khatwa School, the campaign was most obvious in slogans and signs. Dia, the history teacher at al-Khatwa described in the opening vignette, talked with me about the projects she was asked to undertake with students to promote "Jordan First." Primarily she described creating murals and signs with the "Jordan First" logo and related catchphrases: "Because your freedom is first"; "Because our heritage is first"; "Because your country is first"; "Jordan First." When I asked Dia what she understood "Jordan First" to represent, she explained: "You know we have people here who come from elsewhere and for years Jordan has been focused on problems external to Jordan, and now the government is saying, 'No. We need to focus internally on our own development.'"

The detailed program laid out in the "Jordan First" Document was not readily available in school, nor was there much knowledge of it among the general public. However, the thrust of the message was clear to residents of Bawadi al-Naseem: "We need to focus on our own development" and for too long "others" have distracted us from this task. Others in this context typically referred to Jordanians of Palestinian decent. The majority of Bawadi al-Naseem's residents are "East Bank" Jordanians,[12] although Jordanian citizens of Palestinian descent have also lived there since 1948 and others have relocated to this city over the years. Thus, although Palestinian Jordanians are not a majority as they are in Jordan's main urban centers, they live in Bawadi al-Naseem in significant numbers. Jenine, the young woman wearing the "Jordan First" pendant, was a Palestinian recently moved to the area. She told me she wore the pendant to fit in and so as to prevent anyone from questioning her loyalties.

Increasingly the discourse about "others" in Jordan includes Iraqis, as Jordan has an estimated 500,000 Iraqis, most of whom arrived after 2003 (Fafo Institute 2007). In 2008, increased privatization of public institutions and the inroads of wealthy Arabs investors from the Gulf were also a source of disquiet among Jordanians. Unease about these Gulf Arabs was fueled by the widespread concern that the government was selling off national assets to Gulf investors.[13] Indeed the disquiet about the perceived "selling off of the country" reached such heights that the king felt compelled to print a full-page rebuttal (in bold and large font) in the semi-official newspaper, *Al-Rai*, blaming irresponsible journalism for tarnishing Jordan's record of economic accomplishments, while defending government efforts to privatize some national resources.[14]

The "Jordan First" campaign fits distinctly into the regime's efforts historically to construct a national identity through juxtaposition with other potentially threatening national identities, specifically a Palestinian one. Although the regime has presented this as an effort to focus on Jordan's own development while respecting Jordan's diversity, the campaign can easily be extended to support exclusionary and chauvinistic attitudes. A speech made by Nadine, a twelfth-grade student from a neighboring village, at an Independence Day celebration in 2005 demonstrated how such national slogans can take on a life of their own. Although she never used the phrase "Jordan First," the implications of such a slogan were evident in her nationalistic oration.

On this day, Nadine, one of several young women to perform at this event, approached the podium in the municipal hall where the event was being held. She was poised, reciting her words in a loud and clear voice. She spoke in colloquial Arabic and in the local accent, which contributed to the overall nationalistic sentiment she conveyed. Normally at such events students speak using modern standard Arabic, the formal language used for official speeches, poetry readings, and other formal presentations. Her use of the local dialect had a clear purpose here as it emphasized a particular sense of Jordanianness tied to language.[15] Nadine began her speech by describing the physical space of Jordan and its geography, moving from region to region, finally settling on her own geographic identity. Elevating her voice, she declared, "I am a Jordanian from Tel Yahya. I love you my king, my leader." After describing her own town and briefly referencing all the major cities in Jordan, her oration devolved into sentiments that can only be characterized as xenophobic. She pronounced in a powerful voice, "This country is not for strangers [*gharib*]. It is not for strangers and it is not for those who envy us. We will kick them out. We will cut their necks. . . . This country has no price."

From my knowledge of Jordan, Nadine's speech crossed lines of acceptable public speech.[16] Although I had heard similar sentiments expressed before on occasion in Jordan, never had I heard such xenophobia expressed in such a public forum.[17] Ironically, Nadine came to this event accompanied by her principal, who was Jordanian by marriage; in past years, this principal had complained to me that many of the tensions between her and the teachers were fueled by their prejudice against her as a result of her non-Jordanian origins. Furthermore, the audience consisted of some Jordanian citizens of Palestinian and Syrian origin, as well as some Iraqis. Yet I did not detect a discernible negative reaction in the hall. I can only speculate as to why this was the case. First, the term *gharib*, or stranger, may be ambiguous enough that it avoids direct signification; however, it can easily be interpreted to mean those Jordanian citizens of different national origins. The contentious politics of national identity and nationalist sentiment are alive and well in Jordan today, intermittently bubbling to the surface at soccer matches, in the press, and during day-to-day interactions between citizens. Thus, the sentiments conveyed by Nadine's speech were not entirely extraordinary, although the forum and the context were.

"Jordan First" and its attendant nationalist sentiments are parts of a long history of slogans and campaigns through which the regime has worked to construct a national identity and to garner loyalty for the royal family. As early as the 1920s, local elites called for "Jordan for Jordanians" (Massad 2001: 28; Wilson 1987). After the civil war of 1970, in which Palestinian fighters and their supporters were routed out of Jordan, the trend became "East Bankers First" with preference for hiring "Jordanian Jordanians" in the public sector (Brand 1995: 53). During this period, state representatives also renewed efforts to emphasize a uniquely Jordanian history and heritage, drawing on an idealized tribal past. Both Laurie Brand (1995) and Andrew Shryock (1997) point to a renewed emphasis on Jordanian national identity in the early 1990s, with some of its proponents leaning toward ultranationalism. Thus "Jordan First" is not an isolated discourse but rather in keeping with historical efforts to define and redefine what and who Jordan is.[18]

On some level, we can read Nadine's performance as successful nationalist education. She fully embraced the notion that Jordan must be supreme—"Jordan First"—and that those who stand in the way of Jordan's progress should be dealt with harshly. Furthermore, Nadine embodied, at least in part, the narrative of national progress. She exuded great strength in both her voice and her demeanor throughout the speech, exemplifying the image for Jordanian women that the regime, particularly under Abdullah II, has endeavored to embed in a national narrative of development and progress. Yet her message relayed a nationalism that was difficult to contain within ordinary rituals and performances for the nation. As Aurolyn Luykx (1999) argues, "Nationalist ideology depends upon the articulation of popular meanings and pleasures, but these are neither predictable nor easily controlled; the meanings generated by any popular discourse exceed its own power to discipline them" (318). The state may generate the slogans,[19] but what people make of them can be unpredictable and even dangerous. The nationalism Nadine expressed was outside the bounds intended by "Jordan First" but was perhaps predictable given the slippery slope the regime has treaded with respect to inclusion and exclusion in a shifting national narrative about citizenship and belonging (Brand 1995; Massad 2001). The ambiguity surrounding citizenship or, more accurately, the feeling of belonging is thus in some sense deliberate: the haziness is deployed in response to particular events and political realities. Perhaps sensing the need for different sentiments, the regime launched the "We are all Jordan" campaign in July 2006. The slogan conveyed a decidedly different Jordanian sentiment but reflected the regime's continued efforts to engineer national identity and control the nationalist message—a process that the state cannot ever exclusively control.

Enforcing Daily Allegiance

In Jordan, students throughout the country are prompted to do their duty as loyal citizens through the daily performance of the morning assembly, or *tabur* (literally "lineup" or line). This ritual serves as a reminder of the need for loyalty to the king, the Hashemite family, and Jordan, as well as the importance of the Islamic faith and the Arab nation. It also functions as a time for school-wide announcements and admonitions, as well as an opportunity for staff to inspect students to ensure they heed regulations about dress and appearance. Such a morning ritual is not unique to Jordan; daily rituals are part and parcel of states' efforts to build patriotism and loyalty in school systems around the world (e.g., Herrera 1992; Levinson 2001). At the al-Khatwa School, the morning *tabur* began with the *fatiha* (the opening verse of the Qur'an), followed by a student raising the Jordanian flag and chanting "Long Live Jordan" with students repeating after her. The students finished by singing "Hail to the King," the Jordanian national anthem, and another patriotic song, "Mawtini" (My Homeland),[20] a reference to the Arab nation and a link to the Arab Revolt that the Hashemites have relied upon to develop an image as leaders of the Arab nation (Anderson 2001; Brand 1995; Layne 1994).[21] Students also were required to go through the motions of some very brief physical exercises under the direction of one of their peers—always halfheartedly at al- Khatwa. Indeed in all of my time at al-Khatwa, students and the large majority of teachers rarely displayed any interest or enthusiasm at the morning *tabur* unless prompted by some authority.[22]

The symbols embedded in this morning ritual are emblematic of the core tenets of Hashemite claims to legitimacy since the establishment of a Jordanian state. At times, however, representatives of the state altered the symbols to respond to new or local realities. One of my informants, who had been an educator in the region for over twenty-five years, was surprised to hear that the *fatiha* was read during the daily *tabur* as this had not been the case during his career as an educator. Several others with whom I spoke, who had gone to school in the late 1970s and early 1980s, reported that as far as they recalled the *tabur* did not include the *fatiha*. According to an employee of the central office of the Ministry of Education, the official expectation of the ministry is that the *tabur* begin with the singing of "Hail to the King" and the salute to the flag, followed by a reading from the Qur'an. According to this source, these were not explicit policies but rather expectations.

These guidelines, unlike specific directives, leave room for local interpretation of what is required or desirable. Even seemingly rigid official mandates or rules are always open to interpretation, for when the rule is put into practice, there is always the potential of human improvisation intended or otherwise, and states and their policies materialize only through the actions of diverse actors. The order in which the *tabur* is meant to unfold conveys the primacy or priority of king and country. However, at al-Khatwa the order was reversed, with religion being emphasized first, then king and country. In addition, the incorporation of the *fatiha* into the morning ritual was also the outcome of decisionmaking by local bureaucrats and perhaps a reflection of local religious sentiments or official perceptions of such sentiments. Despite being the product of local initiative, it was also in keeping with the regime's efforts to strengthen its religious credentials and to coopt religious symbols and discourse as a counterweight to the many nongovernmental religious organizations or movements vying for the loyalty of the students. Such daily rituals and performances, which seek to inscribe particular national sentiments among youth in Jordan, have existed for decades, but their symbolic content has been shaped and reshaped by local institutions and representatives of the state, educators included, whose job it is to implement the state mandate.[23] But these seemingly innocuous adjustments to this daily ritual are not without consequence, for rituals do not merely reflect meaning, they construct it (J. Comaroff 1985: 125). In addition, even the most mundane and longstanding forms of instilling patriotism and loyalty, such as the *tabur*, do not rest on firm ground, as I discovered one morning at al-Khatwa.

On that morning, I was surprised to find two men standing near the podium for the *tabur*. I soon learned that they were supervisors from the local office of the Ministry of Education on a surprise inspection of the *tabur*. It became clear to me after speaking to several teachers that some of their colleagues, including at least one teacher from al-Khatwa, had made comments at a staff development workshop about the sorry state of the *tabur* in schools and that this was what had prompted the inspection. One of the supervisors went to the podium and admonished the girls for their lack of enthusiasm during the singing of "Hail to the King." He grabbed the microphone angrily and shouted: "Girls, your voices are low. You are singing the anthem of your country. You should sing with feeling." Ironically, the very explicit efforts of these state monitors to enforce the patriotic performance served both to highlight the wavering ground on which the legitimacy narrative being enacted stood and to index competing moral discourses.

The appearance of the monitors at the morning assembly demonstrated the regime's desire to mold young bodies in the hope that "minds will follow" (Luykx 1999: 101). The state's local representatives insisted that the girls should sing with feeling; they should make their loyalty manifest by demonstrating greater enthusiasm. Yet the fact that Ministry of Education inspectors had to come to enforce the morning *tabur* highlighted both the state's power and the need for state representatives to regularly protect it. The expectation of the regime and its emissaries may be that patriotic ideals will flow from these performances; however, rather than create patriotism, enforced patriotism and mandated enthusiasm inadvertently reinforced the tenuous nature of the legitimacy narrative on which this patriotism rests.[24] Yet the potential rupture or dissonance of the intended symbolic content extends beyond the need for enforcement. The content was further challenged in this instance by the exhortation that the girls raise their voices and sing with feeling.

The demands of the *tabur* inspector brought competing disciplinary forces to the fore. For some of the students at al-Khatwa, the command to raise their voices posed a moral predicament for it offended the beliefs of some citizens in this particular community about modesty, gender, and acceptable interactions between males and females. On several occasions, I heard students at al-Khatwa say that a woman should not raise her voice, particularly in the presence of men, because her voice is *'awrah*. *'Awrah* literally means "private parts" or "that which is indecent to reveal" (Berkey 1992: 172). With reference to a woman's voice, the term's use is metaphorical, implying that a woman's voice should not be revealed.[25] The students who expressed this sentiment were those who self-identified as more religious or committed than their peers, and who were labeled as such by others. Sometimes this label was negative when they were considered by others to be too conservative or extreme. The large majority of teachers and students I spoke with did not accept these assertions about the female voice, or their religious basis. But, in this context, with a male education official at the podium, a few of the girls and some parents would have found the demand that they raise their voices immoral and even un-Islamic. Thus, the coherence of the state ideology was challenged by a competing moral project. The objection to the form of the ritual—raised voices—was a critique of the intended meaning of the symbols enacted and specifically of the moral authority of the regime, for the regime seeks to be the primary arbiter of that which is right, good, and Islamic. Enforcing "singing with feeling" elicited morally based objections to patriotic performances and to the moral legitimacy of the institutions that enabled them. At al-Khatwa such objections were also regularly raised about the performances of the "music girls" at patriotic events, as I discuss below. First, I return to another function of the *tabur*, namely, exerting adult authority within the school.

As previously mentioned, the *tabur* was also used as a time for school-wide lectures and admonishment. The principal might lecture the students about repeated violations of the dress code, and at times, as discussed in chapter 4, she would enlist the students in the prayer room committee to give religious lessons that would help support her efforts to enforce school rules. Teachers and staff would inspect school uniforms from time to time during *tabur* as well, as was depicted in the preface. One day Reem, the tenth grader I discuss in chapter 2, lined up for *tabur* with a scarf that had the Palestinian flag embroidered on it. A teacher who was walking the rows inspecting students' clothing promptly pulled it off her neck. Later this teacher told me that political symbols were not allowed. On another occasion, I arrived to find a school administrator, Bashira, screaming at the girls. Indeed she was so loud that at first I could not make out what she was saying. As she went on, however, it became clear that she was particularly incensed about graffiti that had been found in the school bathroom. Although I had not seen this particular instance of offensive graffiti, I heard from a group of twelfth graders that it consisted of obscenities written about particular teachers.[26] Bashira often took on this role as school disciplinarian even if it was not officially her role.

Thus, the *tabur* provided a time and space for collective discipline, both by representatives of the state and by the local school staff—an important reminder that efforts to exert authority are not merely the purview of state education officials and monitors but also localized disciplinary projects. Although Bashira's admonishments were not part of the "patriotic project" per se, they did represent an instance of a local representative in a state school exerting authority over students in the context of what is largely a patriotic ritual. However, disciplinary efforts were not always as explicit as those of Bashira or the ministry's monitors who came to ensure that displays of patriotism were sufficiently enthusiastic. The patriotic rituals in which the music girls at al-Khatwa were engaged also served to bring competing disciplinary projects to light, to challenge the legitimacy of female participation in patriotic rituals, and to highlight the centrality of women in Jordanian national imaginings.

Singing and Dancing for the Nation

In high schools in Jordan, much of the learning and teaching about citizenship occurs around a set of public annual rituals and performances at assemblies and celebrations on national holidays. At the center of many of these public events are student performances that are the culmination of state-directed extracurricular activities.[27] Throughout the course of my research in Bawadi al-Naseem, girls were typically the only performers in such national celebrations.[28] In a region of Jordan where public space was male-dominated and most events were sex-segregated, female students were at the forefront of public events organized to show support for the regime held at the school and in the surrounding community.

At al-Khatwa the music program was the key conduit for such performances. The school music group involved anywhere from twenty to forty students at a given time, and participation was voluntary. Their activities centered largely on preparing for events organized around national holidays. The "music girls" took a prominent place in public national performances, singing patriotic songs, dancing folk dances, and reciting poetry. On several occasions, both teachers and fellow students questioned the participation of the music girls on academic and moral grounds. The music girls' performances were consistent with the regime's efforts to create and display an image of a "modern" Jordan, one with a prominent role for women in its public life. Yet because the role of women in Jordanian society continues to be at the crux of debates about political and moral legitimacy, the performances also served to highlight the contested nature of such images and conflicts among competing forms of religiosity, calling into question the acceptability of the form and, implicitly, the content of these patriotic performances. An account of one such performance will illuminate my argument.

In 2005, I attended the celebration of Independence Day and Armed Services Day at the municipal hall in Bawadi al-Naseem.[29] The hall was filled with educators and students (male and female) who sat and waited for the dignitaries to arrive. The honored guests were the head of the municipality, the director of education for the governorate, and a number of education officials, all but one of whom were men. All of the students who participated in this performance, in celebration of the nation's independence and the armed forces, were girls. The girls wore "traditional" ankle-length embroidered dresses[30] with the exception of one who wore a *jelbab*, an overcoat or robe worn over one's clothes. Other than the girl in the *jelbab* and two of her peers, all of the girls performed without covering their hair.

The event began as most such events do, with the singing of "Hail to the King," in this case to the accompaniment of live music. The director of education talked about history, the Arab Revolt, and Jordanian independence. He also praised the king and his support for education and reform. The master of ceremonies, a student, gave her own speech praising the "miraculous accomplishments" of Jordan in education and development. She also talked about the importance of being "moderate" and moral students.[31] The music group, which at this event consisted of girls from al-Khatwa as well as another girls' high school in the area, sang several patriotic and national folk songs.[32] They were accompanied by music teachers and one of the al-Khatwa students playing instruments. Interspersed with their singing was the recitation of a poem read by an al-Khatwa student called "Oh My Country" and a speech by a student from another school about the need to defend the homeland.

This patriotic event, in which the performance of schoolgirls figured centrally, revealed the obvious ways in which the dominant national symbols were incorporated into such events. The main speakers acknowledged Jordan's progress—the "miraculous" achievements of the Jordanian king—and expressed gratitude to him for this progress. At such events there would often be an accounting of these achievements such as the number of schools that had been built, the number of computer labs recently installed, or the number of new teachers hired. All of this served to emphasize the primacy of Hashemite leadership in the national narrative, reestablishing the link between Jordan and its Hashemite kings. The standard references to the Arab Revolt and Jordan's independence were included as well. Finally, the girls displayed and performed the symbols of Jordan's history—the folk dress and songs that stood for this history, both rural and tribal (Layne 1994; Massad 2001; Shryock 1997). However, a more subtle meaning was also conveyed in this performance via the primary role of girls: the central place of women in the narrative of Jordanian progress and development.

In all of my observations of such events, I noted an absence of boys. Boys were typically in the audience, but in Bawadi al-Naseem, they never performed.[33] When I inquired about the lack of boys' participation, parents and staff usually said boys did not like such activities; given that males had greater mobility than their female peers, they also had other ways in which to spend their time outside the home. Also, many of the local educators and parents said the girls were better students and better behaved. This assertion was reiterated time and time again by parents, administrators, and teachers. Boys were often said to be undisciplined and rebellious, making them undesirable participants from the perspective of the educators who needed to prepare students for such events.[34] Thus, the dominant role that girls held in such performances did not appear to be an explicit policy and was understood to be a matter of boys' preferences. Of course such preferences could clearly be constructed, as music was not even offered as an option for high school boys in Bawadi al-Naseem, assumptions having already been made about their preferences.

However unintended, the fact that some girls play a very central and public role in national performances fit decidedly into the image of Jordan that the regime was struggling to portray, namely, the image of a modern nation with women at its center. Official policy statements and slogans reinforced such images. The education section of the official "Jordan First" document reads: "A new view of the status of women has to be developed among the young, starting with the home, through school and university, and ending with youth organizations" (Jordan First National Commission 2002). The substance of this "new view of the status of women" is clearly still a contentious one, and one intimately tied to the struggles over proper forms of religiosity and their implications for women's participation in public life. Given the controversial nature of such images, the symbolic meaning conveyed through music performances at patriotic events cannot be taken for granted. While the participation of these young women in these public events helped project the image of a "modern" Jordanian woman who was a full participant in her society, they also served to highlight the tensions in the narrative of national and moral legitimacy. Even the folk dress and songs were laden with symbols—meant to stand for an authentic Jordanian identity as well as a uniquely Jordanian history.

Although I never heard of any official objections to girls' participation in very public events (in fact the administration fully supported and facilitated their participation, and the ministry needed schools to participate in such events), some teachers and peers at al-Khatwa regularly voiced concerns about the participation of the music girls in such events. Their objections were focused on issues of academics, female modesty, and proper comportment, as well as the permissibility of music in Islam. Academically, the adults worried that students who participated in music would suffer because they missed too much class. Music practice and performances, like other extracurricular activities, typically were scheduled during the course of the regular school day, so students who participated in music regularly missed class. On one occasion when a teacher and I were talking about an alumna of al-Khatwa who had not scored as high as expected on the *tawjihi*, the teachers said, "She was all over the place with music and theater. She was not focused and her studies suffered." In general, teachers viewed music and other such activities as a distraction and did not believe students would benefit from their participation. Many girls, like Nada in the opening story to this book, dropped out of music in the eleventh grade, because they needed to start "getting serious" in anticipation of the high school completion exam in their final year.

Some teachers and students explicitly raised moral objections about the participation of al-Khatwa students in musical patriotic performances—moral objections having to do with notions of gender modesty and the contested nature of music itself as a respectable or religiously permissible pastime. As Saba Mahmood (2005: 23–24) argues, although modesty as a widely held norm is not new historically speaking, the ways in which the norm is meant to be "inhabited" are fiercely contested. The modesty of the music girls' dress was an issue regularly raised by critics, and girls had to navigate a range of incongruous guideposts in their efforts to understand and define what was proper. As already mentioned, during their performances the girls wore "traditional" embroidered dresses that were full length with long sleeves. Many of the girls did not cover their hair for these performances, and yet the large majority of females in this community covered their hair with a headscarf or *ishar*, a phenomenon that has become widespread in the past two decades in Jordan, as elsewhere in the region.[35] By many people's standards, their dress was modest; however, some manifestations of new religious sentiment frame this folk dress as "traditional" and/or not sufficiently modest and favor a new form of Islamic dress.

The attire of the girls, particularly forms of head covering, during their musical performances reflects the degree of flexibility in forms of dress and covering for some adolescent girls. The decision by al-Khatwa students to don the veil was at times made by parents or other family members but not always. Many of the girls became interested in veiling as they approached middle and high school because veiling was viewed as a rite of passage, a sign that they were "grown up." Some girls at al-Khatwa always covered their hair, while others did so only in certain places. For example, girls might remove their headscarf when they came to school, or they might wear it only in school. On occasion, girls took on the scarf for a short period, an initial trial, and then decided not to wear it anymore, although such "down-veiling" was generally frowned upon.[36] Some of the music girls were students who did not regularly cover their hair or did so inconsistently. Others who participated took their head cover off for the musical performances, and still others performed with their head covered. Not all girls had the freedom to do this switching back and forth; in this city it would be difficult to remain an unveiled woman in the long run, as a Muslim woman would find herself in a tiny minority.[37] Although forms of covering were at times flexible, the very public nature of the music performances and the fact that they were not sex-segregated made performing "uncovered" problematic in the eyes of many adults and students.

The music girls I spoke with responded to such criticism by defending their "costumes" as sufficiently modest. Dia, a tenth grader, discussed concerns about modesty and dress in defending her participation in music. Specifically, she differentiated the music girls' performances from musical performances on television in music videos:[38] "We are not doing anything wrong. We don't get up there like the people who sing on TV, wearing things that are not good. There is nothing *haram* (forbidden)[39] [in our music activities]. On TV the singers, they sing and get dressed in this [objectionable] way. But we all wear the same thing and our sleeves are to here (she pointed to her wrist)." Ironically, Dia watched music videos all the time, as did many of her peers. Regardless of their popularity, music videos were frequently the target of criticism by some teachers and some students. The objections to music videos were not about the music (although for some families this was part of the problem); rather, the most prominent objections had to do with the way in which women dressed in these videos, their appearance with men, and the sexual suggestiveness of many of these videos (Armbrust 2005). One music video in particular, "What do they have to do with us" (*malhum binna ya layl*), became a target of criticism at al-Khatwa, because it features a young woman wearing a headscarf being serenaded by the male singer, Haithem Sa'id, while she sits before him and at times gets up and dances. It is somewhat reserved for a music video, but the teacher whom I heard critique it was incredulous that a woman would appear in a music video wearing the *hijab*. She saw this as a terrible contradiction.[40]

There are clear parallels between the discussion of this music video and criticism of the music program and the participation of students in the celebrations around national holidays. Those who objected to the woman in the music video who wore a headscarf questioned the message that was implied in this performance, namely, that appearing in the music video was compatible with the *hijab*. They saw a clear contradiction between the pious identity implied by the scarf and the immorality they felt was imbedded in such videos. Similarly, girls who typically "covered" and participated in music at al-Khatwa were considered by some to be hypocritical. However, increasingly one finds within the repertoire of music videos available in the region a diversity of mediums and messages that seem in part to be responding to the morally based criticisms to such new media. The music videos of Sami Yusuf are just one example of the use of this medium to emphasize the importance of faith and family, "blending religious world-view with mainstream forms of entertainment" (Kubala 2005: 40).[41]

Beyond the criticisms raised about different forms of dress and cover and the meaning embedded in them, other conflicts emerged surrounding interpretations of religious teachings on music and patriotic songs. The subject of music has entered religious discourse in new ways in the past two decades, with some Muslims identifying a greater religiosity with, among other things, a prohibition on music or particular forms of music (Herrera 2000).[42] Nevertheless, most people still listen to music in Jordan, and many young people expressed ambivalence toward the music prohibition. In fact watching music videos was a favorite student pastime. Furthermore, music was part of the formal curriculum in elementary school and optional in high school. However, some of the students at al-Khatwa, particularly those who were involved in local piety movements, argued that music was *haram* and preached to their peers regularly about the dangers of music. Given her religious convictions, Amina, whom I discuss at length in chapter 4, was adamant that music was forbidden in Islam. She told me that those who listened to music would go to hell, and she regularly shared this perspective with her peers. On one occasion, while I was sitting with her in the schoolyard, a group of teachers passed by carrying instruments, as they were rehearsing for a big event at al-Khatwa. Amina turned to me and said, "It hurts me to see Muslim men and women holding instruments." Some teachers also believed that music was *haram* and conveyed this sentiment to the students. Music, and specifically music videos, are also a focus of intense scrutiny by adults because of their perceived influence on youth and because of adult fears about losing control. Clearly, this type of generational conflict is unique neither to Jordan nor to Islam. Al-Khatwa students had to negotiate the debate about the propriety of music (which music, when, and with whom).[43] After hearing some teachers and students voice criticisms of the music girls during my classroom observations and in the schoolyard, I asked the music girls to discuss objections to their performances with me. A conversation with two eleventh graders who were active participants in music was indicative of how the girls understood the prohibition on music and how they attempted to rationalize their own participation.

FIDA: Do you face any problems because people have the opinion that music is immoral?

HANAN: We hear this kind of talk a lot. For example, the other day the computer teacher got hold of me and said, "Don't you cover your hair? So why music?" But I am not that committed [i.e., religiously]. Should I tell her I am free to do what I want? That would be rude. She will say, "Why do you go to music? Music is *haram*."

FIDA: How do you react to her?

HANAN: I try to take it lightly and joke so as to pull myself out of the discussion.

FARIAL: So that there won't be problems between you and the teacher.

HANAN: Then we go and tell our music teacher, "This teacher said this, this, and that."

FARIAL: We just ignore it. We know what we are doing and music is fine. We listen to music at home.

FIDA: In religion there seems to be a difference of opinion. Do most Muslims consider music to be *haram*?

HANAN: Everyone knows music is *haram*, but there are some who don't pay attention like us and others who do.

FIDA: You mean it is *haram* in religion?

FARIAL: Musical instruments are *haram*. Only the *daff* [tambourine] is not *haram*.[44] But these are [national] anthems? Everything that we do is not *haram*. I just recite [poetry] and Hanan plays the *daff*.

HANAN: Look. It's like [wearing] the *jelbab*. It is not required but there are some people who say if you wear a headscarf that you must wear a *jelbab*.

As Hanan recalled, her teacher argued that if she covered her hair she must be religious, and if she is religious she should not participate in music. In their conversation with me, Farial and Hanan rationalized their participation in music by distinguishing it from other modes of music that were *haram*. Farial argued that because their role in the music performances was limited to recitation in her own case, and playing the *daff* in Hanan's case, their participation was religiously acceptable. She specifically pointed out that they did not play instruments (ignoring the fact that they were participating in a performance while accompanied by people playing on instruments). Thus, Farial did not deny that some music was *haram* but tried to separate her own form of participation from that which would be considered prohibited by some.

Hanan too seemed to accept the premise that some forms of music were *haram*, but she related the prohibitions and her willingness to participate in music activities to different degrees of religiosity, a question of how "committed" she was. The parallel that Hanan made with the *jelbab* here was a pointed one, as it conveyed the reality that people have different interpretations and expectations about how a Muslim should dress, act, and behave. Both girls appeared little concerned about the objections to their participation. They rationalized their participation in similar ways, although Farial invoked distinctions based on religious teachings, while Hanan emphasized different degrees of being "religious."

Most noteworthy here, girls who participated in music also regularly defended their activities in terms of patriotic duty. Performing at such events, they argued, could not be "wrong" as they were events in celebration of the nation and king. Indeed, objections to music participation could be read as a challenge to official attempts to instill national values in young Jordanian citizens, as such performances were almost always in celebration of some national event. In a number of instances I observed or heard about, such objections appeared to be just that—a challenge to the regime's attempts to define the terms of moral life and religious practice—for by sanctioning that which is considered to be *haram* by some, the state or its representatives can be viewed as ipso facto illegitimate or at least as an unqualified arbiter of that which is *halal* (permitted) or *haram*.[45] Hanan argued that a sanctioned school activity of a national and cultural nature must be viewed as legitimate:

HANAN: When there is a music event in the municipal hall you find the whole school there. Isn't it supposed to be *haram*? So why does the whole school come then?

FARIAL: This is something different. This music is national music. It's not something loose [immoral] . . . that which is in their minds . . . that which is *haram*. About love[46] and things like that.

FIDA: Are all music activities nationalistic?

HANAN: Not necessarily. They could be folklore too . . . from Jordanian culture. It has to be that way because we are under the supervision of the Ministry of Education.

Notice that Hanan drew not on nationalist sentiment per se but rather on official power to designate some activities as legitimate and others not. The state not only sanctioned their activities but defined the parameters of acceptable content according to Hanan. The girls distinguished between music about the nation and music that evoked morally questionable sentiments about love and longing (Abu Lughod 2000).[47] Ironically, as I discuss below, the folk songs the girls sang—songs meant to signify a Jordanian national identity—were traditional songs about love and longing. Farial said that her songs were different; they were about the nation and not about love.

Like Hanan and Farial, Aseel, a tenth grader, also emphasized the patriotic nature of the music and distinguished patriotic music from music that elicited dangerous emotions:

FIDA: Do you hear from people that music is *haram*?

ASEEL: A lot. They keep saying it's *haram*. But I don't see what is *haram*. We sing songs about the nation and folk songs. There is nothing wrong with it.

FIDA: Is all of your singing similar to this. . . . About the nation?

ASEEL: Yes. . . . Their [i.e., people's] thought is that music is *haram*. In our religion, the Islamic religion says that music is *haram*. But it is the type of music. Not just any music is *haram*. There is the music on the *daff*; this is not *haram*. It's fine. But the music that has rhythm and sound and things. . . . Some people say it's *haram*. There are people that say also that songs that stir up your emotions that might change you or bother you, that make you cry . . . that this is *haram*. That it makes your soul or self suffer. For some people music in and of itself is the problem. For others it's fine.

In defending her music participation, Aseel singled out music that stirs emotions, implying that nationalistic music does not stir emotions, or at least not the emotions that are considered potentially morally corrupting. Their music sessions, she argued, were patriotic and therefore not *haram*. According to Aseel, her religion teacher had talked to some of the students about such musical distinctions; she clarified that it was music that incited passion which was *haram*.

The characterization of the music performed by the students as nationalistic, and thus not emotional or immoral, is intriguing on a number of fronts. First, the Arab world is home to a long musical tradition that is characterized by deep emotion. In fact, in the Arabic language there is a specific word to describe the "musical affect" or "the extraordinary emotional state evoked by . . . music" (Racy 2003: 74), namely, *tarab*. The term is also defined as the "rapture, ecstasy or enchantment" stimulated by art forms and particularly music (Shannon 2003: 74). Furthermore, the Arab world's most famous singers in the twentieth century sang songs saturated with emotion, most prominent among them female artists such as Um Kalthum and Fairouz, who were incredibly popular. Interestingly many of these highly regarded singers have also produced deeply nationalistic songs. Indeed the emotion exuded in some of these nationalist songs parallels that of the most passionate love songs.[48] Although Arab performing artists whether male or female have always struggled with the social stigma surrounding their profession, a vibrant history of performing arts overshadows these struggles (Zuhur 2005).

Finally, and quite ironically, the music girls actually sang folk songs that were love songs at the celebration I describe in this chapter, as well as other similar events. They sang three Jordanian folk songs: "Wayli mahlaha bint al rifiyye" (Oh, how beautiful she is, the rural girl); "Balla ya ghali salim 'ala walifi" (Please, my dear, give my greetings to my love); and, "Yuma andahalu, shogi marag kheal" (Oh, mother, call him to stop in, my love is passing by on his horse). Two of these songs were explicitly about love; however, they were also *turath* or heritage and as such were central to patriotic performances that drew on symbols of a shared Jordanian past that have been critical to the construction of a Jordanian national identity. Indeed state officials have worked to coopt, transform, and commission music for nationalist cultural projects since the state was first formed, with renewed emphasis on promoting "Jordanian music" in times of political crisis (Massad 2001). Singing folk songs was framed as legitimate expression of sentiment by al-Khatwa students, easily distinguished from the popular music these girls readily consumed but found to be a useful foil for their own musical performances. Yet not all of the actors at al-Khatwa took as a given the acceptability of the folk songs and patriotic performance; some actively critiqued and challenged their legitimacy, calling into question the larger cultural projects that seek to delineate proper displays of sentiment. Thus the everyday enactment of national culture elicited challenges that were part and parcel of contemporary struggles for power in Jordan today.

Music performances positioned these girls at the center of struggles over proper displays of patriotism, appropriate forms of modesty, and accepted religious teaching and practices. Girls grappled with music prohibitions that seemed to clash with a nationalism that is also explicitly Islamic. For some observers, the patriotic performances called into question the "Islamicness" of such state-sanctioned practices. For others it was the state and patriotism that made their activities legitimate. The music girls persisted in an activity they enjoyed even if they were at times forced to justify their participation. Given that their families—the first moral arbiters in a young person's life— approved of their participation, most of the music girls were not particularly troubled by the objections to their participation. Regardless of whether they were committed to the patriotic sentiments on which they sometimes drew, the fact that these were state-sponsored patriotic events also legitimized their participation in their own eyes. However, for those who held serious objections to such performances, these events exemplified the very crisis of legitimacy that these performances served to forestall.

Conclusion

Peter McLaren (1999) has argued that "rituals do more than simply inscribe or display symbolic meanings or states of affairs but *instrumentally bring states of affairs into being"* (41).[49] In this chapter, I have shown how patriotic rituals designed to display the power of the regime and to build loyalty create a "state of affairs" that can undermine this ritual intent. As with any ritual performance, the meaning produced is unpredictable, and the "interpretations of ritual infinitely extendable" (McLaren 1999: 129). I have highlighted the unexpected interpretations that flow from patriotic rituals; the views conveyed by teachers and students with respect to the music girls remind us of the contested nature of state legitimacy, as well as the actuality of state power. Cognizant of that power, the music girls drew on it for moral legitimacy.

From the earliest days of its independence the Jordanian state and, more specifically, the Hashemites sought to construct both a Jordanian national tradition and a vision of what a modern and developed Jordan should look like. Women have played a central role in both these strategies as symbols of tradition and traditional values and as key indicators of Jordan's modernization. In some respects, the religious movements of the last two decades and the increased religiosity of peoples throughout the region have upset this modern/traditional balancing act. For in essence what Islamism and Islamic piety movements have done is force the redefinition of what is traditional, what is modern, what is Islamic, and, after all, what is Jordanian. These religious movements—decidedly modern phenomena—have offered new symbols and practices for dealing with contemporary life in Jordan. These movements have had a significant impact on women—their forms of dress, their education and work, and a range of issues related to living as good Muslim women in Jordan (Taraki 1995). In response, the regime, like its counterparts throughout the region, has worked to enhance its Islamic credentials while at the same time trying to rein in Islamic movements and sentiments that it has perceived as too extreme. Such efforts are apparent in schools where more religious "symbols" have been added to the fabric of daily school life. At the same time, school-based patriotic events underscore tensions that exist between the regime's vision of a modern nation and conflicting conceptions of what it means to be a proper Muslim woman. The differences and conflicts over music are clear examples of this. As I have shown in this chapter, elements of the "traditional" national culture or heritage constructed by the regime conflict in some respects with contemporary religious sentiments, even as they frame the dominant discourse. Rituals work to construct and reinscribe a national narrative with the Hashemites at its center, but in the process of creating and re-creating they leave open the possibility of varied interpretations and the construction of new cultural symbols and meanings.

Drawing on ethnographic research and an analysis of schooling as a set of everyday actions and rituals that are far more contingent than state control of education might lead us to believe, I have shown how national ideals as they unfold in schools through rituals and performance often do as much to unbalance legitimacy as to produce it. As André Mazawi (2002) has argued: "the expansion of schooling is closely associated with a rise in political contestation of the established order" (60), a reality he argues has been often neglected in the scholarship on the Arab world. Schools continue to be arenas in this contest, providing both the space and the material (symbols and signs, civic and national education curricula, a music program, extracurricular events) that draw attention to some of the conflicts surrounding national identity. With their regular performance of symbol-laden rituals, schools also habitually create opportunities for engaging with such conflicts and for constructing new symbols with new meaning.

In Jordan young women are called upon to perform the nation. Their performances (daily rituals, speeches, songs, and dances) convey particular images of the nation—an image of Jordan's idealized past and attendant folklore and, simultaneously, an image of Jordan's progress or development with women as active public participants. At the same time, they bring to the fore tensions and contradictions inherent in this dominant vision for the nation and for Jordanian women. The participation of adolescent girls in such events as participants or observers is never merely an instance of state-imposed ideology; within the very real constraints of what types of activities are permitted in school, and what officially gets taught about the nation, we see multiple levels at which this participation is resisted, interrogated, clarified, and rationalized. At the same time, the school—with its regular performance of important symbols—created opportunities and modeled approaches for engaging with such struggles and for constructing symbols with new meaning (Coe 2005; Starrett 1998).

FOUR

Who Is a Good Muslim? Making Proper Faith in a Girls' High School

We don't want you to think that those girls out there represent the true Islam. We want you to come in here [into the prayer room] and see us. We hope we are examples of good Muslims.

—Amina, eleventh grader, president of the prayer room committee

Attempts to educate students and adults at al-Khatwa about religion were both ubiquitous and obscure in everyday life and interactions in school. All schools in Jordan require formal religious instruction; however, in the space of the school, religious instruction could also be quite informal. For example, one day the lab teacher asked a religion teacher about purification rituals before praying. On another occasion, I overheard a student admonishing her friend for gossiping, drawing on religious grounds. And, in another example, I listened as the principal asked the school community to fulfill their obligation to do *zakat*, or to tithe, by helping to cover the high school completion exam fees of some of the poorer students. My own presence made for much conversation about Christianity. Although discussions about morality stemmed from multiple notions of respectability and progress, which drew on notions of family honor, kin obligations, and tradition more generally, here I take up the very explicit efforts of some actors within the al-Khatwa School to define what is Islamic and, more specifically, what proper Islamic behavior is for girls and young women. Understanding these efforts is critical to providing a broader view of the struggles surrounding religious authority within Jordanian society.

Teaching about Islam in schools goes beyond the official curriculum and entails a set of daily practices, school-based activities, and day-to-day interactions. It involves actors—teachers, students, and parents—all of whom bring a variety of perspectives to any number of pressing questions about what it means to be a good Muslim in Jordan today. As described in the

previous chapter, even extracurricular activities and events designed to instill patriotism and "teach" citizenship could become the subject of religious "lessons" as they at times highlighted debates about modesty and
proper comportment for a Muslim woman, as well as the religious propriety
of music. In this chapter, I analyze the struggles between texts, teachers, and
students to define proper Islamic mores in religion classes and beyond. At
al-Khatwa, the debates about "true" Islamic teaching and what should be
taught about Islam were enmeshed with similar struggles outside of school
and specifically with a local *da'wa*[1] or "piety" movement that made its way
into school.

Competing interpretations of Islamic orthodoxy come to the fore in
schools in unique ways; schools provide a critical lens onto contemporary religious sentiments and the tensions that emerge when contending
religious projects seek to be authoritative. Schools are not isolated from
the debates over religious meaning and practice in which local actors are
engaged outside of school. The boundaries around religious debates in
schools and state institutions are somewhat circumscribed but cannot be
entirely controlled. Moreover, schooling—a project of state development
embedded in global educational narratives—creates new models and expectations for living as an "educated" person that cannot be divorced from
debates about religion and proper forms of piety, particularly for young
women. At al-Khatwa, teachers and administrators gave religious activities
and religious discourse space to flourish. and as a result, the contests over
religious authority flourished also. Indeed, by employing religion to maintain discipline and to point students in the "right" direction, educational
institutions expand the arena for such efforts both spatially and discursively
(Coe 2005; Starrett 1998).

As I have argued throughout this book, schools are particularly significant
in the lives of young women, and this importance extends to their religious
lives. As with young people in many other parts of the world, becoming "a
more committed Muslim" was one way in which some girls at al-Khatwa
sought to demonstrate maturity and to shape their sense of self during a
period of young adulthood (Smith and Denton 2005; Wilkins 2008). Yet
the relative newness of mass education as well as dramatic transformations
in the organization of family, work, and public life in a relatively short
period of time means that religious explorations can be particularly fraught
with the ambiguity that stems from competing perspectives on the role of
religion in public life and the role of women in present-day Jordan. Many
of the public deliberations about proper faith are deeply gendered, marked

by passionate debates about the role of women in contemporary Jordanian society. Girls at al-Khatwa were very much at the center of such polemics.

What became clear at al-Khatwa is that what constitutes being a better Muslim for young women in Jordan today is not always self-evident and is in some instances openly debated. Furthermore, even though the public school is technically the domain of the state, other actors brought their own perspectives on Islam into the school, and the state curriculum (as embodied in the textbooks) did not stand alone. Even the state's own gendered narrative in the curriculum is at times inconsistent, reflecting the competing interests and perspectives of a variety of state representatives. Teachers and students interpreted and deployed lessons from the textbooks, lessons that catalyzed religious debates but did not entirely contain them. At times, they drew on other materials and media sources, or their own religious convictions, as they actively engaged in the day-to-day praxis that is integral to the making of orthodoxy—what Talal Asad (1993) describes as the "(re)-ordering of knowledge that governs the 'correct' form of Islamic practices" to achieve "discursive coherence" and dominance (210). Moreover, schooling itself triggers particular religious debates, due both to its formal presentation of religious content and to its employment of religiosity to promote particular values and behavior (Starrett 1998). Finally, the modern project of schooling provides new images of what a girl's future may hold, and these new trajectories are entangled with debates about what it means to be a pious Muslim woman today.

At al-Khatwa these deliberations were embodied in the preaching of Amina, the eleventh grader who regularly lectured her peers, drawing on the influences of the *da'wa* group in which she was active, her own independent research and reading on Islam, and the religious programs on television that she argued preached the true Islam. The debates also came to life in the directives of Miss Suheil, the religion teacher, who as the official religion expert worked to establish authority by regularly critiquing that which she viewed to be outside the bounds of true Islam, whether it was the extremism of local *da'wa* groups and the conservatism of local tradition, or the "other type of extremism," characterized for Miss Suheil by immoral satellite television programs or the ideas of "feminists" outside the bounds of the religiously acceptable. Miss Jude, another religion teacher, generally let the textbook guide her, but students regularly questioned and challenged the content, and she herself emphasized particular themes and downplayed those that did not fit her particular viewpoint. Others at al-Khatwa similarly engaged in such debates even if they did not take center stage. The textbooks, like television preachers and "immoral" satellite programs, provided important substance for such arguments.

Legitimate Religious Knowledge

"Orthodoxy" is not easy to secure in conditions of radical change. This is not because orthodox discourse is necessarily against any change but because it aspires to be authoritative.[2]

—Talal Asad

Competing projects to define religious orthodoxy characterize religious discourse and practice in Jordan today. With a religious revival in the region that has now spanned nearly three decades, the power to define and monitor religious knowledge has been at the center of struggles between the state, various Islamic groups, and Jordanians who seek to live as good Muslims. Key to constructing religious legitimacy has been official efforts to control religious discourse and define what is religiously legitimate, allowable, and "true." Since Jordan's founding, the Hashemite regime has based its legitimacy to some measure on its Islamic credentials, and this continues to be at the core of Jordan's self-definition as a state. In this vein, the Hashemites have emphasized their status as descendants of the prophet Muhammad and protectors of Muslim holy sites in Jerusalem as the basis for their religious legitimacy (Anderson 2001; Katz 2005; Layne 1994). However, this narrative represents only one dimension of the regime's larger efforts to control religious discourse and practice. The regime has sought to promote a particular vision of a moderate Islam in Jordan (and in the region) by sponsoring conferences for religious scholars, by emphasizing its vision in public speeches and policy statements, and by seeking to control the production and transmission of religious knowledge within Jordan and beyond.

In November 2004, during the month of Ramadan (the Muslim holy month of fasting), King Abdullah II delivered the "Amman Message," an official religious platform for the regime, which emphasizes that Islam is a religion of moderation, peace, and progress:

In this declaration we speak frankly to the [Islamic] nation, at this difficult juncture in its history, regarding the perils that beset it. We are aware of the challenges confronting the nation, threatening its identity, assailing its tenets . . . and working to distort its religion. . . . Today the magnanimous message of Islam faces a vicious attack from those who through distortion and fabrication try to portray Islam as an enemy to them. It is also under attack from some who claim affiliation with Islam and commit irresponsible acts in its name. ("Amman Message")

The Amman Message was a response to internal concerns about the growing strength of militant Islamic groups that threaten the regime, as well as religious extremism in the region more broadly (International Crisis Group 2005; Wiktorowicz 2001).[3] After the public launch of this message, the regime initiated an ongoing initiative under the framework of the Amman Message, which aims to take leadership in authoring and delimiting legitimate religious discourse in all its dimensions in Jordan and the region. The message specifically emphasizes the importance of education in this regard: "Hope lies in the scholars of our Nation, that through the reality of Islam and its values they will enlighten the intellects of our youth. . . . The scholars shield our youth from the danger of sliding down the paths of ignorance, corruption, close-mindedness, and subordination. It is our scholars who illuminate for them the paths of tolerance, moderation, and goodness, and prevent them from [falling] into the abysses of extremism and fanaticism that destroy the spirit and body" ("Amman Message"). Thus, in Jordan as in many other states, the proper education is considered critical to preventing religious extremism among young people. To this end, the regime has also sought to keep close control over religious public spaces, religious teaching, and preaching in mosques and in Islamic centers (Antoun 2006; Wiktorowicz 2001).

The regime's efforts in this regard have been in response to competing religious narratives and authorities. Throughout the Middle East since as early as the 1970s, religious movements of various persuasions, from those with overtly political agendas to those concerned with encouraging greater piety and promoting new interpretations of what it means to live as good Muslims in the contemporary world, have gained prominence and popular currency. As discussed in chapter 2, the increasing prominence of Islamist movements in the region and the growth in religious sentiment among the population have led to a new politics of identity, with debates about religious practice and politics at the center. Private Islamic organizations, most notably those affiliated with the Muslim Brotherhood, have been in competition with the state over the authoring of religious discourse.[4] These developments challenge the regime's attempts to control and shape religious discourse and the model of Jordanian and Islamic citizenship the regime has put forth. Perhaps one of the most underexplored avenues for the regime's efforts to control religious discourse is mass public schooling, the institution that acts as the primary purveyor of a state discourse of religious authenticity.[5]

Jordanians have access to a variety of Islamic centers of education throughout the country where they can go to learn about Islam, Islamic teachings, and living their lives as good Muslims. These institutions include formally registered ones under the auspices of the Ministry of Religious Endowments and Islamic Affairs as well as private centers. The Muslim Brotherhood has also been active in providing its own private religious education through a network of Islamic centers under its umbrella.[6] Many of the young women at al-Khatwa had attended or were currently attending some form of religious education outside of school, particularly for Qur'anic recitation.[7] For the school-aged population, such centers supplement the religious education that they receive in school and at home, as is the case in other countries (Boyle 2006).

Although there are many contexts for learning about Islam in Jordan, schools are critical spaces for examining the efforts to secure orthodoxy (Asad 1993). Textbooks, which are synonymous with curriculum in this context, are the most palpable tools in this endeavor, presenting "official wish-images" about proper faith and religious practice (Limbert 2007: 121). In Jordanian state schools, religion is a formal subject that all Muslim students must take from first grade until twelfth grade.[8] In high school in 2005, all students took at least three periods of religion a week, and students in the literary or humanities track took an additional three periods in the eleventh and twelfth grades.[9] The religion class is more specifically an Islamic religion class, and so Jordan's Christian minority is exempted from this subject throughout their years in the public school system.[10] At al-Khatwa, Christian students typically left their classroom during religion class. On occasion, Christian students remained either because they wanted to stay indoors out of the cold or because they were curious about the religion lessons.[11] The form and content of the religious curriculum vary from year to year and for the different academic tracks after the tenth grade, although one finds a significant amount of repetition and revisiting of particular themes and topics within and across textbooks.[12]

Topics covered in these textbooks range from the more "technical" matters of religious doctrine, specifically the methods and principles of jurisprudence, or *fiqh* and Qur'anic interpretation (al-Sawa et al. 2001), to lessons about the implications of religious teaching for a range of day-to-day matters from marriage and family life, to work, economic systems, and professional unions.[13] Although all the textbooks make religious references, the relationship between religious doctrine (in the form of verses from the

Qur'an or *ahadith*) and many of these day-to-day matters is less than direct. This is most evident in *Islamic Education*, the eleventh-grade text, which deals with a range of contemporary topics outside the specific purview of Islamic teaching, such as a discussion about unions in the chapter on Islam and labor (al-Dughmi et al. 1996: 203).[14] Even when the authors of such texts do not draw on particular religious teachings to verify or contextualize a particular topic, they frame lessons in the textbook such that they read as *the* Islamic teaching on this topic so as to establish "textual authority" (Anderson 2007; Messick 1996).

Yet textbooks provide us with a limited view of what happens in schools, what teachers and students do with official texts, and how they interpret them. It is misleading to speak of a singular state vision for religious education, since state bureaucrats (some of whom are directly involved in developing curriculum) hold divergent perspectives on the shape that Islam should take in public education, and this miscellany is reflected in part in inconsistencies in the official narratives and in the broader curriculum. In addition to the formal and intended curriculum, I observed myriad ways and spaces—in the classroom, prayer room, schoolyard, and teachers' room—within which actors in school attempted to teach others about religion, religious practices, and living piously. I draw on observations from religion classes and some reference to the curriculum to show how the curriculum provides a foundation for discussion in religious studies, one that is in turn shaped by students and teachers. Most importantly, such deliberations were not limited to religion class, as teachers and students worked to convey their vision of true Islam in many other contexts in the school. Not all these efforts were equally fruitful; however, they all represent significant dimensions of this account, both because they aspired to be authoritative and because they are indicative as well as constitutive of the struggles surrounding proper faith in Jordan today. As the school's official authorities, teachers were central to the debates about being a good Muslim in school.

Miss Suheil's Distinction

Teachers, both educators and civil servants, are at the forefront of state educational efforts. As representatives of the state, they are charged with implementing state curricular goals (goals they have little say in delineating, like teachers in most countries),[15] but in many respects they are the farthest removed from the centers of power in the offices of the Ministry of Education and other related state institutions.[16] Instead, they act as mediators of the textbook in schools and as the main arbiters of what can and cannot be said in the classroom. Miss Suheil, a religion teacher at al-Khatwa, was one of the most popular teachers among students and regularly engaged them in discussions about how Islam should guide their lives.

When queried about their most accessible teachers, students almost unanimously mentioned Miss Suheil. Her distinction as a favored classroom teacher also stemmed from her pedagogical technique. She employed teaching methods typically associated with "progressive" pedagogical theory, including small-group exercises, role playing, and skits.[17] For example, on one occasion, drawing from a lesson entitled "The path to seeking knowledge" (al-Dughmi 1996: 153), Miss Suheil had her students develop skits to demonstrate how early Islamic scholars traveled about in search of knowledge. I observed one skit prepared by six students who acted out the travels and interactions of Abu Ayoub al-Ansari (155). The students were engaged, and the excitement in the classroom was palpable. Miss Suheil asked two classmates to comment on the quality of the skit and the lessons embedded in it, concluding by reminding the students that they all had the obligation to pursue knowledge. Then she asked the students to discuss what they would like to become when they grew up. Samar responded that she would like to be a journalist, while Ayesha said she wanted to memorize the Qur'an in its entirety. Jumana answered, "I want to be on *Star Academy*," which led her classmates to erupt in laughter. Miss Suheil reminded the class that they should not laugh at anyone, although it was clear the girls were laughing because Jumana was once again having fun at Miss Suheil's expense.

Pedagogically speaking, such exercises were unique at al-Khatwa, and despite the jesting of students like Jumana, the students appreciated Miss Suheil's efforts. Although students found Miss Suheil's exercises enjoyable and her classes interesting, the opinions of her colleagues were not always as generous. Some teachers found her presumptuous and felt that her extra efforts in class were meant to paint their own practice in a less than positive light, a tension common to many workplace settings. They seemed threatened by her pedagogical authority; her work outside of school as a researcher and writer may have compounded this resentment.[18]

Miss Suheil's role in the classroom was critical both because she was the arbiter of the curricular content presented in the text and because she aspired to be authoritative. As an educator, she explicitly took part in struggles over religious authority in her own community (Bawadi al-Naseem), juxtaposing what she believed to be true Islam with what she viewed as illegitimate. She also typically used her religion class to launch into a social critique of Jordan and the Arab world more broadly. She found much to be lacking in the education system, criticizing teaching methods and the particular types of knowledge valued in Jordan. She also believed that employing progressive teaching methods was indispensable for the confidence and moral edification of the high school girls who were her charges.

In her work to define proper faith, Miss Suheil frequently commented on the problem of tradition, various forms of "extremism," and the ways in which they denied women their rights and corrupted true Islam. Miss Suheil defined true Islam by juxtaposing it with what it was not: Islam was to be found in neither the traditions that oppressed women, nor the conservative views of religious elements in her community, nor the depravity of some television programs. True Islam gave women the right and responsibility to pursue education, work outside the home, and contribute to society. True Islam enabled a woman to be a full participant in her society while remaining within the bounds of what was good and moral. For Miss Suheil, the process of defining the terms of moderation was critical to conveying her vision of Islam to her students.

For an educated and pious woman her perspective was not atypical. Some of the most vocal female Islamists throughout the region have argued that it is the corruption of Islam that has denied women their rights.[19] Miss Suheil was not involved in any religious organization or movement; however, being a committed Muslim was central to her sense of self and purpose. She drew on the topics raised in the textbooks to launch into broader conversations about education, progress, Islam, and women. All of these were part and parcel of her efforts to point young women in the right direction and to defend her authority as teacher when it was challenged by other voices of religious and moral authority.

Da'wa: The Call to Islam

In the spring of 2005, I attended a lesson on *da'wa* in Miss Suheil's Islamic culture class.[20] As previously stated, *da'wa* refers to the responsibility of individual Muslims to call others to be good Muslims, although it can also include calling non-Muslims to Islam. In the past few decades, however, *da'wa* activities have been central to the formal activities of Islamic organizations, "encompass[ing] a range of practical activities that were once considered outside the proper domain of the classical meaning of the term," such as establishing neighborhood mosques, social welfare organizations, Islamic education institutions, and printing presses (Mahmood 2005: 58). Saba Mahmood argues that "while many of these institutional practices have historical precedents, they have, in the last fifty years, increasingly come to be organized under the rubric of *da'wa*" (58). *Da'wa* activities have been central to the mission of the Muslim Brotherhood in Jordan, as well as those of other Islamic organizations, including the Jama'at Tabligh (Islamic Missionary Society), whose explicit goal is missionary activity within Jordan, "enjoining friends and strangers alike to practice Islam" (Wiktorowicz 2001: 136).[21] The responsibility to do *da'wa* was described as a duty for all Muslims in religion textbooks, but it was also evidenced in the myriad ways that actors within the school worked to call their fellow Muslims to follow the true Islam. What this duty consisted of could be a matter of debate, as became evident in Miss Suheil's class on *da'wa*.

The topic of *da'wa* was a full unit in the *Islamic Culture* textbook for all eleventh graders, and I sat in on several classes during which it was discussed (Jabr et al. 2004). The unit was in turn divided into three sections: *da'wa*; the methods of *da'wa*; and the goals of *da'wa*. In the first lesson of this unit, the authors discuss the duty of all Muslims to engage in *da'wa*: "The Islamic calling is a responsibility to be borne by all Muslim men and women within their ability to do so and within the limits of their knowledge. Thus, the responsibility of the great scholars is greater then the responsibility of others and the responsibility of the ruler greater than that of his followers. . . . However, the responsibility is that of all Muslims within the limits of his or her knowledge and abilities" (169–70). Upon beginning this unit with a group of eleventh graders in the science track, Miss Suheil summarized some of the main points of the lesson but quickly branched out to other topics:

MISS SUHEIL: The call should go out to everyone, but each person should have a chance to decide. For example, you can talk to your friend about the importance of the *hijab*, but she must decide on her own. . . . What are people's rights in *al-da'wa*? People have the right to hear the message but with respect. We must respect people's choices even if they go the other way.

By the way, those involved in *da'wa* here [in Jordan] don't follow these guidelines. They think they are the only ones who know the truth. They pressure people. For example, regarding women covering their face, only one of four religious scholars has called for it. The *da'wa* people say women should cover their face. They say cover your face to fight imperialism.

Miss Suheil began by discussing the proper methods and ethics of *da'wa*, which were expressly discussed in the text (180). She criticized those involved in such activities for failing to follow these guidelines, accusing them of being aggressive and of believing they had a monopoly on the truth. She used the example of women covering their face, a practice uncommon in Jordan but increasingly being practiced and encouraged by some groups involved in *da'wa*. Again, she worked to bolster her own authoritative message about Islam by critiquing that which she saw as unacceptable or illegitimate.

As class discussion continued, prompted by a passage in the textbook about calling non-Muslims to Islam, Miss Suheil talked about the perception of Islam in the West:

MISS SUHEIL: There are those in the West who accuse Muslims of being terrorists. This does not represent the true Islam but rather a small group that claims to be Muslims.

STUDENT: And there are those who say that Islam oppresses women.

MISS SUHEIL: Can you believe that they say that the *hijab* closes minds [she says this as if she thinks this notion is ridiculous and some of the girls laugh with her]. There was this woman who used to write this in the newspaper. She wrote that the *hijab* closes minds.

STUDENT: What was her background? Is she Muslim?

MISS SUHEIL: She is a Jordanian, a Muslim. Such attitudes are wrong, but so are those who follow their religion too strictly. For example there are those who believe that girls can't go to the university because it is mixed [coeducational]. There are girls like that here [in the school].[22] I tell them, "Is it better to stay home and not influence people at all?" She is worried about mixing with males. Well, we walk down the street with males. We all studied in the university [i.e., the teachers]. Did things fall apart? No.

We should be rational. Being extremely open and extremely closed or strict leave us with the same result. You decide how to behave at the university. You can decide to sit on the other side of the room. . . . A girl can be anything. She can be a journalist, a doctor, a teacher. . . . In Saudi Arabia they are too strict. . . . To a degree that is wrong.

Shortly thereafter she returned to the topic of the *hijab* again:

MISS SUHEIL: In the prayer room, some girls say that a pink *ishar* is wrong. That is ridiculous. It's okay to wear colors and different styles. After all, God made beautiful things and God likes beauty, but with limits.

STUDENT: A lot of people believe this. They believe the *ishar* has to be white and the *jelbab* black.

A lesson on the Islamic *da'wa* was made into an opportunity to discuss the importance of moderation and to criticize those whom Miss Suheil considered to be extreme in their religious beliefs and in their efforts to convince others of the superiority of their beliefs. The class discussion also served to put Miss Suheil in the position of arbiter over what is "true." The call for moderation was not unique. In fact, as discussed above, moderation and tolerance have been the hallmark of the current regime's platform on Islam, and these themes have been threaded through most official pronouncements of the Ministry of Education. Furthermore, the concept of moderation is found throughout the religious curriculum, with a full lesson in the tenth-grade Islamic education textbook devoted to the topic. In some respects, Miss Suheil buttressed the state position on the need for religious moderation. However, she was not merely mimicking official discourse but rather appropriating it to address her own sense of what was corrupting Islam. Miss Suheil's deployment of this discourse and the way in which she related it to the everyday realities of the girls at al-Khatwa made moderation a tangible ideal—one more directly linked to the lives of the students than somewhat abstract slogans in an official speech.

In the class discussion I reference above, the notion of "moderation" specifically led to a commentary on women's dress and access to higher education. Miss Suheil criticized members of the *da'wa* movement for pressuring women to cover their faces, but she defended the practice of covering one's hair, a practice widely accepted in Bawadi al-Naseem.[23] However, unlike some other teachers at al-Khatwa, she never told students who did not cover that they should wear the *hijab*. She criticized those in the West and Jordan who considered the *hijab* to be oppressive. The student who responded to the claim that the *"hijab* closes minds" was almost indignant, assuming that such a statement could come only from an outsider: "What is her background?" the student asked. Miss Suheil clarified that it was a Jordanian who had a criticized the *hijab*. Miss Suheil rarely leveled her criticism at "outsiders" (although she often compared Jordan and the Arab world with the West), reserving her censure for her own society. Indeed, on a number of occasions, I have heard elite Jordanians complain about the *hijab* and "the closing of minds." On one occasion, a Jordanian who worked with teachers complained about the prevalence of veiling among them. She wondered how teachers oppressed by the *hijab* could be effective educators. Thus, the struggles surrounding the terms of Islam, education, and progress for women were very much local ones enmeshed with other contests for power and influence. Young women in Bawadi al-Naseem were situated in a particular place vis-à-vis these local debates.[24]

In this vein, Miss Suheil's criticism often turned toward actors within the school, where the struggle over religious authority was most immediate for her as a religion teacher. Thus, when Miss Suheil argued that it was possible to be modest and fashionable (as in the color-of-*hijab* discussion), she was responding to lectures that had been given on campus in the prayer room about proper forms of dress for Muslim women, where females who wore colorful headscarves were criticized. At times, she specifically challenged beliefs articulated by the student president of the prayer room, Amina, although Miss Suheil never mentioned Amina by name. As the religion teacher and the in-school religion "expert," Miss Suheil may have felt personally challenged by other efforts to teach about Islam in school.[25] Miss Suheil responded to the challenge posed by Amina, as it was critical to establishing her authority as a teacher. Amina's challenge was both individual and institutional, as Amina both functioned as an unofficial authority in the school and was linked to a *da'wa* movement in the community. Amina had made it clear to many in the school that she would not go to the university on moral grounds because all of the universities were coeducational. Miss Suheil completely rejected such grounds for not pursuing higher education. First, she argued, if one (a female) wanted to be in a position to influence people (as in the case of the *da'wa* preachers), being out and active in places like the university was important. Second, with sarcasm she said, "[Will] things fall apart?" In contemporary Jordanian society men and women often found themselves sharing public spaces, and moral chaos had not ensued; Jordanian society did not fall apart.

The religion textbooks generally emphasize the importance of knowledge and the pursuit of knowledge for all Muslims, as long as one approaches learning with seriousness of purpose, puts forth real effort, and remains ethical in his/her interactions with teachers and students (al-Dughmi et al. 1996: 144–62). The twelfth-grade Islamic text (Jabr et al. 2004) specifically addresses coeducational institutions in a lesson called "The Provisions for the Mixing of the Sexes" (108). In this unit one can sense some ambivalence about the propriety of young women going to coeducational institutions, although it is not forbidden by any means. The lesson outlines the conditions under which it is acceptable for men and women to be together.[26] Among the acceptable situations, the textbook highlights three: at times of war; to go to the market; or for the pursuit of education (Jabr et al. 2004; 108). However, two pages later the authors say that the pursuit of knowledge in a coeducational setting "is permitted only under the condition that the environment is completely devoted to learning as in the atmosphere of worship in a mosque or during the pilgrimage" (110). Although the textbook states that Islam permits attendance at coeducational settings, it emphasizes the need for seriousness of purpose, as well as modest dress and demeanor. For Amina, the textbook did not go far enough. In fact, many families were concerned about the potential for moral corruption (typically a reference to relationships with the opposite sex) at the university, and rumors about immoral behavior at universities were rampant. In light of these concerns, many parents insisted that their daughters attend classes and come right home, in keeping with the directive of the textbook to stay focused on the educational imperative. At the same time, some parents were willing to send their daughters to other cities to study and to live in dorms. Thus, "seriousness of purpose" was open to interpretation.

In many respects, the fear among some Jordanians that moral corruption is threatening their way of life is at the crux of the struggles that Miss Suheil's students face in Jordan today. Betty Anderson (2007: 72), in her analysis of Islamic education textbooks in Jordan, charts a narrative of change as threatening. According to Anderson, students are instructed that "individual transgression will lead to disintegration of society" and that Western influences will corrupt the Muslim world intellectually and culturally (81–82). Just as Amina and others in the *da'wa* movement seek to convince young women and their families of the moral perils in contemporary Jordan (at universities, in schools, on television), the official "wish-images" in textbooks sometimes foster similar sentiments. Even Miss Suheil, who sought to temper the crisis mentality of people like Amina, found the "foreign" influences in media excesses to be a threat to the moral edification of youth. However, she did not necessarily frame such media as Western, and many of the programs or pop stars criticized by adults at al-Khatwa were Lebanese or Egyptian. She also framed the West in positive terms, particularly with respect to education and intellectualism. Furthermore, her pedagogical outlook meant that she preferred to engage her students in discussion about various forms of media rather than preach about dangers and hellfire. Using her authority in the classroom, she sought to empower the girls but with the intention of guiding them toward her vision of correct Islam and the rejection of other perspectives.

My observations of religion classes and Miss Suheil's class in particular reinforced my conviction that textbook analysis is a limited way to understand what happens in schools. The teacher had a significant role in conveying the curriculum, and students at times shaped the content of the lesson as evidenced in Miss Jude's class, which I discuss below. More important, the religion classes I attended did not conform to the stereotypical picture of religious education, and Islamic education in particular, shared by many in Jordan and in the United States; my research shows we cannot assume that religion classes by default stifle thought.

Answer Our Questions and You Will Get "Points from God"

Miss Jude was a young substitute teacher who at times struggled with classroom control. She was a deeply religious woman who had married shortly after finishing high school. After a few years of marriage, she convinced her spouse to support her in pursuing a bachelor's degree; she had only recently graduated before coming to al-Khatwa. Her approach to teaching religion was more traditional than Miss Suheil's. Like Miss Suheil, she typically started with the lesson in the text and at times made links between the texts and everyday life. However, she primarily talked *at* her students and often admonished the girls for behavior she considered to be un-Islamic, although always in a gentle and friendly way, never raising her voice. However, Miss Jude did not completely determine what happened in the classroom, as the students questioned her and at times challenged her. Also, because she was a new teacher who conveyed a sense of insecurity, some of the older students took advantage of her by being disruptive and making it difficult for her teach.

I observed fourteen of Miss Jude's religion classes and spoke with her on a number of occasions. One thing I noticed in Miss Jude's classes was that she often began class by asking girls to cover their hair. Some of the students at al-Khatwa wore headscarves only outside of school and had headscarves with them. Some of these girls responded to Miss Jude by covering their hair. However, others disregarded her, and some did not even have a headscarf to begin with. In some classes (such as an unruly group of eleventh graders) she did not even broach the topic. The tenth graders had the best rapport with Miss Jude, and the students liked her. Although she was not always the most engaging teacher, she was kind. One day I joined a group of tenth graders for a lesson on "moderation in Islam" ('Oweidhah et al. 2001). The lesson in the textbook began: "God made the Islamic community [umma] the best community, distinguishing it with the most perfect law [i.e., religious law] and the soundest method, and made the community moderate. What is moderation then?" (210). This opening statement is followed by a Qur'anic verse related to the lesson, which is the case in every lesson in this textbook. The remainder of the lesson addresses moderation in one's faith (belief), in (Islamic) law or legislation, and in spending, eating, drinking, and punishments (i.e., for sins and/or crimes). Drawing on the lesson, Miss Jude began a discussion about what moderation meant for religious practice and in one's life:

MISS JUDE: What does moderation in Islam mean?
IBTISAM: You should not just pray all the time and do nothing else.
MISS JUDE: Yes, you need to take care of your body too. Islam makes adjustments for those with physical limitations. So a traveler does not have to fast, nor does a pregnant woman. You need to take care of your body and spirit. *Zakat* [tithe] puts you at ease . . . but even *zakat* should be moderate.[27]
We should also show moderation in other ways. We should show respect for teachers and not overdo our friendliness. It is overdoing it when you start calling teachers by nicknames like "Tutu."
LENA: Miss, that means you would be "Ju Ju."

Miss Jude's reference to the need for moderation in teacher-student relations was her own and perhaps stemmed from her own efforts to assert authority in the classroom as a new teacher. Shortly after Miss Jude discussed the importance of not being too friendly with one's teachers, Deema got up from her seat to throw something in the wastebasket and then proceeded to walk by Miss Jude's desk and pinch her cheek. The class all laughed at this excessive friendliness. Even Miss Jude could not contain her smile. The students were comfortable with Miss Jude, perhaps too comfortable in her view.

At times, however, Miss Jude tried to get the girls to take their religious lessons more seriously. One week she brought a DVD to school, what the girls called the "the death DVD" as it was filled with scenes of accidents, funerals, and deaths, with subtitles about the afterlife and at times the voice of someone preaching about the afterlife. The DVD was clearly meant to put "the fear of God" into these young women.[28] The following week she asked the girls if they had been affected by the DVD: "How many of you started praying as a result of watching the DVD?" Two of the girls raised their hands. One girl joked that she no longer went to the market as she was afraid to be hit by a car. But other girls said the DVD made them cry and fear the loss of loved ones. Miss Jude continued, "Who began wearing an *ishar* as a result of the DVD?" None of the girls raised their hand. Miss Jude frequently discussed the need for head covering and at times addressed particular girls who did not cover their hair, asking them when they would start covering. I had heard one other teacher, a math teacher, ask a student the same question. Students told me that for the more religious teachers (not necessarily the religion teachers), this was to be expected. Even the official religion curriculum explicitly addresses the need to cover one's hair.

The religious curriculum included passages that explicitly addressed modesty in dress for men and women and provided Miss Jude with an opening to emphasize the need for a woman to cover her hair. Lesson 37 in the tenth-grade religion textbook explicitly addresses clothing and modest dress in Islam for men and women ("Clothing and Decoration in Islam"). Although this lesson does not include an explicit discussion of veiling, it references a saying attributed to the Prophet (*hadith*) that is interpreted to mean that women should cover everything but their hands and face ('Oweidhah et al. 2001: 174). The last lesson in the tenth-grade textbook specifically enjoins women to cover their "wrists, arms, neck, ears, and the hair on their heads" (242). Miss Jude reiterated the passages in the lesson on women's dress, adding that the need to cover one's face was debatable.[29] For the most part Miss Jude stuck quite closely to the text. However, she added her own assertion that unrelated men and women should not shake hands. I found no mention in this lesson (or other lessons I had read in the religion textbooks) of a prohibition against handshaking, and in my experience such beliefs were considered to be too conservative by many Jordanians, including students and adults at al-Khatwa. However, like covering one's face, handshaking between the sexes had become another marker of a new form of public piety in Jordan, a development closely associated with new religious movements and sentiments in the region (Deeb 2006). These piety movements have worked to redefine the requirements of living Islamically in a contemporary era, in ways that are not necessarily in tandem with the public discourse of the regime, although the textbooks—the official state religion curriculum—contradicted this discourse at times.

Many girls raised their hands during this lesson and began to ask questions: "Who should you shake hands with? What if you have friendly relations with your neighbor and he is like your brother?" Ibtisam asked if it was acceptable for men to look at women uncovered on television. However, before Miss Jude could answer her questions, the girls began debating this among themselves. The discussion then shifted to marriage (the final paragraph in this lesson was about marriage), and one student asked out loud, "What about women marrying women?" Miss Jude ignored her. The student behind me, whom I did not know, kept muttering things that the teacher could not hear. At one point, when Miss Jude was talking about the immodest dress of people before Islam, this student said, "They were smarter then." This student also said something about never getting married. Miss Jude seemed uncomfortable with questions but the students persisted.

During another classroom observation, Miss Jude seemed particularly uncomfortable with student questions. On this day, Lena initiated a discussion about fate, destiny, and free will. The lesson itself began with a brief synopsis of the previous lesson on moderation, but Lena raised her hand and said, "There is something that I have been wondering about." She went on:

LENA: If people are destined and God gives grace [ziraq], then it's not fair to judge them if their fate is written.

RITA: If God made us and knows what we will do, then what is left?

MISS JUDE: It is not that God will determine what you do. It's just that God knows what you will do. There have been many debates and judgments made about this among religious scholars so we don't need to repeat this.

Miss Jude seemed bothered by the questions, and Lena sensed this. She responded to her teacher, "We are just using our minds." Miss Jude in turn said, "Use them for something useful. Read books [for example]." Rita raised her hand to add to this conversation; the teacher ignored her, even joking to the class about ignoring troublesome students. After Rita had been standing and waving her hand for almost five minutes, Miss Jude said jokingly, "Oh. Rita. Do you have a question?" Rita, bothered by the teacher's actions, said, "Just forget it. I don't want to ask anymore, but, Miss, it's not right to cut me off."

Miss Jude tried to refocus the class on herself. She asked two girls why they were not wearing an *ishar*, neither of whom responded, and then she began talking about prayer and the need to focus on God during prayer. Some students were not paying attention at all; I saw Kareema and her friends looking at pictures of movie stars cut out of a magazine and then passing them to their friends. But others continued to ask questions, and Miss Jude remarked, "Your questions don't end." Deema responded, "Miss, they are questions about religion. You will get points with God [for answering them]. You will go to heaven." Miss Jude seemed a bit overwhelmed by all the questions but kept smiling. Then Majida, who was usually somewhat quiet in class, asked a question Miss Jude seemed more comfortable with: "Miss, I don't wear an *ishar*. I pray. I don't do anything wrong. Will God judge me?" Miss Jude responded, "Everything will be judged for its own right. Being stubborn about something is wrong. It's like disobeying your parents just to be stubborn." The class ended on this note, but this group of tenth graders persisted in their questions in the coming week.

I found many contrasts between Miss Suheil's classes and those of Miss Jude. Most significantly Miss Suheil was more experienced and explicitly experimented with different pedagogical techniques. Both were concerned with the moral education of their students, but Miss Jude's directives were more specific and related to particular "Islamic" practices and behavior, most consistently the dress and composure of females. Miss Suheil, on the other hand, gave more general advice and was more broadly concerned with inspiring and encouraging her students to be confident and strong as well as moral beings. Thus, although each of these women was quite religious by local standards, their vision of what this required of them as teachers varied. Each teacher shaped the content of religious lessons in the classroom by deciding what to emphasize from the text and what direction to take the textbook lesson. Yet neither completely defined the parameters of those lessons, both because the text and religious doctrine as portrayed in the text created a framework for discussion and because student responses were varied and at times exigent.

The place of religion in the assessments that determine students' future educational opportunities is also relevant. *Al-tarbiyya al-islamiyya* (Islamic Education), the curriculum and textbook for eleventh graders in the humanities track, is a case in point. Because the girls would not be tested on this particular text in the *tawjihi* exam, Miss Suheil could veer from its contents without too much concern about jeopardizing the students' scores. This was also the case with Miss Jude and her tenth-grade classes. The twelfth-grade religion teacher, in contrast, was focused on helping her students pass the high school completion test, which required memorizing the contents of their text. Thus, the possibilities in the class were in some sense shaped by the structures of the school and assessment system.

At some level, religion class is more conducive to discussion and debate than other classes because of the way in which it relates to questions about proper living in the contemporary world. Gregory Starrett (1998) has argued that this process of making religion applicable and useful to everyday life in state religious curricula—what he calls "functionalization"—has unintentionally supplied the tools for a counterdiscourse of Islamic opposition in the Egyptian context: "In order for compulsory schooling to relay knowledge of the 'legitimate' religious culture sufficient to attain its goal of social control, it must use pedagogical techniques that work to undermine the authority of the holders of religious legitimacy by marginalizing the means of cultural production that they possess" (187). Starrett argues that this process of functionalization serves to undermine not only the state's dominance over the interpretation of religious knowledge but that of the traditional religious authorities as well,[30] in essence popularizing or democratizing processes of attaining and making meaning in religion. The way in which religion is objectified and then functionalized in state schools has a powerful albeit unintended effect. The curriculum in Jordan similarly functionalizes religion. However, the clearest models of these pedagogical techniques at al-Khatwa were Miss Suheil, Miss Jude, and Amina, the sixteen-year-old *da'iyya*, or preacher. The textbooks are meant to impart orthodoxy, the accepted account of proper faith, but their transmission is dependent upon the work of the actual actors in the school. Proper behavior and comportment, legitimate textual references, and acceptable belief are communicated through the practices and narratives of individuals in the space of the school. The practices and discourses that vie for this authority are many, and not limited to religion class, but not everyone is accorded equal authority, as I will show in the example of Maysoon later in this chapter.

Amina: An In-House Preacher

Amina's vocation was *da'wa*. She wanted to show her peers the "true" Islam and thus was engaged in actively trying to define that truth. Amina was an average student who, as already discussed, regularly announced that she had no intention of going to college because it was coeducational and, hence, immoral. She was one of a handful of girls in this school and a small minority of women in Bawadi al-Naseem who wore the full *khimar*. In Jordanian colloquial, *khimar* refers to a long and loose robe, usually black, and a head covering that completely covers the face. Amina's father had been a religion teacher for decades, and her family was active in *da'wa* activities. Such a family history was not a given, however, for students active on the prayer room committee. Dunya, Amina's friend and a prayer room committee member, came from a family that had only very recently become more observant, prompted by the "conversion" of her older sister, who became more religious and then preached to her own family, calling on them to be better Muslims.

Amina considered herself to be a *da'iyya* in training; in fact, she was already a preacher at school, taking any opportunity she could find to preach about being a good Muslim. In addition to giving lectures in the prayer room, she gave impromptu lectures in class if a teacher did not show up or if a teacher ended class early. She also had a tendency to turn an answer to a teacher's question into a ten- or fifteen-minute monologue. Although Amina placed much weight upon her influence over students, on the few occasions where I observed her "lecturing" her class, the majority seemed to lose interest quickly, and some seemed annoyed. The teachers at most encouraged her and at least tolerated her. At least one student who had been active in the prayer room committee quit because, as she said, "the girls go only when Amina is there, and when they are not in the prayer room they are fooling around outside. . . . The point is they act all nice and well-behaved around Amina, but the minute she's not around they are like a zipper that's wide open." This student also bore some resentment because of Amina's dominance in the prayer room.

However, Amina did seem to hold sway over some students. Khadije, a twelfth grader, was a follower of Amina, and Amina's influence led to major changes in Khadije's dress (she began to cover her face) and in her behavior (she stopped listening to music). Khadije was socially awkward, had few friends, and was from a desperately poor family. She found much comfort in the attention she received from Amina and her peers. By discussing Khadije, I do not mean to imply that only someone so marginalized could respond to Amina's preaching. Research around the globe has shown that becoming more religious, or seeking new religious experiences, is often part of the search for meaning or purpose in young people (Smith and Denton 2005; Wilkins 2008). Khadije followed her because she was looking for friendship and because she sought some status or recognition from her peers and maybe even her teachers. Although many of the students were ambivalent toward or even openly dismissive of Amina, some students clearly found her knowledge of Islam useful in their own struggles to make something meaningful in their lives, to help them get through problems at home, or just to make friends. Like their peers around the world, for some of the girls religion figured strongly in their coming-of-age process.

One of the primary venues for Amina's work was the prayer room, a small one-room building that had been constructed some time in the mid-1990s. Students who prayed regularly and wanted to do their midday prayers at the prescribed time were allowed to go into the prayer room to do so.[31] In addition to being a space to pray, the prayer room was the site of lectures organized by a student committee during the midday break, and interested students could come hear a fellow student or a teacher speak on a particular topic related to Islam. According to Amina, it was her initiative as the student president that led to the lunchtime lectures in the prayer room.[32] The number of students in the prayer room at lunchtime could be anywhere from fifteen to thirty, although their attendance seemed to trickle off as the semester progressed. The prayer room committee also held a number of contests or competitions of Qur'anic memorization and knowledge of the

Qur'an. Students worked under the guidance of one teacher, Miss Majida, who provided books and sometimes money as prizes for such competitions. Although Majida acted as an advisor, the students seemed to have almost complete control over the activities held in the prayer room, in distinct contrast with all other such "extracurricular" activities at school.[33] Amina and Dunya corroborated this, stating that they received very few directives for their work.

Al-Khatwa administrators, like many Jordanians, viewed the influence of religion and of more religious members of their community as positive and in line with their efforts to ensure that girls behaved, respected their teachers, and followed school rules.[34] The principal talked about the role of the prayer room committee as supportive of the school staff's goals:

> I tell them [the prayer room committee]: "Keep your focus on student behavior, manners, and discipline. Focus on these things so we can cut down on the problems in school." If I notice that we [the school] are in need of a particular lesson, I will tell them, "Talk about this or that." For example, sometimes I ask them to talk about makeup. Sometimes about lateness, absences, or the behavior of the girls in the street. These are the things on which we focus.

The prayer room committee was seen as an ally in keeping the students in line. The staff and administration took the view that these girls, and especially Amina, were calling their fellow students to Islam and encouraging them to behave better, which had to be positive from the perspective of a staff trying to keep nearly six hundred students under control and out of serious moral trouble. To this end, Amina was free to act and preach as she saw fit, even though Amina represented a minority perspective, one that was considered overly conservative and even extreme by some. The independence given to this space and to the students involved in managing this space was uncharacteristic of the way in which business was normally conducted at al-Khatwa and in state schools.

The leeway given to these students may have been a function of several dynamics: Amina was a student and not a teacher; the prayer room was an informal space; the primary actors were females. Had a teacher taken on the same role as Amina, her divergence from the official curriculum might have raised more concern. Indeed, Miss Suheil had been active in the prayer room prior to my arrival at al-Khatwa, and according to her, she had been discouraged by the administration from taking this role. Of course, a teacher could deviate from the official curriculum in the privacy of her own classroom.

However, preaching in the prayer room constituted a potentially more visible deviation. Indeed, the religiosity of teachers is a concern in Jordan, as it is in other countries such as Egypt (Herrera 2000), and the Muslim Brotherhood has long emphasized the importance of teaching and education.[35] Furthermore, not only were these merely students, they were females. The specter of extremism that circulates in the region and around the globe is a decidedly male image. Although there has always been a role for women as religious authorities in Islam, the dominant image and reality of religious authority is male. The activities of adolescent girls like Amina are viewed as less authoritative and less threatening than activities undertaken by males.

Amina and her peers were given the autonomy to pursue their *da'wa* activities because these activities did not seem to openly contradict mainstream religious ideas and because they might be helpful in maintaining order in the school. However, in many respects Amina's Islam did challenge other perspectives on the truth and the authority of others in the school to define what it means to be a good Muslim. By preaching outside the parameters of religion class and, in some instances, conveying a message that was different from that found in the classroom (e.g., concerning gendered modesty and the implications for women's participation in public life), she posed a challenge to the official attempts to control religious discourse in schools and to propagate standard narratives about women and development. Furthermore, as depicted in the previous chapter, by constructing certain activities sanctioned by the state as *haram*, she indirectly challenged the regime's religious legitimacy. On at least one occasion she also acted to monitor the realm of acceptable religious discourse, which I will explore now.

Maysoon and "Unorthodox" Islam

The terms of acceptable debate about Islam were limited, as I discovered in the case of Maysoon, a student who was almost expelled for her ideas about Islam. Maysoon was a sensitive eleventh grader easily brought to tears by an admonishment from a teacher. She seemed interested in religion—she read religious magazines and at times sung hymns in class—and usually went to the prayer room during break. When Maysoon did not show up for school for several days, I asked about her and heard conflicting stories about what had happened. One of her classmates said her parents took her out of school because she "caused problems." Another girl told me that Maysoon had been transferred to another secondary school because of a disciplinary problem.[36] She said she had heard that Maysoon had had an argument with

Miss Majida. Another student said they transferred her because she was sitting with groups of girls and talking with them about "strange" ideas; I tried to find out more about what had happened:

FIDA: What kind of ideas?
STUDENT: Well, she is in this religious group called al-Habashiyya.
FIDA: Are they Muslims?
STUDENT: Yes, they are, but they are not accepted by Islam.
ANOTHER STUDENT: They follow 'Ali.
FIDA: Isn't that Shi'a?
STUDENT: Yes, they are Shi'a.
FIDA: I didn't know there were Shi'a in Jordan.
STUDENT: They are from Palestine.
FIDA: I didn't think they had Shi'a in Palestine either.

No one responded to my last comment and the period soon ended. What eventually became clear after repeated inquiries was that Maysoon had somehow gotten involved in a controversial Islamic movement called al-Habashiyya. She had been speaking to her peers about the al-Habashiyya movement, and this had led to her expulsion. Al-Habashiyya, which literally means Ethiopian, or al-Ahbash, is the commonly known name for the Association of Islamic Philanthropic Projects, an organization and movement established in Beirut by Shaykh 'Abdalla, an Ethiopian Islamic scholar. Al-Ahbash are known for their emphasis on moderation and coexistence with Christians (Kabha and Erlich 2006: 525). They draw on some Sufi practices, although Mustafa Kabha and Haggai Erlich argue that Sufism is not central to the identity of the movement (2006: 525).[37] Their movement has spread throughout the region, with a particularly strong presence in Lebanon and among Muslim minority populations in Europe. Al-Ahbash have been in direct conflict with Wahhabi scholars, and Saudi clerics have issued fatwas against them, accusing them of being "deviators" from Islamic orthodoxy (Kabha and Erlich 2006: 527).

I never learned what ideas Maysoon had sought to share with her peers, but I discovered that the student prayer room committee and Amina in particular had brought these "unacceptable" ideas to the attention of their advisor, Miss Majida. Thus, what most students came to know about Maysoon's expulsion was that she had had a disagreement with Miss Majida. On a couple of occasions, I tried to learn more about this incident from Amina and some of her peers, but they seemed determined to keep the details quiet, and I respected their wishes. When I asked Miss Suheil about Maysoon, she did not explicitly discuss the incident, saying: "I do not like to just reject a student's ideas. I don't like to just disregard them. I like to approach them through discussion. I try and convince them." Thus what made Miss Suheil unique as a religion teacher was not that she did not seek to be authoritative; rather, it was her pedagogical perspective, which viewed rational debate and discussion as the best means to "true" religious knowledge.

To my surprise, Maysoon returned to school after several weeks. When I asked the principal what had happened, she explained: "Maysoon was talking about some religious movement, al-Habashiyya, in school with the girls. We do not allow new ideas that are not acceptable to society, especially ideas about religion, in school." The principal explained that she and Maysoon's father had agreed to let the girl think that she was expelled and then allow her to come back to school if she promised never to discuss such things again. The principal said that Maysoon's parents had thought their daughter was going to "ordinary" religion lessons at someone's house and did not realize that these ideas were being taught. Although al-Habashiyya has a small presence in Jordan (Kabha and Erlich 2006: 523–24), the group was clearly considered outside the realm of the acceptable.

The staff and teachers in tandem with students worked to prevent the emergence of a different religious perspective—one outside the bounds of the dominant Sunni narrative. The al-Habashiyya movement was made "unthinkable" (Asad 1993: 35) by the power of this dominant narrative, and the move to silence Maysoon was swift. Maysoon was disciplined because she challenged the bounds of acceptable religious belief, in this case the dominant Sunni narrative. Amina seemed angered by Maysoon's transgressions and even demanded an apology from her upon her return. In speaking with me, the principal did not convey any personal sentiments about al-Habashiyya, but rather a concern with her role as moral arbiter of what was socially acceptable at the school. Miss Suheil took a slightly different stance; although she did not question the premise that Maysoon's new beliefs were problematic, she argued that the adults in the school should approach the project of guiding Maysoon to the right knowledge differently. Despite the prevalence of debates about proper faith within the school, the terms of such debates were limited by the power of a dominant discourse, even if the terms of that discourse were regularly tested.

Conclusion

Teaching about Islam was part of everyday efforts to point others in the "right" direction and fulfill the personal responsibility to do *da'wa* within one's capacity. Given the increasing number of Jordanians involved in *da'wa* or piety movements, schools are logical places for such activities. The Muslim Brotherhood has long seen education and teaching as among its most important vocations (Wiktorowicz 2001). Even the leftists and nationalists of the 1940s and 1950s saw schools as critical recruiting grounds for their efforts to create an Arab nationalist ethic (Anderson 2005; Kharinu 2000). The piety movements are a new manifestation of these historical efforts to shape young minds, beliefs, and practices through school. They are less about recruiting members to formal political organizations and more about calling Muslims to be better Muslims. However, even for those not formally involved in any religious organization, pointing young people in the right direction and teaching them to be moral and good people are clearly within the realm of what schools do. Thus, this struggle to participate in the moral edification of youth is not limited to the efforts of organizations that challenge the state but is also about teachers and administrators who want to control students and maintain orderly schools as well as work to shape moral citizens and community members. However, these are clearly political contests as well. Ultimately debates about proper forms of piety and legitimate forms of religious knowledge are deeply political (Mahmood 2005).

As I have shown in this chapter, although educators at al-Khatwa accepted the centrality of Islam in this process of edification, different ideas about what constitutes proper faith circulated within the confines of the school. Furthermore, these debates were entwined with the gender deliberations that have characterized contending discourses about progress, development, and authenticity in Jordan. Competing interpretations of the proper modesty and comportment of women, of the proper Muslim family, and of legitimate gender roles and relations are all central to religious discourse in Jordan today, as they are to public images of what a girl's future may hold. At al-Khatwa, these struggles were manifest in the competing efforts to be authoritative in the space of the school. The state's curriculum is the dominant narrative and has the most resources at its disposal. Educators are state representatives, but they are also social actors with their own experiences, lives, and intentions. Their struggles to be authoritative are not contained by state designs. I do not mean to imply that they are always in opposition to the state. Indeed, Miss Suheil's teaching was in many respects in step with the official narrative, as was Miss Jude's. But the "wish-images" of the textbooks are limited in their reach and the discourse of public figures distant and abstract. It is in the teaching and day-to-day interactions that such sentiments are made actual.

Furthermore, the teacher is not alone in her teaching. Amina was a prominent student educator and one whose lessons directly challenged the authority of others in the school. Amina's work also highlights the porosity of the school's walls and, as a result, official authorities' inability to control the terms of religious discourse. Yet it was not just Amina and her *da'wa* group that entered this space, for the sources of religious authority were multifarious, albeit not equally powerful. Even the constant questions from students such as Deema, Rita, and Lena served to challenge teachers' lessons and the text. From the al-Habashiyya movement that almost led to Maysoon's expulsion, to the television preachers who conveyed a range of doctrinal perspectives, to the satellite TV programs that functioned as a foil for what is right and good, the religious material and sentiments that flowed through the school were many, and the attempts to interpret, foreground, and forbid particular visions of true Islam were persistent. In the next chapter I follow some of these themes as I examine competing notions of gendered respectability and related discourses about love, marriage, and relationships that drew on multiple notions of morality not exclusively religious in nature.

FIVE

Making Girls into Respectable Women

Gender Lessons

The al-Khatwa School is completely surrounded by a wall, save for a gate at the main entrance that is left open during operating hours. In 2005, the school had a guard who could be found standing just outside the main entrance in the morning. The wall that surrounds the school was tall enough to keep this public institution somewhat private.[1] In practice, however, many people came and went throughout the day. Education officials, salespeople, parents, and other adults came to see the principal, teachers, or whomever they might have business with in the school. Teachers sometimes went on errands when they had free periods or if they had official business to undertake elsewhere. Students also could be seen going to buy candy or ice cream at the nearby candy store or just strolling nearby even though this was expressly forbidden.

Despite the presence of the guard, the principal was often at the gate in the morning and, at times, during dismissal to make sure students entered promptly in the morning and went right home at dismissal, and to ensure that any unwanted visitors, namely, teenage boys, stayed out. Technically this was part of the guard's duties, but he, despite his tall stature, was timid and rarely spoke to the students. Furthermore, the local male youths had little respect for the school guard and paid no heed to his presence. Thus, the principal was at the gate as a guard of sorts. Yet her "guarding" duties were not limited to the school gates. One day while she was en route to school the principal saw a girl wearing a pink shirt over her uniform getting out of a pickup truck near the school. She did not recognize the girl but was concerned that she might be an al-Khatwa student and had suspicions about whom the girl had been with in the truck (i.e., she suspected it was not one of her male relatives). When the principal arrived at school that day, she asked that all the teachers look out for a girl wearing a pink shirt and send any girl fitting this description to her immediately.[2] This incident was indicative of how concerned some of the staff at al-Khatwa were with monitoring the behavior of their young charges even outside the confines of the school. The staff at al-Khatwa worked to ensure that students were not engaged in any immoral activity, particularly during the hours in which the girls were their responsibility, for the reputations of the girls in turn built the reputation of the school. Many teachers were also motivated by concern for the girls, discouraging them from behavior that could anger their families or tarnish their reputations.

Schools are in many respects "disciplinary institutions" with the purpose of molding young minds and shaping young bodies (Foucault 1977). In Bawadi al-Naseem, teachers and parents alike conceived of school as an extension of the family—as an allied social institution that in addition to teaching academic subjects was entrusted with the upbringing or *tarbiyya* of young women, according to a set of generally shared moral values. Most school officials took this responsibility quite seriously, and given the time girls spent in school, gender lessons at school were salient dimensions of their upbringing. Educators worked to monitor and control the behavior of students and to shape respectable young women. Monitoring the behavior of students at al-Khatwa was not limited to teachers, however, as students too worked to keep the behavior of their peers in check. Yet for both teachers and students the terms of gendered respectability—the appropriate gender lessons—were not always self-evident. Indeed, both students and educators were actively engaged in defining the terms of gendered respectability through their everyday talk and practices.

Janise Hurtig (1998) defines "gender lessons" as "the daily teaching and learning of gender as a kind of social practice; the different ways in which gender is practiced and learned in different places and contexts" (17). At al-Khatwa, girls were not merely taught gender; gender was constructed through the day-to-day practices and interactions with parents, teachers, and peers. Many of these processes were so mundane that their express work as gendered projects was obscure. However, some girls and teachers actively worked at gender—to define the ideal or authorize the appropriate gender lessons. Some girls tried to subvert or circumvent existing gender standards. More often, students at al-Khatwa worked to "pass," or fit in, pushing at some boundaries. Even when young women accepted the dominant norms, their efforts to live by them also worked to define and at times transform gender meanings, for to embrace is also to imbue with meaning through one's actions (Butler 1988, 1993; Mahmood 2005). For example, as discussed in chapters 3 and to a degree chapter 4, modesty was one such norm; however, what it meant to be modest in a variety of new social situations—new to the girls as they matured and faced new circumstances and new to Jordan by virtue of social transformations under way—was not expressed in clear rules but rather was negotiated in day-to-day practices, situations, and interactions.

At times, community expectations surrounding gendered respectability seemed quite clear and inviolable.[3] Adolescent girls should be modest and should not bring unnecessary attention to themselves. Girls should be reserved and convey a seriousness of purpose when in public places and in school. They should avoid contact with unrelated males and should not develop a relationship with a male until they were ready to marry, and then only under the auspices of their families. Marriage in many respects was the desired outcome of a life lived respectably. Marriage in turn accorded respect; it was the marker of adulthood for women more than for men. Although for some Jordanians respectability was expressed largely in religious terms, for many in Bawadi al-Naseem it was discussed in more general terms related to propriety, "our" culture and customs, and class and economic status. All of these in turn were closely tied up with family and kin obligations and reputation. However, as in any society, no ideology or dominant narrative is entirely consistent, nor is it the "only game in town" (Ortner 1996: 19). Gendered norms are complicated by new economic and social realities; education constituted a powerful force in this regard. Being educated is inextricably linked to contemporary notions of respectability, and these links are manifest in unexpected ways. Education constructs new forms of respectability with the value accorded to being educated and to particular forms of education and thus creates new forms of hierarchy and exclusion alongside new opportunities (Levinson and Holland 1996). In Jordan, this was most apparent in the school tracking system, discussed in chapter 2, and the moral valuation of particular fields of study and academic performance more generally.

Struggles surrounding respectability and a girl's reputation were readily apparent at al-Khatwa. In Bawadi al-Naseem, sex segregation was a key component of respectability and a girl's reputation; as a result, school officials were particularly concerned to prevent "relations"[4] between boys and girls. Adults' preoccupations with the behavior and respectability of students were also intertwined with concerns about marriage (shared by many of the young women as well), particularly given the perception that Jordan was witnessing a "marriage crisis." This crisis typically referenced the inability of young people to get married due to economic difficulties, or as a result of gendered social transformations that led women to wait too long to marry.[5] The perception of a crisis was also fueled by regular media coverage of the topic. Ironically, strict sex segregation at times seemed to stand in the way of marriage. At the same time, stories about love, boys, and relationships permeated much of day-to-day adolescent conversation, alongside a discourse that found such talk immoral and objectionable. Today these preoccupations with love are increasingly influenced by the global mass media, which present new modes of marriage and love for young people. Not only do tensions between respectability and love play out in schools in stark ways, but schooling opens up new possibilities for social interaction and exposure to discourses about love and marriage. While the curriculum specifically addresses the institution of marriage and marriage as a moral imperative in Islam (Jabr et al. 2004), schools themselves construct new forms of respectability through the status accorded to the educated person. Schools in this respect are important sites of negotiating gender boundaries and gender lessons.

Keeping Boys and Girls Apart

One norm that was held up as particularly important was the separation of the sexes. In Bawadi al-Naseem, the relations between unmarried young women and men who are not members of the immediate family are typically limited to the most necessary interactions.[6] However, contemporary social and economic transformations have rendered this social precept somewhat ambiguous. On the one hand, some Jordanians now practice greater sex segregation owing to new perceptions of the impropriety of mixed-sex gatherings tied to new forms of religiosity.[7] Furthermore, throughout the last century (and even more recently in Bawadi al-Naseem), some women have experienced less mobility and access to public spaces than an earlier generation as a result of the increased settlement of peoples who were previously more mobile and a decline in agriculture and husbandry, as well as urbanization and attendant transformations (Abu Lughod 2000; Tucker 1985). On the other hand, women are marrying later, going to the university in numbers greater than men, and entering the formal labor force (albeit at relatively low levels).[8] As more women enter the spaces created by such transformations, they encounter and interact with unrelated males. In many respects, then, the realities of "modern" urban life mean that some men and women are in greater contact with each other and have new occasions and/or spaces for interaction, especially in urban areas.

For high school girls in Bawadi al-Naseem, there appeared to be much less ambiguity about the mixing of the sexes and gendered spaces than for university students or working women. Adolescent girls had little occasion for sanctioned everyday interaction with males outside the family. Schools were sex-segregated, and there were few if any opportunities for socializing outside of school. This made it easier to monitor the behavior of adolescent girls. The efforts in and around the school to keep boys and girls apart were manifold, albeit not always effective or consistent. On at least three occasions while I was at al-Khatwa, I was surprised to find adolescent boys wandering around the school grounds. More frequently they could be found hanging about the school gates waiting to catch a glimpse of the girls leaving the school. For this reason, the principal often stood near the gate at dismissal, as well as at the beginning of the day. The reaction to these "incursions" by the teenage boys was either anger (and threats to call the police) or an attitude of "boys will be boys." The remarks reserved for the girls were typically less charitable. When boys came on campus and I inquired about these incidents, students and teachers blamed the girls for attracting unwanted attention. The concern with keeping boys and men outside of female spaces was an ongoing public preoccupation outside the school as well, with accompanying rumors about men sneaking into girls' schools or colleges sometimes dressed in female garb.[9] Rumors of one such incident at the al-Khatwa School circulated while I was there but were unsubstantiated.

For a girl, charges of talking or flirting with boys were quite serious. Yet many girls talked about boys endlessly, and some hoped to see particular boys on their way home. A few girls even managed to have some type of relationship. At times it was limited to a phone relationship, but some actually managed to see a boy they were interested in, although this was deemed unacceptable by the overwhelming majority of people in this community. Indeed, in my conversations with students, they often described "bad friends" as those who distracted a girl from her studies and led her to vice, the most serious vice typically being framed as engaging in a relationship with a boy. The school authorities' concerns about this issue extended even beyond the school's gates. This was not official policy but rather something the principal felt it necessary to take upon herself. On one occasion, she complained to me that colleagues at other schools did not similarly see this as their responsibility, and therefore girls would arrive from middle school already involved in such "relationships." Some of the students complained about being monitored outside of school, but even more complained that the school was too lax in its duty to keep girls in line. In part they were concerned that if the school developed a reputation as morally lax and its students as ill behaved, this would reflect negatively on them. Nevertheless, another discourse went alongside this one about "bad" girls and relations with boys —a discourse about "relations" and love as legitimate and natural and, in the eyes of some, a necessary part of securing a marriage partner. Even a seemingly unambiguous prohibition on adolescent male/female relations was regularly violated on some level, and although the discourse that treated such relations as immoral was dominant, it was not the only one that existed.

"Do They Love in America?": Talk about Love at al-Khatwa

> We must not imagine a world of discourse divided between accepted discourse and excluded discourse, or between dominant discourse and the dominated one; but as the multiplicity of discursive elements that can come into play in various strategies.
>
> —Foucault

One day Jenine, an eleventh grader, came up to me with an entourage of seven or eight friends clinging to each other and with a dreamy-eyed look said, "Miss, do they love in America?" I laughed, thinking as I did many times while at al-Khatwa that there was so much that was similar about being a high school girl in Jordan and being one in the United States. I replied, "Yes. Do they love in Jordan?" She replied in turn, "Yes, that's all we do." The girls at al-Khatwa frequently spoke of love, relationships, and marriage. For many of the girls, everyday conversations, arguments, hopes, and disappointments consisted of adolescent dreams of love. Some girls labeled such talk as silly, while others criticized it for being immoral. The girls held different notions of what constituted a relationship and to what degree, if at all, any such relationships were acceptable, moral, or honorable. Many so-called relationships between males and females were merely talk, and relationships could be as limited as fleeting glances in the market as the girls walked home. However, some girls pushed the boundaries which prohibited relationships with boys, even if they faced serious consequences. Given how sex-segregated life in Bawadi al-Naseem appeared and how severe the consequences could be for a girl found to be in a relationship with a boy, I assumed that even if "relations" between girls and boys existed, girls would make every effort to be discreet. Yet talk of relationships and love was constant.

School was a logical place for talk of love since it was a space in which adolescent dreams and desires were shared, created, and criticized. Boys and romantic relationships—real or imagined—were the subject of secrets, gossip, shared imaginings, and jealousies; "sentimental education" was the subject of everyday discourse, peer interactions, and friendships at al-Khatwa.[10] At al-Khatwa, educators also engaged explicitly with issues of love, marriage, and relationships in the "gender lessons" they sought to impart to young women. They gave advice about the future and acted as "filters" or interpreters for information and rumors that made their way into school. Finally, because educational attainment is intertwined with narratives about good marriage prospects, being in school is linked to talk about love and relationships through discourses about the future, adulthood, and success. However, the association between education and marriage/respectability is not always so predictable in an era when marriage is in crisis and educational success is defined locally and globally in increasingly narrow terms.

The al-Khatwa students listened to love songs, dreamed about movie stars, and wrote sentimental letters to each other. They had also been exposed to different conceptualizations of love, relationships, and marriage than an earlier generation through mass media that today have few limits. Such images of love and romantic relationships are not entirely new (Armbrust 2005); the difference is in the reach of global media conglomerates, the range of potential images now readily at hand, and the space that such media have come to fill in people's lives. Images of love and romance from the media were frequently the subject of discussion and criticism among teachers and peers, whether in the classroom, in the schoolyard, or in the graffiti found throughout the school. Students talked about movie stars they adored, music videos they loved, and a range of satellite programming from American movies to television shows like *The Oprah Winfrey Show* and *Friends*. Lebanese satellite programming such as *Star Academy* and *Super Star* were also high on the popularity list. These shows often present women dressing less than modestly, performing for public audiences, and putting their bodies on display. They also construct an ideal image of romantic love as the path to marriage that diverges significantly from the way most marriages are made in Bawadi al-Naseem, as I will discuss further. Teachers also engaged with such images, at times condemning the visions of life and love being presented in the popular media and cautioning the girls to be discerning in their viewing of such material and, in some cases, admonishing them for wasting their time on such programs.

Talk about love and relationships has always existed in the Arab Muslim world, the subject of poetry, stories, and songs centuries old.[11] However, historically a distinction between romantic love and marriage has been clear.[12] Today many Jordanians still reject the notion of "marrying for love," but romantic feelings could not always be controlled. Talk about love and romance filled the space created by youthful longings and physical attractions, serving as an outlet, one that some adults encouraged. Tensions surrounding love and romantic sentiments were also intimately tied to conceptions of marriage and fears about not getting married that dominated public discourse about marriage. Twenty years ago the majority of girls the age of the al-Khatwa students would be married or preparing to marry soon. Today, the overwhelming majority of adolescent girls are in high school, and most hope to go on to a community college or university. Whereas in the past, adolescent physical attractions and emotions were channeled into early marriage, today young men and women marry much later. In 2008, the Jordanian Department of Statistics reported that the average age of first marriage for females was 26.3 and for males 29.8.[13] Diane Singerman (2007) highlights some of the social repercussions of delayed marriage: "These repercussions are reflected in the rise of new discourses and debates about sexuality and morality, generational conflict, the rise of a 'marriage black market,' and conflicts about identity because youth are negotiating and trying to reconcile contradictory public and private norms, values, and expectations" (8). Some school officials were cognizant of such conflicts and worked to control girls' movements and their talk, to ensure that girls did not risk their own reputations or that of the school. Yet such efforts could be shaped by divergent discourses—discourses about adolescence, love, and the imperative to get married.

Despite a seemingly hegemonic discourse in which love and romantic relations were taboo, a "multiplicity of discursive elements" circulated at al-Khatwa about love, marriage, and relationships (Foucault 1990: 100–101; Abu-Lughod 2000). The competing discourses, which I heard and observed, can roughly be categorized as three. Those with the most rigid perspective on these matters believed that girls should not talk about love, boys, desire, or relationships. Such talk itself was dishonorable and worse yet could lead to immoral activity. The clearest example of this was found in families who prohibited their daughters from listening to love songs or watching television shows or romantic movies. Fedwa, an eleventh grader, told me that she had watched the movie *Titanic* in secret as one of her older brothers forbade her to see romance movies. Some people feared that the sentiments conveyed by such romantic media as films and song might incite immoral or unacceptable behavior. Some of the concerns about music discussed in chapter 3 also allude to such fears.

A more practical discourse guided others at al-Khatwa, who considered silence or censorship as unhealthy and unrealistic. Their rationale seemed to be that it was better to air such thoughts and feelings, recognize them, label them, and teach girls to refrain from acting on them until they married. One staff member at al-Khatwa discussed the need for mothers to understand that their daughters' attractions to the opposite sex were normal;[14] she encouraged mothers not to let girls feel as if this was something bad or wrong.

A third perspective was not as explicit but emerged in the course of my research. This perspective held that if a girl was to ensure that she would marry, she needed to be strategic about increasing her "prospects." This meant that some adults might look the other way if a relationship was budding or intercede to ensure that it remained "honorable" and resulted in marriage. In part, this approach was related to beliefs about the superiority of companionate marriage that had their roots in a modernizing discourse that first emerged in the region a century ago (Abu-Lughod 1998; Najmabadi 2005), as well as perceptions that divorce had increased dramatically in Jordan.[15] It also stemmed from the contradiction between strict sex segregation and the need to become known as an eligible and desirable bride. Going to school could both help and hinder one's marriage prospects. Going to school made a girl who might otherwise spend most of her time at home more visible, even if it delayed marriage. Also, by conferring the status that today comes with increased levels of education, schooling increased the prospects that a young woman would marry well. However, going out to school also had its risks, as girls could be susceptible to the influence of their peers and might jeopardize their reputations.

The story of Ghaliye, an eleventh grader, reveals some of these tensions around love, marriage, and respectability. Ghaliye stopped me in the schoolyard one day and asked, "When will it be my turn to sit and talk with you?"[16] The day I met with Ghaliye, she told me, "I sought you out because I need someone to talk to. Here in Jordan there is no one to talk to. You can't talk to your parents. Nobody sits and talks with you. There is no one to talk to." I knew that Ghaliye had been in trouble at school. She had been caught with a cell phone, which was forbidden. This was one of the school rules that was strictly enforced. At the time, many adults were wary of allowing girls to possess cell phones, for fear that cell phones would facilitate relationships with boys.[17] However, many girls did get a phone by the time they finished high school, especially if they went to the university.[18] Ghaliye, in fact, had been talking with a boy, as she proceeded to tell me:

I was caught talking on my cell phone and the principal called my father. When my father questioned me about the phone, I told him that all of my friends brought cell phones to school. When my father came to meet with the principal, he told her, "Look, Ghaliye says all her friends have phones. Why is she the only one getting in trouble?" I was there and the principal told me to name the girls who had phones and I told on my friends. They managed to hide their phones and so they did not get caught, but my friends won't talk to me now because I told on them.

I asked if indeed she had been talking to a male, and she said that she had developed a phone relationship with a twenty-two-year-old man, Hussam:

One day he called my father's phone—he had dialed a wrong number—and we began to talk regularly. Eventually I got my own phone. He is from Amman, and when I go to Amman with my family, I tell him where I will be so he can see me. He says he loves me, and he came to ask for my hand but my father refused. My father said he was not mature enough and that I was too young.

Yesterday, Hussam called me to say that he cares about me but that it is over. I was very upset and I called him back from my home phone three times. My father saw his number on the caller ID and threatened to punish me if I talked to him again. I didn't tell him I had called Hussam, and it will appear on the phone bill at the end of the month, and I am afraid of what my father will do when he sees it. But I am even more afraid that my uncle will see the bill. He works with my father, and the bill comes to their store. My uncles are very strict. My father is very gentle and understands me, but my uncles are the ones I am afraid of.

As evinced in Ghaliye's situation, extended families and in particular paternal male relatives can have significant authority over their female relatives. The degree to which this is the case can vary though and depends on relations among extended family members and the preferences of the girl's father. Some of the girls at al-Khatwa were clearly at the mercy of brothers who were only a few years older than they were, and sometimes even younger than they were. Many were monitored by their uncles and cousins. However, some fathers made it clear that only they had authority over their daughter's comings and goings.

As my discussion with Ghaliye continued, I learned more about her family, her friends, and her feelings about school. Ghaliye complained that other girls were jealous of her because she was a good student and she was pretty; she believed that girls resented her because she was fair-skinned. Fair skin in Jordan, as in many parts of the world, is considered a sign of beauty. Ghaliye stated, "Girls will get you into trouble if they are jealous of you." Her family gave her greater freedom of mobility than many other families of al-Khatwa students, allowing her to visit friends frequently and go on outings with their families. Some of Ghaliye's disapproving classmates felt this excessive permissiveness had led to Ghaliye's relationship with Hussam. In voicing their disapproval, these girls worked to define what was appropriate or acceptable for a young woman, just as Ghaliye's teachers did. Some of the girls did indeed envy the freedoms that Ghaliye enjoyed, but others explicitly rejected such choices.

I never found out how Ghaliye resolved the phone bill issue and was surprised to find out that she had left school about two weeks later. She had gotten into an argument with two of her classmates because they were spreading rumors about her relationships with boys. Ghaliye was none too careful about hiding her story, yet she was angered when her former friends talked about her having "relations" with boys. When Ghaliye spoke with me about her relationship with Hussam, she felt the need to defend herself. She said, "All the girls love. They talk to boys but they point the finger at others all the time." Even though she was outraged that her classmates would talk about her (much of her anger seemed to have to do with the falling out they had had over the cell phone incident), she also seemed somewhat proud about the fact that a twenty-two-year-old from Amman was interested in her. The principal confronted Ghaliye about the argument with her classmates and the rumors about her relationship. Some of Ghaliye's classmates said that school officials had forced her to transfer. Later when I asked Ghaliye's friend Samar about what had happened, she said that Ghaliye's father was the one who took her out and enrolled her in another high school, preempting the school's punitive transfer.

Interestingly, Ghaliye's father continued to support her and take her side against that of the school administration despite her having transgressed the most significant taboo for girls her age. In part, this was because her "relationship"—a phone relationship, which as far as I could tell never resulted in their actually meeting and talking in person until Hussam came to ask for her hand in marriage—did not go all the way in violating this taboo, and her father seemed to understand that her desires were to be expected at this age. In other families, the reaction might have been different. Even within Ghaliye's family the reactions varied; she told me that her paternal uncles acted in a much more severe manner to a similar incident when she was in the tenth grade, physically beating her for talking with a boy.

Another student at al-Khatwa, Manar, had been pulled out of school by her father permanently for similar transgressions in the previous year. Yet there were other girls whose "relationships"—however limited by cultural constraints—proceeded discreetly and, for some, eventually led to a marriage approved by the girl's family.

Ghaliye's "boyfriend" Hussam tried to transform their relationship into a legitimate one by going the route of asking for her hand. He faced the obstacles faced by many young men his age in Jordan today. Ghaliye's father deemed him too young and unsettled to fulfill his obligation as a man and a husband. Hussam's story was not a unique one. For a young man in love with a young woman whom he has met outside the bounds of the family-orchestrated marriages that are the norm in Bawadi al-Naseem and much of Jordan, asking the girl's father for her hand in marriage is the only culturally sanctioned way to proceed. However, high youth unemployment and the economic situation of most young men decrease the likelihood that they will be taken seriously if they are young and not financially established. Since males are still considered the primary breadwinners in Jordan, they must demonstrate the ability to provide for a family before they marry.[19] Given these demands, it is assumed that the male will need to be older than the female. Indeed, in Bawadi al-Naseem, many of those I spoke with did not consider it appropriate for men and women to marry age mates.[20] However, in practice some people do marry age mates, and female economic contributions to the household are becoming more significant and necessary. Thus, although this ideal continues to be narrated, practice is more nuanced. The reality of delayed marriage and concerns about youth, moral corruption (i.e., that which some assume will flow from the lack of marriage), and the reputation of girls have led some families to choose a marriage outside the ideal of the financially secure older male as the option for their daughters.[21]

From the perspective of the school administrators, Ghaliye's actions were a threat. They could not tolerate girls hiding in the bathroom talking to boys on the phone. It was detrimental to the reputation of the school, set a bad example for other students, and could lead to more severe repercussions for the school and the girls if the situation were to escalate. Schools were obligated to protect girls, and part of this protection was guarding their reputations. The school in turn had its own reputation to be concerned about. Another reason the school desired to be rid of Ghaliye was that her classmates had become increasingly difficult to handle.[22] Not all the adults in the school were in agreement about how to handle such problems. Ghaliye had confided in Miss Suheil, who had kept her problems secret. Miss Suheil did not agree with the way in which the school dealt with her. She believed that the adults in the school should try to counsel girls like Ghaliye, show them the right way rather than push them away or punish them.

It was Ghaliye's father who pulled her out and transferred her, not giving the school the opportunity to punish his daughter. Although he was unhappy about his daughter's relationship, he came to her defense when the school authorities found her with a cell phone. He resented his daughter's being singled out for discipline when "all the girls were doing it." This fit clearly into the complaints of teachers and administrators that parents blindly took the side of their daughters, even when their daughters were clearly in the wrong. However, as I discuss below, there was more to this looking the other way: concerns about getting one's daughter married were linked to a discourse about modern marriages and conjugal unity that has a long history in the region.

Stories about love, boys, and relationships permeated much of day-to-day adolescent conversation, alongside a discourse that found such talk immoral and objectionable. The sheer fact of bringing so many adolescent girls together in one place made this inevitable. Schools facilitate such talk because they create a space for romantic talk and actions—for the consumption and enactment of romantic images (Illouz 1997). Again, these preoccupations with love are increasingly shaped by the bombardment of mass media images and models for marriage, love, and romance for young people. Not only do some of these tensions play out in schools, but the space of the school also exposes young women to varied discourses of love and marriage. Schools in this respect are important sites of everyday gender lessons.

Love and Marriage

One day a group of eleventh graders begged their teacher to let me take them outside to talk so they could get out of class. Since it was near the end of the year and teaching had all but ceased, their teacher relented. When I was with them in the schoolyard, I asked, "So what were you all so anxious to talk with me about?" One of the girls responded, "Love." "What is it about love that you want to discuss?" I asked. The girls took over, yelling out to each other. Jumana, her voice rising over the din, shouted, "Who of your parents married for love?" Kareema informed us that her father was madly in love with her mother. "My father went with a homemade bomb to my maternal grandfather's house and threatened to blow them all up if he did not agree to give him my mother's hand in marriage." The girls were surprised to hear the equally dramatic story of my own grandparents. I told them how my grandfather was intending to ask for my grandmother's hand when he received word that one of her cousins was going to preempt him by asking her father first.[23] My grandfather rode by this cousin's house on a horse, shot his rifle in the air, and shouted something along the lines of "Stay away from Wadi'a. She is mine!" The girls laughed and then Jumana told the story of her parents: "My mother was a nurse, and my father brought his uncle to the hospital one day. My mother came to measure his blood pressure, and my father saw her and started talking to her. My mother, who thought he was cute, told him if he had serious intentions that he should come to her home to ask her parents for her hand." Kareen chimed in, "Hey, my mom was a nurse too, but she married one of the doctors." Khulood, who had been silent up until then, said, "My mother never saw my father before she married. She was sent from Syria to Jordan to marry my father." Batool's parents had a similar story.

More stories circulated and we switched to talking about their own future marriages. One of the girls said that even if suitors came, her parents would not let her get engaged until she finished her studies. Others agreed with this. Jenine turned to me and said, "Hey, what about you, Miss Fida? How did you meet your husband?" I responded briefly, "He was my tutor," and then tried to change the subject. "But did he love you?" Not wanting to get into my own story at the moment, I asked, "Do you need to love to marry?" Samar responded, "I will only marry for love. That's why I want to go to the university." Nasra smiled and said, "Is there anyone who does not want to love?" Ibtisam responded, "As for me, my parents completely reject the idea that I will have a love relationship before marriage. All my sisters married in the traditional way and that is the best way." Then the bell rang; the period was over and we left our talk for later.

Among the targets of twentieth-century modernizing projects in the Middle East was the institution of marriage. The modernizing rhetoric emphasized the bourgeois ideal of the modern family with preference for the nuclear family with the conjugal couple as its center. Tied to this shift in the conceptualization of the preferred family unit was also a new conceptualization of marriage, namely, a preference for companionate marriage (a marriage based on companionship, compatibility, and even love) over arranged marriages (Abu-Lughod 1998; Baron 1991; Najmabadi 2005).[24] Despite the passage of over a century since the onset of this discourse about "modern" families and companionate marriage, for girls in Bawadi al-Naseem the struggle to define the most appropriate forms of family and couple continues. In some respects, contemporary ideals have been adopted.

For example, young women expressed a preference for living in a nuclear family unit, and the tenth-grade civic education textbook profiled the nuclear family, juxtaposing it with the traditional extended family, as an example of social change (al-Masad et al. 2004: 58).[25] However, in practice most marriages in Bawadi al-Naseem were "arranged" by family members, and many young women, like Ibtisam above, accepted this as the appropriate means of getting married.[26]

In Bawadi al-Naseem, marriages usually occurred through a process of matchmaking and personal connections: a man and his female relatives see or hear about a prospective bride, come to inquire about her, and then come for a visit to see the potential bride. Depending on the family, there might be limited opportunity for the prospective couple to get to know each other. Often the period of engagement[27] serves as a period of sanctioned courtship. Because a significant percentage of Jordanians (20–30 percent) still marry their cousins, brides and grooms can also be found among one's relatives (Hamamy et al. 2005; Khoury and Massad 2005).[28] The potential bride could also be a neighbor, a friend of one's sister, or a relative of an older sibling's in-laws. One important venue in which potential matches are found is weddings; at such events, mothers and sisters of men interested in marrying keep an eye out for eligible and attractive young women. Young women interested in getting married also view wedding celebrations as important spaces in which to display their beauty as well as their manners. In recent years, the presence of women in universities and in the labor force has increased the possibility of initiating marriages without the assistance of family matchmakers. At times a match might be sparked by fleeting glances exchanged in the street or with a neighbor. Jamileh, a tenth grader, was almost engaged to a soldier who had been on duty near her home and with whom she had exchanged glances. On a recent visit, I found out that one of the girls I knew in 2005, who had just graduated college, married a young officer she had been courting from afar. Another young woman who was a student at al-Khatwa when I first visited in 2002 met her fiancé through a colleague at work. However, for young women in Bawadi al-Naseem, even if such connections began independently, they quickly moved to the sphere of family matchmaking.[29]

The fear of not getting married could be a source of anxiety for families and for some of the girls. Throughout the time I was in Jordan, the local press ran articles about the increasing problem of unmarried women (e.g., *Al-Rai*, February 2, 2005; March 21, 2005), and people held the opinion that this was a crisis of growing proportions. Never marrying was a fate feared by most young women, as being married is key to one's status as an adult woman. The transition to full adulthood is tied to marriage for males also, but for most females not getting married left one dependent on one's fathers and brothers. Single women increasingly have options for financial independence and in some cases help to care for their parents. However, even when they have independent financial means, their male relatives continue to function as their guardians. Indeed, legally speaking unmarried women are dependents (Amawi 2000).[30]

The anxiety about unmarried "girls"[31] was also tied to concerns about their honor and that of their families. Since premarital sexual relations are expressly forbidden[32], an unmarried girl is a potential risk. Of course families differed as to their perspectives on these issues. All families were concerned that their daughters marry, without exception. However, some felt girls should go to the university and work for two or three years first. Others felt that they should marry as soon as they completed college. Still others—parents or the girls themselves—might make the assessment that marriage made more sense after high school or (for a smaller percentage) after tenth grade, the last year of compulsory schooling. Often a family might decide that one daughter should drop out of school and marry while another should try to go to college. This assessment involved any number of factors, among them the daughter's grades, the daughter's behavior, the number of daughters in the family, and the family's economic situation.

A girl's own assessment of her family's economic situation, the economic situation in the country, and her standing as a student figured into her appraisal of her marriage prospects. In my conversations with Rashida, a staff member at al-Khatwa, about the challenges facing schools and young women today, she discussed the desire of some girls to marry early, alluding to a confluence of factors—the media, the economic situation, the example provided by teachers, and the students' grades—to explain this desire. On a number of occasions in Jordan, I heard that a girl who was not doing well in school might make the calculation that she was better off getting married while she was young, given that her prospects for completing her education and getting a job were limited. A girl who knew her parents could not afford to pay for a university education might make the same assessment. However, Rashida provided a more complicated picture of what was entailed in such decisionmaking. According to her, a girl's grades and her economic situation were influencing factors, but so was a new conceptualization of "love" marriage that Rashida argued the girls were getting from the media:

RASHIDA: There are some ideas [which the girls get from TV] which are very dangerous in terms of the society. The economic situation exacerbates this.

A young man needs to marry a woman who works, but the girls say, "I see my teachers; they have their work and their home and they are not happy. So I should cut it short—what's the point of studying? I should find myself a guy and that's it." So this can lead to delinquent behavior. She becomes concerned with grabbing the attention of the *shabab* [young men], hoping one will marry her.

You say to them, "Your brother, your cousin . . . will he marry someone who is not educated, who does not work?" She says, "Maybe. If he loves her . . . So why don't I get the *shabab* to love me, so that I save my time [and trouble]." She says, "Maybe I will finish my studies. Maybe my parents can't pay for my education. And even if I finish, I won't get a job. I know I will sit for five or six years waiting.[33] In this situation I am not attractive to a guy. Now if I fix myself up [i.e., make myself attractive] . . . maybe he will pick me, choose me."

FIDA: I heard that some girls are open to getting married now but their parents are opposed.

RASHIDA: Yes. Lots of girls cause problems. She wants to get married and her parents refuse to let her. They say, "She is too young. We want to educate her. We want her to grow and mature some, to take on responsibility for a home." The girl says no, she wants to follow the model she sees on TV. She believes that a girl must find a partner in life by any means.

Rashida alluded to several influences that she believed led girls to consider early marriage. First, she pointed to the "negative" example provided by the teachers. Some girls saw their teachers as models of what *not* to follow. Their teachers' lives appeared to be unhappy ones. They were tired, overworked, and, according to Rashida, "did not take care of themselves" (i.e., their appearances). Thus, some of the students did not see the lives of their teachers—working women—as an appealing alternative despite the widely reproduced narrative that working women were more marriageable, to be discussed further in chapter 6.

In addition to the economic constraints, she argued that the media cultivated in some girls the idea that they needed to find a partner in life. For Rashida and even some of the students, the notion of love marriage and of finding one's partner (rather than waiting for one's family to find one's partner or consulting with them) was still a "foreign" idea and a dangerous one, given the kind of behavior it might lead to when girls sought out this partner. Staff and teachers also generally believed the girls to be too young and immature to make responsible decisions about a matter as serious as marriage, and in Bawadi al-Naseem relationships were meant to lead to

marriage. Nevertheless, the prohibition on male/female relations sometimes came into conflict with the concern of families and the girls themselves that the girls get married. This could lead to reactions on the part of
parents that conflicted with those of the adults at the school, whose concern
it was to maintain the reputation of the school and the respectability of the
students under their watch, as was evident in the case of Ghaliye.

For school administrators and staff, who regularly monitored the movements of girls in school and at times outside of school, the seeming acquiescence of some parents in what they viewed as misbehavior created a
disjuncture between the school and families. On a number of occasions,
school staff complained that they were trying to "raise" students to be respectable while the parents worked against them. Usually such complaints
were in reference to minor matters such as failure to follow the dress code
or disrupting class. On the surface, there seemed to be little discontinuity
in areas of greater significance—such as a girl's reputation and the critical
importance of sex segregation. However, this was not always the case. Sara,
an al-Khatwa teacher, described an incident that had occurred in a nearby
rural school in which she had previously worked that highlighted the tensions between schools and families:

FIDA: Do you see any contradiction between what the girls learn in school and
what they learn at home?

SARA: Sometimes, with some of the families. Not in terms of the curricular content but more in terms of social customs. We faced this in the villages. Once
we found a love letter with a girl and we called in her parents to discuss this
with us since she was at a delicate age; she was sixteen. We advised her in all
the ways we could because this is a relationship that would have a negative
effect on her life. Since she was still young and did not comprehend what she
was doing, we called her parents. And what was the result? They encouraged
her and they did not care. What was the response of the mother? "Leave my
daughter alone to pursue her fortune." Sometimes they [parents] say that
because the principal or teacher is not married, she resents the girls and does
not give them the opportunity, and accusations like that. . . . They accuse the
principal or teachers and they say, "Just because you failed . . . does not mean
that you have the right to advise our daughters."

Sara alluded to the willingness of some parents to let their daughters
"pursue their fortunes" and seek out a marriage partner.[34] Sara also discussed how such willingness created conflict for the school—teachers and
staff—with parents accusing school staff who had never married (who had

"failed") with interfering in the marriage prospects of their daughters. The large majority of the teachers at al-Khatwa were married, but the prospect of an unmarried daughter could produce such tensions. For although most families desired educational success for their daughters, without marriage a girl could never completely be successful. Sara's comments above also indexed some of the assumptions embedded in geographical hierarchies, with rural girls being perceived as particularly vulnerable to "immoral" behavior because of their ignorance, the sheltered lives they led before coming to the town or city, and/or their lack of discipline.

For their part, school officials found the responsibility of watching over adolescent girls to be a heavy one (girls who, according to the adults in the school, differed significantly from those of earlier generations and whose worldview was shaped in large part by the infiltration of regional and foreign media), and they approached this responsibility with a "be safe rather than sorry" attitude. Any indication that a young woman was involved in a relationship with a young man would be investigated. The school's efforts were not out of a desire to prevent girls from "finding their fortunes," as some parents intimated, but rather out of concern for the school's reputation, the girls' reputations, and fear of the repercussions for the school and possibly for the girls if the situation got out of hand. A school that appeared unable to maintain discipline and order reflected negatively on the administrators and teachers.

Most of the teachers considered early marriage to be a mistake and conveyed this to their students. They also often became the filters for information, rumors, and misinformation about marriage and relationships. For example, during my time at al-Khatwa there was much controversy and rumors about *zawaj 'urfi*. *Zawaj* in Arabic means marriage, and *'urfi* literally means customary. *Zawaj 'urfi* refers to a marriage that meets all of the religious requirements but is not registered with the state and has no public announcement or celebration. Initially the rumors were that *zawaj 'urfi* or some distorted form of it was rampant at the local university. At some point during the year, rumors emerged that girls at al-Khatwa had been involved in *zawaj 'urfi*. These rumors spread quickly, to the point that even I was being queried by acquaintances outside of the school as to what was going on at al-Khatwa. The principal found it necessary to address these rumors directly at the morning assembly. In a conversation I had with her later that day about these rumors, the normally serious and composed principal laughed out loud at their absurdity. At the same time, several of the teachers advised the girls about the dangers that lurked behind *zawaj 'urfi*. Some teachers told them that *zawaj 'urfi* was *haram*. However, the religion teacher clarified to students that if it met all of the requirements of marriage in Islamic law, then it was a legitimate form of marriage. However, she and others cautioned the girls that what was happening in Jordan and in places like Egypt was the corruption of *zawaj 'urfi* and represented in fact attempts by men to trick girls into engaging in relationships that were immoral.[35] Girls were regularly warned to be wary of males who were out to deceive them.

Of course the school staff (teachers and administrators) individually could take different positions vis-à-vis marriage matters. When the engagement of two tenth graders was announced at al-Khatwa, most of the teachers reacted negatively, viewing early marriage as outdated and inappropriate for teenage girls of this era. In almost every instance when someone told me a story about a girl who had gotten married at the age of fifteen or sixteen before finishing school, it was framed as a negative thing. However, when Jamileh almost got engaged, a few of the teachers thought that given her poor performance in school and her apathy toward school in general, perhaps getting engaged was not such a bad idea. Thus, it is important to consider the ways in which students' academic performance figured into the assessment of early marriage and, on a related note, how a girl's academic performance was related to perceptions of her respectability.

Tracking Respectability

Education, or one's educational status, is in and of itself an important marker of respectability for women in Jordan. Whereas an earlier generation may have assumed an educated woman to be of questionable respectability or worried that too much education would make her too willful and not sufficiently cognizant of her responsibilities as a wife, for the overwhelming majority of Jordanians I spoke with this was clearly not the case any longer. However, this newfound status for educated women has had contradictory effects. Females now have easy access to schooling and schooling is valued. As a result, however, not being educated or not doing well in school can now be considered a deficit and is often tied to implicit assumptions about a girl's behavior and respectability. Such assertions are also clearly classed, as certain forms of education (tied to particular careers) are viewed as lower-class alternatives, and because socioeconomic status affects a student's academic performance and access to quality education, tutoring, and similar supports.

If a girl was a poor student, it was frequently assumed that this was a result of her laziness and her preoccupation with matters that were frivolous and possibly even immoral. Such insinuations were usually made when a girl appeared to be perfectly capable of doing well in school. If a student had no obvious disability[36] the assumption made by most adults and even fellow students was that this student was lazy, uninterested, or distracted by other matters such as TV, music, clothes, or friends who were bad influences. At worst, a girl could get the reputation of someone who was distracted by boys.

Assumptions about the poor behavior of weak students were most prevalent when the girls in different academic tracks were compared. At al-Khatwa there were two academic tracks—the humanities and the scientific track.[37] In Bawadi al-Naseem, all of the vocational tracks were housed in separate schools, one school for girls and one for boys, so that students in the academic tracks were completely separated from those in the vocational tracks after tenth grade. Most people held a clear bias in favor of the scientific track, in keeping with the general preference for and higher value placed upon the sciences and mathematics. Furthermore, the prestige surrounding mathematics and sciences is not as distinctly gendered as it is in places such as the United States, where females enroll in these fields in comparatively lower numbers (Adely 2009a). It was assumed by most Jordanians that academically successful students would pursue such fields, regardless of their gender. Indeed, the educational system was structured to reinforce if not create such preferences. Students in this track were considered to be more serious and better behaved, more respectful of school rules and teachers. In contrast, the girls of the humanities track, or *banat al-adabi*, were frequently criticized as a group and disparaged by teachers at al-Khatwa.[38] The correlation made between the various tracks and degrees of respectability proved to be a source of anxiety for tenth graders who had to obtain the grades needed to get into the desired track. At least one student told me her brother would not let her continue school if she was placed in the vocational track. Families were known to use their connections to get a girl out of the vocational track.

Being in the vocational track in Bawadi al-Naseem was viewed as particularly problematic, because of both the poor reputation of the vocational education school and the perceived uselessness of that degree. In addition, only the poorest-performing students ended up in this track.[39] Vocational education shares a similar stigma in the United States. Associated with trade and blue-collar jobs, it has been considered a lower-class option by most Americans. Indeed, vocational education was initially developed for the express purpose of controlling a subclass of students (Villaverde 2003).

The Girls Vocational School in Bawadi al-Naseem had a terrible reputation. People insinuated that the girls were morally "loose," that they violated the most basic moral principles of the community, and that the administration had no control over the school. One of the al-Khatwa teachers, Hind, had previously taught at the vocational education school, and she spoke with me about her experience there: "I was shocked at what I saw there. Those girls did things that I thought I would never see—things that went completely against our conservative society. They would leave the school, go with *shabab*, and pretend to be at school all day. It was terrible and I didn't know what to do and I realized it was too late for these girls. There was nothing I could do for them. They were lost." When I asked Hind if it were really possible that all the girls in this school behaved in this fashion, she said even the girls who were not inclined to such behavior were easily swayed by their peers because they were not very intelligent: "Because of that experience, and other experiences I have had with students, I am convinced that the smarter students have better morals and better behavior. It's as if the students who are not smart are not smart enough to make the right moral judgments. They are not conscious enough or they are easily corrupted [morally]." Although I had never heard this assertion made quite so explicitly, the link of education type with degree of smarts and moral standing was frequently insinuated.

The high status that people attached to formal education, and certain fields of study in particular, was exemplified in a most extreme fashion in the situation of Siba, a twelfth grader whom I came to know at al-Khatwa. Siba wanted desperately to study medicine. In fact, much of our time together consisted of her imploring me to find ways for her to study medicine abroad despite my being clear that I could not help her.[40] What is most relevant here is why Siba wanted to be a doctor. Siba's family had faced a major crisis that had led to a split in the family, with the result that her mother and sisters had left their home. Primarily as a result of her assessment as to what would be best for her reputation, she had decided to stay with her brothers.[41] She was no longer on speaking terms with her mother or sisters and was clearly quite shaken by the whole situation. She was also very concerned that her family's reputation—and, by default, hers—had been tarnished by this incident and the manner in which her mother had managed it: "She [her mother] created a problem for us and everyone knew. She hung our dirty laundry out for everyone to see. The problem in this society is that people label you and then write you off. That's why I want to study medicine—to improve my situation." Siba was desperate to become a doctor because she believed that the prestige associated with studying medicine and being a doctor would overcome the gossip and the labels that her community had imposed upon her as a result of her family situation. For Siba, a career as a doctor appeared to be the only means to repairing her damaged reputation. For many lower-income families, education continues to be the only means to class advancement. Their hope is that education will provide both the financial means and the cultural capital for improved status, but their limited financial means already put them at a disadvantage.[42] Furthermore, as an abundance of previous research in the West has shown, for families with limited assets and connections, cultural capital is much harder to come by (e.g., Bourdieu and Passeron 1977; Willis 1977), and increased levels of education, if they are attainable, are no guarantee of upward mobility.[43] Indeed many scholars of education have argued that schooling actually serves to prevent advancement and to reproduce inequality.[44] Siba hoped to gain respect through education and a high-status professional job in medicine, but she lacked the grades needed in the rigidly tracked education system or the resources to buy her way out of it.[45]

A girl's respectability was not only monitored in school but also constructed there, as her social status was intertwined with being an "educated person." Although the value of particular types of knowledge and degrees is closely tied to the perceived economic benefits of certain careers over others, the worth ascribed to varied forms of education was not limited to economic returns. Particular forms of education held greater social value than others. This was also a concern for boys, particularly in their marriage options and their ability to convince a girl's family that they were worthy suitors; they needed to be good providers, but the status of their profession also mattered, especially for more well-off families. This economic assessment was of increasing importance to girls as well.

For a young woman, then, imagining a desirable and respectable pathway was both shaped and complicated by education. A girl needed to be respectable to get married, and she needed to be good student to be respectable. She needed to be educated to marry well but might seek marriage if she was not performing well academically. She should not interact with boys, but some students and at times even their parents believed they needed to do so in order to attract potential suitors. She should not equate romance with marriage although images of romantic love abounded. A girl should keep her feelings in check—control her emotions—but the presence of nearly six hundred high school girls in one place created a space for "sentimental education," and the gender lessons permeated the space and the life of the school. The education of al-Khatwa students was also an education in navigating these tensions in their school lives and beyond its walls.

The global narrative of education for development and female empowerment neglects the unexpected ways in which education has transformed basic conceptualizations of successful personhood, morality, and progress. In the opening pages of chapter 1, I described how the World Bank's gender assessment of Jordan (2005) depicted the high levels of education for women in Jordan as paradoxical because of the failure of women to progress along particular development indicators, namely, fertility and labor force participation. The examination of schooling, respectability, and marriage prospects in this chapter shows how the logic of the World Bank can be turned on its head, as people have appropriated the imperative of education for their own status concerns and needs, a reminder of the limits of the power of global development institutions.[46]

Contemporary state schooling complicates notions of respectability, because it constructs new forms of status and respectability while guarding "traditional" ones. The value of being educated has become as integral to local constructions of modernity and respectability as to a national narrative about progress and development. Yet the perceived "marriage crisis" in Jordan means that many young women and their parents worry that they will not marry. Even though schooling may afford new status, marriage is still a major preoccupation. Marriage and schooling are further entangled because of the common perception that an educated girl is more marriageable, particularly if she hopes to marry a man of similar or better status. In this respect, schooling has become critical for one's marriage prospects.

Competing discourses about the necessary foundations for a marriage also complicate these processes. Family-orchestrated marriages predominate, but girls in Bawadi al-Naseem love, they talk about love, and many wish to find love—a "partner." Furthermore, they see people "loving" on TV in American movies, *Friends*, Egyptian soap operas, and Lebanese music videos. Much of what the media present are models far removed from their reality. They also hear about love from their friends, their neighbors, and from the rumors that abound. What they are allowed to say and do with respect to these desires is subject to much monitoring and control by school authorities and families alike, but the discourse about forbidden love or love as shameful is not the only available one.

Despite hegemonic conceptions of gendered respectability and the concomitant lessons about love, marriage, and relationships, the image of womanhood and proper relations between men and women has changed—

often in paradoxical ways. Schools and schooling experiences are key forces in the shifting of the winds. Education creates new forms of gendered respectability that are not only reliant on educational status but also intertwined with an educational hierarchy that places some forms of education—mathematics and science—above others. The education of women—and the uses to which their education is put—are also pivotal in national and global narratives about development and developed Jordanian women, as I discuss further in the next chapter.

SIX

Education for What? Women, Work, and Development in Jordan

The Ambiguities of "Success"

I walked into Dr. Sumaya's waiting room one day. She was expecting me because an old family friend, Ustadh[1] Yahya, had arranged for us to meet. In fact it was at his urging that I decided to interview her. She was from the nearby village where I had initially explored my interest in education, girls, and development. The people of her village were regularly heralded as "developed" or "advanced" for they had embraced the education of their sons and daughters before other villages in the area. Ustadh Yahya was one of the first teachers in her village. He had bragged to me that it was he who convinced Dr. Sumaya's father to send her abroad to study medicine when she was awarded a scholarship to do so. I came to learn more about her experiences.

It was a busy day in her office, and I sat in the waiting room until the doctor was available to see me. Many people came and went, some without appointments. I waited nearly an hour, and when we finally began to talk, Dr. Sumaya seemed uncomfortable with my interest in her story. I mentioned that I had heard about Ustadh Yahya's role in her education as a doctor and that I knew she was considered a trailblazer for women in the community. Before I could proceed further, she said, "I wish he had never done so. I told Ustadh Yahya that I wish he had never interceded with my father to let me go study medicine abroad."

"Do you really regret it—regret having gone abroad to study medicine?" I asked. "Well, it's just that I feel bad for my kids. I don't have enough time for them. What adds to this is that my husband is also a doctor who travels, and so he is not even here during the week. My oldest is only in the fourth grade. Our financial situation is quite good because my husband and I both work, but our work is very demanding. It's difficult."

In the previous chapter, I ended by pointing to the ways in which a girl's moral standing—her respectability—is increasingly enmeshed with her status as an educated person. Like Dr. Sumaya in the opening vignette to this chapter, educated women were frequently held up as pillars of their own communities. Nonetheless, this relationship is not a straightforward one. In the day-to-day life of the school, a girl's academic performance is an important part of the way she is assessed by her peers and teachers. Her parents look to her grades to ascertain how serious she is about her studies, and this in turn figures into decisions about further investment in her education and the delay of marriage, particularly for poorer families. Indeed, a young woman herself may make similar calculations and at times conclude, "There is no point in continuing my studies." However most young women and their families hold onto the promise of education, for they see education as key to their success, progress, and ability to live a good life. Yet how this progress is conceptualized *and* the role that education might have in achieving it can vary and upset our very basic understandings of what education does for young women who have been framed by a host of observers as "oppressed." Today, the primary raison d'être for the characterization of these women as oppressed is their failure to pursue waged labor.

From the perspective of global development institutions, education has not delivered what it should for young women in Jordan and the Middle East more broadly. To come back to the opening pages of this book, the great paradox of women's increased education in the Middle East is its failure to "empower" women. More specifically, women in the region have not entered the waged labor force, and this is regularly pointed to by development agencies as evidence of the malfunction of educational development.[2] Since women in the region and in Jordan more specifically have not sufficiently followed this path, their education is viewed as a development aberration. However, for the young women at al-Khatwa and the adults in their lives, the desirability of waged labor was not a given, and as is the case for women and men everywhere, it was shaped by a range of material and ideological factors. Many did see education as a source of power, but this power was not strictly tied to economic returns.

The value placed on getting an education has long had recognizably gendered dimensions. Debra Skinner and Dorothy Holland (1996) argue in their analysis of schooling for girls in Nepal that "girls' understandings of the educated person and their vision of schooling as opportunity more explicitly intersected with their gendered identity" (285). For both young men and young women in Jordan, the expectations tied to education are clearly gendered; however, the gendered implications of educational status are decidedly more ambiguous for a young woman in Jordan. For young men, educational success is closely linked to expectations that they will be the primary breadwinners for their families, despite the reality that many men are finding it difficult to do so alone. Another related pressure is securing enough resources to get married. Many young men face great obstacles to getting married because they cannot secure the funds needed to establish a household, pay for a wedding, and prove their capacity to be good providers to the parents of potential brides. Some opt out of education to become breadwinners sooner, especially if they are poor and not succeeding academically.

What is distinctly different about the "education for what" question for girls is that women's roles and the expectations that come with women's education have changed significantly in the past few decades. This does not mean that the conditions for men have not changed—they have. Furthermore, the changes that women are experiencing have serious implications for gender relations (Hasso 2007). However, in some sense, what males face most prominently is a disconnect between the image of what a man should be and the realities that limit what is possible. For females, there is the added complication that the images or possibilities for an educated woman are still decidedly ambiguous, often contradicting each other and requiring a great deal of negotiation. Increasingly, Jordanians talk about the need for two-income families. Yet, as I show in this chapter, an understanding of women's work outside the home as valuable or beneficial is not shared by all. The ambiguity of the contemporary context is strongly gendered in its manifestations, and given the politicization of gendered symbols in religious debates, as well as debates about modernity and authenticity, the struggle to define proper pathways or images of womanhood is a struggle for power.

While conducting fieldwork, my questions about education and the al-Khatwa School led to many discussions about the purpose of education. Women's labor in and outside of the home was a logical outcome of such discussions. In this chapter, I highlight the range of discourses that circulated at the school, in the curriculum, and among students and teachers about women's work outside the home and the purpose of education. Although I was regularly told by Jordanians that contemporary economic circumstance demanded that a woman work, both men and women expressed ambivalence about women's labor force participation. These issues were taken up explicitly in school textbooks and at times in class discussions.

More informally, young women learned from their mothers, sisters, and teachers what being a working woman might entail and tried to make sense of often competing narratives of what education was for.

The Benefits of Educating Girls

A plethora of research points to the particular benefits that come from educating women. At the most basic level, studies have demonstrated a correlation between increased levels of education and decreased child mortality, decreased fertility, and increased life expectancy.[3] Even when statisticians control for factors such as income and geography, the relationship between increases in girls' education and improved health outcomes persists, although the relationship to lowered fertility rates is less consistent (LeVine et al. 2001; Watkins 2000). It has been more difficult to establish *how* education leads to such outcomes. What are the actual characteristics of schooling or education that contribute to such benefits? Answers typically fall into three categories. First, some research relates these outcomes to the characteristics of the girls. For example, girls who go to school tend to be healthier, less likely to suffer from malnutrition, and thus more likely to have healthy pregnancies and give birth to healthy babies (LeVine et al. 2001; Watkins 2000). Second, some researchers link improved outcomes to the curriculum, which presumably provides information and skills that help young women make more informed health decisions.[4] Related to this second category are arguments about the ability of educated women to "process" new information, the assumption being that formal schooling makes them more adept at this task (Watkins 2000). Third, some studies argue that education increases the confidence of young women and/or empowers them to control decisions related to their fertility and health and that of their children (LeVine et al. 2001; Watkins 2000). In other words, girls who attend school will develop more confidence and, as a result, be more likely to assert themselves with male partners or to seek out medical care and feel more at ease in their interactions with health care providers. Robert LeVine, Sarah LeVine, and Beatrice Schnell (2001) found that the relevant skills (for health outcomes) garnered in school had less to do with individual confidence and more to do with learning the "academic registry" needed to function in bureaucracies, the school being a bureaucracy itself. The authors argue that this effect is particularly significant in contexts where the extension of state bureaucracy is relatively new. Most important, they argue, females learn to obey official authority and expertise in school, and this ability transfers to their interactions with the health bureaucracies.

Jordan overall enjoys higher rates of school access and completion than most countries in the region. In 2008, the net enrollment of females was higher than that of males at all levels of education (primary, secondary, and tertiary).[5] Many of the supposed health benefits of education have been documented. Yet, as much of the research on this topic has shown, it is impossible to attribute improved health indicators to education alone (LeVine et al. 2001: 3). In Jordan, state extension of health services occurred simultaneously with the expansion of education, making it difficult to attribute improved health outcomes to the expansion of schooling for girls. Despite high levels of schooling for girls, Jordan continues to maintain a comparatively high fertility rate[6] and significantly low rates of labor force participation, leading to its representation as a "gender paradox" (World Bank 2005: 61).[7] Juxtaposing such representations with the experiences of al-Khatwa students illuminates the limits of contemporary development narratives and measures of women's development through education.

A plethora of literature exists that examines the problem of women's low rates of labor force participation in the Middle East. The bulk of this research is quantitative and seeks primarily to measure women's work and to delineate patterns of economic activity throughout a woman's lifespan in relation to her level of education and geographic location. However, even in this respect—measuring when and where particular women work—the picture presented is incomplete. Nadia Farah (2006) argues that measures of female labor force participation grossly underestimate actual women's involvement in the labor force and that the reliance on these measures in indices of female empowerment or development is problematic (38).[8] For example, she points out that in the two measures used by the United Nations Development Program— the gender empowerment measure (GEM) and the gender-related development index (GDI)—income is defined in nonagricultural terms (38). Farah continues: "The bias toward the urban sector is bias towards the pattern of development relying on the familiar modernization model. Agriculture in advanced industrial countries is a capitalist enterprise and is highly mechanized; it employs a very small number of the population" (39). As a result, Farah concludes, women's participation in the economy is grossly undercounted, especially in Arab countries with significant rural populations. Her assertions are also corroborated by the Arab Fund for Economic and Social Development (2003), which found that "the smallest gender gaps in participation in the labor force were located in less developed countries with large agricultural bases," while the gap was significantly higher in wealthier nations (142). Indeed, most development documents and the broader literature on women's labor force participation acknowledge the limits of official statistics in capturing the true extent of women's economic contributions, let alone their important labor in maintaining households and families. Yet these documents continue to assess women's development and economic opportunity based on these limited categories, data, and definitions of work; and in some instances these assessments explicitly devalue forms of work that are not easily measured (N. Farah 2006).

Beyond efforts to measure economic activity, much of this research also incorporates explanations as to why women do not work, or fail to work in nontraditional (i.e., male-dominated) fields. Many explanations fall in the realm of the cultural, laying blame on family, culture, and traditions (Moghadam 2005; Sonbol 2003; UNDP 2006).[9] Some of this literature also points to state policies, arguing that a better legislative environment is needed to encourage women to work (Sonbol 2003; World Bank 2005). Other explanations are economic in nature. One important economic explanation for the comparatively low rates of women's participation in the labor force is the existence of oil wealth, which contributes to both high wages for men and generous state services for citizens in some Middle Eastern countries (Moghadam 2005; Ross 2008).[10] These economic analyses are in some respects a refreshing departure from the cultural determinism of much of the research on women in the region. However, the desirability of work for women continues to be taken as a given, the links of such work to progress assumed. Thus, for example, such economic analysis bemoans the lack of low-level manufacturing jobs for women in the Middle East—jobs that in other regions have provided an entry point for women in the workforce. However, the exploitative nature of such jobs is given little space in this analysis.[11]

In my own interactions with women in Jordan, uncertainty surrounding work outside the home emerged frequently. I met many adult women who conveyed the ambivalence expressed by Dr. Sumaya in the opening vignette of this chapter. Although her circumstances were quite different, Nur, the grandmother of an al-Khatwa student who had retired from a low-level civil servant position as a typist when I met her, also expressed conflicting sentiments about her work outside the home and her own experiences as a working woman. She was the mother of eight children and entered the workforce only when her oldest child went to the university. Her spouse was a schoolteacher, and they could no longer make ends meet with the university-related expenses. In many respects, Nur felt frustrated and disempowered by circumstances she felt had forced her to work. When she started working outside the home, she was no longer able to care for her children in the way that she wanted. Until she came home, they would be out in the streets play-ing. She also missed the time she used to spend visiting with the women in the neighborhood. However, on other occasions she conveyed that being able to make decisions about purchasing items without having to go to her husband was valuable. She believed it gave her some independence.

Although Nur found that work isolated her from her social networks, many of the teachers I spoke with in the course of my research (most of whom were significantly younger than Nur) found that working outside the home gave them the opportunity to socialize with peers and colleagues that they would not otherwise have enjoyed. Asked if she would like to retire, Mariam, a science teacher, said, "No. I would become too isolated if I stayed at home." Several teachers told me they feared they would become too immersed in cooking, cleaning, and taking care of the home and chil-dren, leaving them no time to see their friends. Going to work gave teachers a reason to be out of their homes and the opportunity to socialize with other women. At the same time some teachers, especially those with young children, wished they did not have to work. The existence of extended fam-ily nearby to help in caring for children and home influenced women's perspectives on the desirability of working, an important reminder that family is not usually viewed as a burden or obstacle but rather as a critical support system, particularly when state services are virtually absent (Hatem 2005; Olmsted 2005b).[12] Thus, the desirability of work outside the home, although framed as necessary in economic terms, and as a positive experi-ence for some women, was not a given. How a woman assesses such oppor-tunities, not surprisingly, has much to do with her circumstances.

The assumptions that underlie discourse about gender, education, and development lead to conclusions that are too simple to capture the com-plexity of Sumaya's, Mariam's, or Nur's experiences. Conflicts can and do exist between economic pressures that force women to work and women's own perceptions of what is valuable and/or powerful. Given economic deterioration in the region and the effects of neoliberal economic policies on the most vulnerable citizens, many women do not have choices about waged labor. But given the choice, not all want to work; they may find the existing jobs exploitative and disempowering rather than desirable. Or they may find their "jobs" as mothers and wives sufficiently meaningful. Some who want to work outside the home may not have the choice, as husbands may pressure them to stay home, especially once they have children. Under Jordanian law, the husband has the right to prevent his wife from work-ing under certain conditions. As a result, a woman's right to work (or not work)[13] is often the subject of premarriage negotiations and agreements.

These competing perspectives on the value of work outside the home and its relation to childrearing and caregiving are not unfamiliar ones. The desire to balance work and home and the weight of the "double burden" upon women's shoulders are regularly the subject of public debate and discussion among middle- and upper-class women in the United States. One example is instructive for comparative purposes. In a *New York Times* opinion piece of April 25, 2007, Linda Hirshman argues that the tendency for women with young children to leave the labor force in the United States is problematic because of both lost economic potential and productivity for the U.S. economy and the lost wages for women who choose to reenter the labor force later. Also, Hirshman points out, these women tend to be highly educated and are most frequently the spouses of high-wage-earning men. Most interesting about this piece was the response that it elicited. Two days after its publication, nine letters were published in the *New York Times*, all of which criticized Hirshman's devaluing of some women's decisions to stay home with their children. The letter writers (all women) questioned her assertion that "participation in public life allows women to use their talents and to powerfully affect society," while staying at home to raise children does not (Hirshman 2007). One writer argued that feminism should have taught "us" that "choice is key."[14] Of course the women who are at the center of Hirshman's analysis come from among the middle and upper-middle classes, as the letter writers most likely did. Their choice then is shaped by this socioeconomic status. The point here is that while middle-class and elite women in the United States continue to debate issues of waged labor, motherhood, and opting out of the labor force, such debates are given no credence in the literature about the Arab world. Rather, similar debates and choices are framed exclusively as the product of oppression or false consciousness (Adely 2009a).

"A Diploma Is a Weapon in the Hands of a Girl"

In her discussion about the desire for education in the Old Moshi region of Tanzania, Francis Vavrus (2003) argues that it can be explained in part by the "search for security at a time when global capitalism heightens a sense of insecurity" (10). In many respects, the Jordanians I met—students along with their families and teachers—thought about education very explicitly in terms of security. Their concerns about the future were two-pronged. Most immediately, they saw education as critical to securing a "good" marriage, typically a very classed notion. As early as 1960, Richard Antoun (1972), in his ethnography of a village in Jordan, reports that residents considered girls with even a few years of education to be more desirable brides who warranted higher dowries. Along much the same lines as the American concept of "marrying up," girls or their families wanted their daughters to marry an educated and professional man of financial means. His family's reputation was equally important in this community where marriages were still in many respects marriages of families, but his ability to "provide" generously for his wife's well-being was critical in the assessment of his status as a potential marriage partner. In order to marry up it was believed that a girl needed to be educated. On one level this was tied to the belief that an educated man needed an educated woman as a partner in life to better relate to him, raise his children, and care for his household.[15] However, increasingly men saw educated and potentially employable brides as necessary and desirable to make ends meet and ensure a decent quality of life.

Although a diploma was deemed critical if a girl was to secure a good marriage partner—one who could adequately provide for his family—it was also seen as a form a security, "a weapon" should things "go bad" in the future (Adely 2004).[16] "Going bad" typically referred to one of three things: never marrying, divorce, or the death or incapacitation of one's husband. Despite assumptions about the links between a diploma and a girl's future economic and marital security, many Jordanians still conveyed ambivalence about women's work outside the home and the types of work that are acceptable or suitable for women. Some argued that a woman's place was in the home, and most women still considered it to be a man's responsibility to support a family financially even if a woman helped.[17] However, others felt that in today's world a woman needed the financial independence that working would provide her, enabling her to make her own financial decisions.[18] Thus the relationship between education and work outside the home was not a given, nor did I find any unanimity about the terms of this relationship.

Both Willy Jansen (2006) and Mary Kawar (2000) in their research among families in Jordan find that while parents attach a great deal of value to their daughter's university education and actually garner prestige from her educational status, the perspective of parents on waged labor varies. Jansen argues that a girl's prestige and that of her family might actually be enhanced by not working:

> In the Jordanian context, not only women's dress and jewelry, but also their education, can be seen as a form of conspicuous consumption. The fact that a girl's education is not put to direct economic use increases its value as a symbol of wealth and prestige. Her education . . . shows that she is from a good

family; it enhances her attractiveness and makes her worthy of a good partner. It brings prestige to her father, and to her future husband, and secures her position within the family. And, as with a golden bracelet, it is an insurance that can bring an income in difficult times. (2006, 485–486)

Although prestige was clearly part of the picture, many of the families I spoke with were also concerned with the economic benefits that their daughters' education might accrue in the future, as well as in the present. Indeed, some of the al-Khatwa families were dependent on the income of older daughters, and so the economic returns to the family were immediate. However, many Jordanians spoke poorly of families who they believed exploited their daughters by taking their income and delaying their marriages. In the next section, I profile some of the families of al-Khatwa students in order to better explicate how this notion of security was articulated and how the desire for security through education was pursued.

What Families Hope For

I first met Um Samir in 2002 when her daughter, a high school student, invited me to their home. After some small talk and tea, I asked Um Samir about her own education, and she responded, "My father, God forgive him, he never let me get an education." Hers was not unlike many such statements of regret and sometimes blame that I heard from several of the mothers of al-Khatwa students who had not completed their own education. She was taken out of school in the third grade and was married at the age of fourteen. However, her three oldest daughters had all finished high school; one had a master's degree and two were enrolled in the university last time I visited them in 2008. Recall also Hiba's mother in chapter 2, who was quite well off but regretted that both she and her husband had not completed their education. I had also heard similar sentiments from men in the course of my research. One man, who had been a teacher in the 1950s, asked me to stop recording our interview at one point because he was gong to say something that was embarrassing to him. He did not want me to record that his family had forced him to leave school in the sixth grade so that he could help support them by working on the family farm. The sense of regret conveyed by adults about not finishing their own education translated into a deep desire to see their children receive an education, and increasingly a university education was a minimum. At times, it seemed that their daughters' education was more important to them than their sons', because of the sense that a young man could manage without an education. They might disagree about what the daughter should study, but the sense that "getting an education" was critical for her future as a woman in Jordan today transcended families' economic status and background. Some families felt that high school was sufficient, particularly if a girl was not a particularly good student and had little chance of getting into the university. However, most of the parents I spoke with saw higher education as key to future success and security in whichever way they might define that.[19]

Selma, Science, and Community Prestige

Selma was a shy eleventh grader, whom I sat and spoke with soon after my arrival. When I learned that she came from a village with which I was not familiar, I asked her if I could come visit her family sometime, and she invited me over one day. By car, Selma's village was not too far, but using public transportation (there was one minivan that went back and forth from her village to Bawadi al-Naseem), it took us nearly an hour. Selma was one of twelve children—nine brothers and three sisters. She was ninth in the sibling order, and the youngest daughter. Her oldest sister, Flaha, left school in the tenth grade because at the time there was no regular transportation to Bawadi al-Naseem. She had already been traveling to a nearby town for tenth grade (she said she walked with a group of local boys), but the trip to Bawadi al-Naseem was not possible without transportation. Now she stayed at home and helped her mother take care of the household. The next daughter in line had failed *tawjihi* but was encouraged by her family to keep trying until she passed. Two of her older brothers had gone on for higher education and were employed. Her oldest brother was a religious sheikh who had married soon after high school. Abed, the brother closest in age to Selma, had just failed the high school completion exam the previous year and refused to repeat it.

Selma's family was Bedouin, and they had been settled from a more nomadic lifestyle for only thirty years. The government had offered their tribe land in the village as an incentive for them to settle. Selma's father had finished primary school and joined the army. He was retired, but his service in the army entitled his children to scholarships in the public universities if they received sufficient grades.[20] Her mother never went to school and was married at the age of eleven. The family had high hopes for Selma. When I asked Selma what her future plans were, she said, "I want to be a journalist, but everyone encourages me to consider medicine." In fact, according to Selma her whole community encouraged her to complete her studies: "[It's] not just my parents. My neighbors. My previous teachers. They all want me to be a doctor. I told one of my teachers maybe I will do journalism and she said, 'No. It must be medicine or pharmacy. You are smart. Don't underestimate yourself.'" Selma's community encouraged her to become a doctor—a high-status profession—as this would reflect positively on this village that had never had a doctor emerge from among its members, let alone a female doctor. Studying medicine, like engineering, was held in high prestige, and the pressure to succeed academically went beyond her parents and siblings and to the larger community, many of whom were her extended kin. Given that her grades were only in the upper 70s, these pressures to succeed specifically as a doctor seemed unfair, although Selma did not seem bothered by them.

The Family of Amal and Tamara

Amal was a quiet and extremely polite student, who was known by her classmates as a loyal friend. Had she not been my neighbor, I might never have gotten to know her since she kept such a low profile at school. She and her sister, Tamara, came from a large and poor family. The family had moved to Bawadi al-Naseem many years before because of her father's job in the military. They often went back to their village on weekends, as many of their relatives still lived there, as did the family's older daughter who had married and settled there. The father, Abu Mousa, had left primary school to join the military. The mother had never gone to school.

Amal was in the eleventh grade at al-Khatwa, while Tamara was at home studying to repeat *tawjihi* a third time, having failed it twice. They had four older brothers and two older sisters, as well as three younger siblings. The oldest sister had gone to the university and was a schoolteacher. Another older sister, Kareema, had failed *tawjihi* and had a low-paying job at a local hospital. At such a low salary, a job that required travel would not have justified the trouble, but given that it was in walking distance, she and her family agreed the job was worth it. In 2005, their brother passed *tawjihi*—the first of the brothers to do so. However, he did not score high enough to qualify for the military scholarship that his family would have had to rely on to send him to the university.

Tamara was always studying during the time we were neighbors, and I was overjoyed to hear that she had finally passed the *tawjihi* exam in 2006. I received word that Amal too had passed, and the family now had two daughters who had earned a place in the university in the same year. Amal's tuition would be covered by scholarships for sons and daughters of those in the military. Tamara, despite scoring well on the exam, was too old to qualify for the scholarship. However, the family was determined that she go to the university. They worked the channels of their personal contacts to see if they could get around the age limit. When these efforts failed, they insisted on finding a way. Despite their difficulties making ends meet at times, they decided to pay her tuition by pooling the incomes of her father, brothers, and her sister Kareema and borrowing when they needed to. In her second year at the university, Tamara married a man who agreed to pay her tuition so that she could complete her university education. She had initially been studying law, but according to her sister, her new husband convinced her to switch to education. According to Tamara, she had already been considering switching majors before marrying, as few jobs in law could be found in Bawadi al-Naseem. She was a university student and an expectant mother when I saw her last.

Jenine, Eleventh Grader: "The Husband Is a Diploma, Gold, Everything"

Jenine was the sensitive and funny eleventh grader who asked me about love in America in chapter 5. She loved the Arabic language and sometimes read poetry in her spare time. Jenine's family was Palestinian-Jordanian. They had lived in Saudi Arabia, where her father had been a teacher, until the First Gulf War, when they were forced to leave for Jordan. I never met her family, as Jenine was not comfortable taking me to her home. I learned about her family through her. Her parents were paternal cousins; Jenine's mother was twelve and her father twenty when they married. They were divorced when I met Jenine, and each parent was remarried. Jenine's mother was married to a man of little means from a local clan, and her father and his new wife lived in Amman. Jenine was living with her mother and siblings in a nearby town. It was unclear to me how the family was supporting itself, but there were many indications that they were struggling.

Jenine was one of twelve siblings—four girls and eight boys. She was the seventh child in the family, with four older brothers and two older sisters. None of her older siblings had gone on for schooling beyond high school, and most left school before finishing high school. Her younger sister (younger by one year) left school in the eighth grade and married at the age of sixteen. Jenine said this sister did not like school and never did well in her schoolwork. Jenine was an average student but showed enthusiasm for her studies. She said she planned to go to the university but admitted that her family did not have the financial means to support her education. Furthermore, her mother believed that the primary concern of a girl at her age should be getting married. According to Jenine, her mother would always say, "The husband is a diploma, gold, everything in life." I asked her if she thought her family would pressure her to get married before she finished school, and she said her father never forced his daughters to do anything they did not want to do.

In her extended family, none of the girls had gone on to the university.[21] According to Jenine, the rest of her family was conservative and found these coeducational institutions to be socially too "free" for their daughters. Jenine insisted that things would be different for her: "I want to finish [my education]. No one studies *tawjihi* to just sit at home." She joked that if a decent suitor came along she might give marriage a thought but again emphasized that education was her top priority because "it is a difficult situation in this country, and one does not know what will happen moving forward. A girl sees what happens with her family and has to be prepared for whatever might come her way in the future." Jenine kept emphasizing that all she needed to do was pass her high school completion exams and she would find a way to finance her university education.

When I inquired about Jenine on a return visit in 2008, Sara, one of the teachers who had stayed in touch with Jenine, said she had passed the *tawjihi* but had not done as well as she had expected. Passing with a low score meant that she would have to pay a higher tuition at the university, if she could even secure a place there. Sara, however, was trying to help Jenine get to the university. "Fida, I am trying to find her a good groom who will pay for her to go to the university, because her parents cannot afford it." The first groom that Sara had tried to arrange for Jenine did not work out, but Sara said she had other prospects. Sara was acting as a matchmaker for Jenine, but the goal of the match was education.

Most of the families I interviewed thought educating their daughters beyond high school was desirable if not critical for the future. Some, such as Jenine's, found the coeducational setting of universities threatening to their efforts to maintain the respectability of their daughters and sisters. However, rarely were such reservations separate from other considerations—financial, academic (whether their daughters had the academic ability to succeed), or personal (divorce, family breakup, dislocation). For example, Jenine's family had faced many tribulations. They had been made refugees by the 1967 War and the Israeli occupation of the West Bank and Gaza, leaving them officially stateless. She and her parents had been dislocated once again at the onset of the First Gulf War when they were forced to leave their jobs and homes in Saudi Arabia. Personal crisis, namely, the divorce of her parents, had compounded this difficult situation, and the realities of poverty were threaded through these events and exacerbated by them. Jenine always expressed hope that things would work out and that she could finish high school and go on to the university, but her cognizance of the formidable obstacles sometimes tempered her optimism. She had adopted the discourse of education as security, but her family, in the midst of great uncertainties, seemed more convinced that marrying Jenine off soon would be best for all. In the end marriage might do both if Jenine's teacher is successful in finding the "right" groom. Indeed, one of my most surprising findings in my subsequent return trips to Jordan is the reverse phenomenon—marriage to get an education rather than education to get married—whereby girls and their families seek suitors who will enable them to complete their education.

All the families I interviewed shared the belief that education provided for a more secure future. Again and again I heard people say, "In Jordan today a girl needs a diploma," "A girl needs to depend on herself," or "One never knows what will happen." Yet all had slightly different perspectives about what education could provide for their daughters and their families, which reflected their personal circumstances and histories. Amal's family was struggling financially and hoped that their daughters, at least for a time, could help support the family. Her parents also were worried about their daughters just sitting at home and feared they might not get married. There were many other families in this situation—such as the families of Batool, Rand, and Yasmine—also struggling with poverty, who wanted to spare their children the difficulties that they had endured in life. As with Dr. Sumaya, whose story opens this chapter, Selma's academic success was also viewed as a matter of community pride, for not only was she one of the few girls from her village who had gone to the city for high school but she was in the scientific track and could even become a doctor.

All of the families profiled here had at least one daughter who had not completed her education and was not married. Thus, in part a family's concerns for their daughters currently in high school were related to the situation of older daughters who were at home, having neither finished school nor married (and some had little prospect of marrying). Jenine's mother, a divorced and recently remarried woman with a large family and little means of supporting them, seemed particularly concerned that her daughters might become "old maids." The presence of unmarried daughters in the house motivated some families to ensure that younger daughters went on to the university; other families tried to get their daughters married before it was too late.

Economic status and educational background could not always predict what families hoped their daughters could achieve from their education.

Mothers who did not work, or who worked at a number of informal jobs to scrounge together a living for their families, were often vehement about wanting their daughters to go on to the university because of economic hardships they faced. For some, the hope was that their daughters would work and be able to gain some financial independence; for others the assumption was that education would ensure that their daughters could marry someone who was well off so that they did not have to work. Some working mothers discouraged their daughters from the idea of studying to work, as they were too tired from work and all the other responsibilities they had to bear. Still, they felt that going to the university was important for their daughters' status and marriage prospects. The school was an important space in which young women grappled with the competing images of education for marriage, motherhood, and work. In school, they interacted with working women daily—their teachers—and they were exposed to official lessons about work and family life in the curriculum.

Salaried Employee Wanted

In school, both the state (via the curriculum) and the teachers (state employees) contributed to the polemics surrounding women's work outside the home. On several occasions at al-Khatwa, I observed debates about women's work. When I spoke with students about their future plans and wishes, some explicitly engaged with these debates, drawing on a range of personal experiences and information that circulated in school, the media, and the everyday conversations of the adults around them. Girls framed the issues by drawing on varying considerations: religious acceptability, moral propriety, economic circumstances, women's desires, and the practical difficulties of working outside the home. A conversation I had with two friends (tenth graders at the time of this interview), Anwar and Lena, about their expectations for the future conveyed some of these sentiments:

FIDA: Anwar, what would you like to study?

ANWAR: If I get a good average I would like to be a doctor—a gynecologist. If not, then engineering. If I can't get into engineering, then math.

LENA: I always say that engineering is not a job for a girl here in our society. What will a girl do if she becomes an architect or something like that? We have a computer teacher who is a computer engineer. But what did she become in the end? A regular teacher. She did not benefit from engineering.

ANWAR: My cousin is working as an engineer at the university.

LENA: But it's difficult for a girl.

FIDA: What's difficult about it?

ANWAR: Here [in Bawadi al-Naseem] they prefer teachers.

LENA: As soon as she gets married, she herself without anyone telling her will start taking care of her children. Her husband does not like her to go out. An architect always has to go out. But a teacher, she only needs to be out of the house for five hours. Then she comes home, cleans her house, and that's it.

FIDA: If the situation is like this, what is the motive for a girl to go study engineering then?

ANWAR: In the ninth grade everybody wants to be a doctor or an engineer and things like this. In tenth grade it's less and eleventh grade even less. Then you get to *tawjihi* [in twelfth grade] and you just want to get the grade. A lot don't get the grades. They just want to go to the university; it becomes about the university. They see the university as some big deal because it's open and coed . . . shameful things. You ask a girl why she is studying and she says because she wants to go to the university. Then she wants a groom. The potential groom . . . the first thing he asks is: "How much is her salary?" He wants her to help him.

FIDA: But you said when a woman gets married she stops working. So what is the benefit from the salary in the end?

ANWAR: A woman who is an engineer won't marry a laborer. People will typically come and request the hand of someone of the same class.

FIDA: So a doctor should marry an educated woman?

LENA: Yes. So she will understand him.

FIDA: So about the salary . . . I still don't understand. They want a woman with a salary, but they do not want her to work?

ANWAR: She will go and get him a salary. Then she has a child and then he needs childcare; he needs to send them and bring them, and he needs to send his wife to work, and they need to send food to the childcare. [He thinks] Let her stay at home and cook for the kids; it's better for her. Childcare takes all of the salary.

LENA: Also, now there are a lot of women who work, and they see the women who do not work living a life of luxury—not tired. They start thinking about retiring or quitting. My mother [a teacher] was like this. She used to see her friends. They did not work, but they were living, going out with each other. My mother was very stressed. She took her job very seriously. Not all teachers do. Some just go to school for a change of scenery. But my mother would come home worn out and tired. When she would see the women sitting at home, she would feel as if something were missing from her life.

FIDA: Your mother would tell you this?

LENA: Yes, and she retired. She says it is nice to sit in the house.

Lena and Anwar alluded to multiple considerations in defining ambitions and strategizing about the future. They pointed to the difficulties young women face in getting to the university and the desire of most to "just go to the university." Through her description of her own plans for the university and her reflections on what "everybody wants," Anwar reminds us how much of a girl's future is determined by her grades, as getting the grade is critical in determining if and what a young woman will study beyond high school.[22] In the end, Anwar did "get the grade" for medicine as she desired, but she was unable to afford the high tuition for studying medicine and instead opted for engineering, which cost considerably less. Lena, on the other hand, did not get grades high enough for engineering but chose to study engineering at her parents' expense. Thus future pathways were circumscribed by economic factors as well.

At my prompting, Anwar tried to explain the contradiction between the perception that men want to marry women who work, or at least who could potentially work, and the reality that few women work outside the home. Both Lena and Anwar alluded to the inconsistency between the pressures to excel in school and to go into the more prestigious fields like the sciences and engineering, and the perceived reality that even if men want women who work, they prefer women who are teachers, because their jobs enable them to more easily balance their responsibilities at home and at work. However, as Anwar points out, the prestige of studying engineering is important in its own right, both for the social status it affords young women and for the potential marriage partners it might attract. As discussed in chapter 5, degrees in scientific and mathematical fields are held in high regard independent of their economic utility.[23]

Lena's mother was a schoolteacher, while Anwar's mother was a widow who took in children to supplement her income. Although Anwar's mother would not be counted in the official labor force statistics, her work to supplement her late husband's pension reminds us that women in difficult economic circumstances, particularly where the man is not bringing in an income or is deceased, find ways to help their families survive and have little choice about the matter.[24] Um Waleed, the mother of Yasmine whom I discuss in chapter 2, faced similar challenges. Yasmine's father was a migrant worker who came and went from the Arab Gulf states and occasionally worked in Jordan. However, he seemed unable to hold a job or to save money to send to his family, and so Um Waleed supported the family through multiple jobs with limited help from two older sons who had left high school to work. She had a low-level janitorial job at one of the local ministry offices in the late afternoons. To supplement this meager income, she baked bread and sold it to townspeople for special occasions like weddings and funerals; she made juice and sold it to children at a nearby school; and during the day she took care of three or four children of working mothers in her neighborhood. Her daughters, particularly Yasmine's older sister who had dropped out of school and was at home, helped her with these multiple income-generating initiatives. Yasmine, however, thanks to the hard work and determination of her mother, went on to the university; I discuss her situation further in the next chapter. Lena's mother, on the other hand, was educated, married to a doctor, and, ostensibly, did not have to work. She had gone to the university, had a professional job as a teacher, and given that she had only one child, did not have a heavy domestic burden at home. Nevertheless, according to Lena, she was unhappy with the life of a working woman. Like most women, Jordanian women struggled with the "double burden" of work in and outside the home, and this was a subject that came up frequently in talking to teachers about their own lives and with young women about their future plans (Hochschild 1990).

The majority of mothers of al-Khatwa students did not work outside their home, but in this day and age all of the girls would have encountered a working woman in some sphere of their life—at the very least their teachers, even if the career paths of their teachers at times seemed undesirable. Hanan, an eleventh grader responding to her teacher's assertion that she would be a teacher someday, replied: "No, not if the teachers say, 'Damn the day I ever became a teacher.'" The most immediate model of a working woman was not always an appealing one, and many students claimed that their own teachers discouraged them from this path, primarily by their complaints about the hard life of a teacher and a working woman. Some teachers, such as Miss Suheil, encouraged the girls: "A girl can be anything. She can be a journalist, a doctor, a teacher." Other teachers, however, felt it was their role to temper what they viewed as unrealistic aspirations. For girls in Bawadi al-Naseem, where few other employment opportunities were available that did not require travel, this could be practical advice. However, there were women in Bawadi al-Naseem who were doctors and lawyers; over the years I also heard about more young women traveling to Amman to work or living in dormitories for single female workers in the capital. Thus, although work outside the home was often framed by Jordanians as necessary owing to the contemporary economic situation, and by some as a positive experience for women, its desirability was not a given. A woman and her family assessed such options—when they were indeed options—in light of their circumstances. Most important, taking care of a family's financial needs was still viewed as the primary responsibility of a man, even if in practice women have always worked for the economic benefit of their families.

National Narratives of "Social Change" and Women's Work

The national and civic education curriculum for tenth graders provides an official perspective on women's education and work outside the home and the implications of their work for shifting gender roles. In a lesson entitled "Social Change: Definition, Elements, Manifestations and Problems" in the *National and Civic Education* textbook for tenth grade (al-Masad et al. 2004), among a list of the manifestations of social change is a reference to women's work outside the home: "The view of society toward women's work has clearly changed, especially because their work contributes toward increased production and an improved standard of living for the family. Notice that the percentage of the labor force who are women in Jordan has been increasing in the last period" (61). This section of the textbook is followed by a list of "problems" associated with social change. One of the problems listed is the "breakup of the family" (62).[25] Amongst the reasons listed for the breakup of the family is the "change in men's and women's roles in the family" (62). Further along in the textbook, a passage explains the conflicts caused by changes in men's and women's roles through the concept of "cultural gap" (63). The authors describe the double burden faced by women who now must carry all the responsibility for work in the home, as well as contribute to the building of society and to the family's income through her work outside the home. They argue that this represents a failure of cultural beliefs to change or keep up with the reality of more women working outside the home. A selection from this passage reads: "As long as both men and women work outside the home with the goal of meeting the needs of making a living, then there is no choice but for there to be cooperation in the housework" (63). Thus, the authors of this textbook acknowledge a problem that students at al-Khatwa seemed well aware of, namely, the double burden faced by women who work outside the home; the authors explain it in terms of a cultural lag.[26]

The *National and Civic Education* text depicts women's work outside the home as a necessary, if not positive, development. This is in keeping with the public stance taken by the regime in recent years supporting women's work and the regular initiatives to ready women for the workforce and make jobs available to them. The National Social and Economic Plan for 2004–6 expressly stated its commitment to enable more women to join the labor force (World Bank 2005: 15). Almost daily the press highlights job-training programs,[27] microfinance schemes for female-headed small businesses, new factories that will employ women,[28] or women working in traditionally male professions.[29] The stories are often accompanied by photographs of royal women, more often than not the queen or Princess Basma, the king's aunt. Nevertheless, even at the level of the official discourse of the state, as embodied by the curriculum (the textbook and the curriculum being one and the same), the lessons were ambiguous. In the religion textbooks I reviewed, I found no explicit passages about women's work, but treatment of this topic could be deduced from the lessons on the mixing of the sexes and the rights and responsibilities of husbands and wives. For example, in the *Islamic Culture* textbook under "the rights of the husband," a woman's responsibility for taking care of house and home is clearly delineated (Jabr et al. 2004: 266). In the same unit, in keeping with Islamic teachings, the authors emphasize the husband's responsibility to provide for his family. This passage gives no hint as to the need for sharing domestic responsibilities. In addition, the passage also states that a woman must obey her husband and ask his permission to leave the home. In practice, the latter is then interpreted to mean that a woman may not work without her husband's permission.[30]

Such inconsistencies are reflective of the multiple voices with which the state speaks; state bureaucrats do not necessarily convey a coherent message, and the Jordanian regime has long worked to maintain a delicate balance of power by appeasing social conservatives in order to protect their own interests as a regime (Brand 1998). Furthermore, the authors of religious education texts approach the textbook writing process from a different perspective than do the authors of the *National and Civic Education* textbook. Thus, to speak of the Jordanian state and its representatives is to speak of a politically heterogeneous group of actors that also includes members of Islamic political groups (Antoun 2006).[31] The socialization of young people with regard to gender roles and expectations is considered by many in Jordan to be key to issues of cultural authenticity and political autonomy. The inconsistencies in the official language of the state give us a sense of the competing projects to shape young women.

Yet as with the religion classes highlighted in chapter 4, the textbook does not fully contain the lesson at hand. Indeed, several debates ensued in different tenth-grade classrooms regarding this lesson about social change and women's work. In one section, Lena argued that the problems alluded to in the text were caused by "women taking men's place." Indeed the dominant ideology surrounding gender roles was so strong that even women who strongly supported women's entry into the labor force often spoke in terms of "women becoming men."[32] However, the response of Lena's classmate Rita challenged the construction of such gendered roles:

RITA: A woman can work and take responsibility for her family, but it does not mean that she becomes a man. She works like a man, but she hasn't become a man. Maybe the man can't work or won't work.

DIA (the teacher): In World War I and II women worked in factories while all the men were at war. This helped Europe come to respect women. They came home and found things in even better shape. This is not about changing women into men but women taking men's roles. King Faisal of Iraq used to say women are half of society. He was saying this in 1932. He said, "Can a man cut off one hand and still be productive?" No, and so neither can society do so.

LENA: I was trying to say that in our society men are the strong ones. They control things. If a woman controls finances, it creates problems.

RITA: But this is not a situation God created. Men used to be the ones who worked, and so that is what we have become used to. So it is not that women have become men, it's just that we are not used to women working. Women might even do a better job—be more productive.

Rita objected to her classmate's characterization of women's work, arguing that it is not divinely ordained that men should be the providers. Rita's critical perspective on this issue was likely enabled by the experiences of her own family. Her father had died when she was a child, and her mother had recently died, leaving her and several siblings orphaned. Her mother had been the sole family provider for many years, and now her older sister and brother were. Her teacher, Dia, also came to the defense of women who work, citing the example of women in Europe and the critical role they played in meeting labor needs during the two world wars. Dia also referred to Faisal, a member of the Hashemite family, arguing that as early as 1932 this Arab leader was advocating for women's equal participation in society. However, she also responded to Rita's enthusiastic defense of women sarcastically:

DIA: Rita, you are with women. Why are you so emotional? We are all with women. The Jordanian constitution says everyone is equal irrespective of race, ethnicity, or sex. . . . They used to bury girls alive in the *jahiliyya* period.[33] Islam respects women. In her home she has full respect, but now the situation requires women to work. Even before [in the past], men and women worked side by side farming. A woman may become a colonel or a general, but is it accepted? No. Not even in Europe. Here we are more respected than there.

Dia asserted that both Jordanian society and Islam protect the rights of women. She also responded with the official discourse of the state about equality and opportunity for women in Jordan. This was no surprise given how openly patriotic Dia was. An image of Jordan as modern and forward looking is critical to the regime's national vision, and Dia saw this discussion about women's work as an opportunity to reinforce this with references to Faisal (a Hashemite), the constitution, and Islam. Teachers played different roles in this respect, both in the things they said and in the example they provided as working women. However, teachers too could be an uncertain model.

For girls in Bawadi al-Naseem the job prospects were limited. Furthermore, despite the contention that they needed to work to become attractive marriage partners, many women and men in Bawadi al-Naseem still found women's work outside the home to be undesirable and/or unacceptable. Despite this ambiguity, models of working women were all around, most immediately in the example of their teachers. For women from diverse socioeconomic backgrounds in Jordan, the question of women's work outside the home is complicated, just as it is for women in the United States (hooks 1984). Um Waleed, for example, had no choice but to work menial and low-status jobs to ensure that her family survived and her children were educated. In addition to her salaried job in janitorial services and multiple small trading schemes, she used her spare time to work the networks of the more powerful in her community to help her sons find a job and secure a scholarship for Yasmine.[34] But even women who appeared to have many choices, such as Dr. Sumaya in our opening vignette, expressed ambivalence, if not regret, about insufficient time with her children and the tiredness that came from trying to balance it all.

Conclusion

Most girls at al-Khatwa had high hopes for completing their education and finding contentment and material comforts in their lives, but they struggled with the expectations that education created and the shifting realities of women's lives around them. Schools provide spaces for girls to negotiate conflicting pressures in twenty-first-century Jordan, while also complicating this process by creating new expectations and placing value on new forms of knowledge and newly constituted status positions. Yet the deterioration of

160 / Chapter Six

the economic situation in most of the region has closed many of the doors they thought had been opened, while, ironically, their participation in the labor force is believed to make them more attractive marriage partners. At the same time, for some young women, debates about sufficient modesty, new forms of Islamic dress, and the propriety of interacting with males in the workplace also complicate attempts to define and navigate acceptable and respectable future pathways.

The young women I spoke with were cognizant of the restrictions on their options—economic, cultural, and personal—and struggled to negotiate the opportunities and limits they faced as they matured and moved on beyond al-Khatwa. The school provided a critical space for teaching and learning about their place and potential in Jordanian society, but it was modern schooling that had raised new expectations, some of which appeared unattainable to many girls from al-Khatwa. Schooling has transformed the terms of national, religious, and gendered identities, making education desirable but its desired effects contested. The visions of what education could provide these young women were not necessarily in accordance with a global narrative about women's development through education. Nevertheless, families connected many of their aspiration for a better future for their children to the promise of education. Some families' needs were more immediate, as parents hoped that a son or daughter with a degree could help support them and younger siblings. Although parents did not express the language of gender equality or empowerment common to much of the national and global discourse on women's development, they were concerned that their daughters have the *power* to care for themselves and their families.

SEVEN

Conclusion

In January 2006, soon after I returned from spending eight months at al-Khatwa, the Regional Bureau of Arab States in the UNDP released the *Arab Human Development Report 2005: Towards the Rise of Women in the Arab World*.[1] I was asked by a colleague to read the report and participate in a public forum to share my reactions to it. Reading this report with the memories of al-Khatwa's students and their families so fresh in my memory was startling. The report bore little resemblance to the day-to-day realities I had observed and gave no sense of the struggle of families, often against insurmountable obstacles, to secure a future for their daughters through education. Instead, the report's authors argued that the Arab world faced a gendered educational crisis, that education had failed women, and that families were the primary obstacle to women's development. Perhaps it is inevitable that such a report, which seeks to paint such a geographically expansive and heterogeneous space with broad brushstrokes, should fall short. The danger lies in the effects of such discourse—in its dehumanizing tendencies. Despite the best efforts of the authors of *AHDR 2005*, one is left with an image of powerless and subjugated Arab women whose families and culture are repressive (Adely 2009a).

Many factors limit and shape young women in Bawadi al-Naseem, Jordan—geography, economics, culture, and politics. However, like human beings anywhere, they are not completely determined by these structures. Young women also actively engage in the making of their future possibilities—by getting good grades, by attracting the attention of young men who may marry them, by resisting the entreaties of potential suitors because they prefer to study, by teaching others about Islam, or by singing at musical performances on the king's birthday. Young women do not act independently of their families' counsel, but nor are they necessarily in conflict with their families; they are products of the same environment and as such share many of the same beliefs and ideals. Typically their families are a source of support, advice, and even inspiration, even as they impose limits and enforce particular gendered expectations. I have endeavored in this book to capture the complexities of life that a variety of young women in Jordan face as they move through secondary education and grow into adulthood. I have also incorporated the stories of their families where I have been able, as the narratives of these young women are not separate from those of their kin. As I have shown here, central to the narratives of these young women is education—as a space of deliberation in their lives, as part and parcel of national and local ideals of a developed woman, and as a project with substantial material implications (Bartlett 2003).

Through this ethnography, I have highlighted the ways in which the ideology of education is interpreted, negotiated, and made in schools, as well as within families and their larger communities. What schooling offers to these young women—status and respect, future educational opportunities, the promise of mobility and economic security—is also inextricably linked to their passage to adulthood, decisions about marriage, and careers. Additionally, the decisions that young woman face today are equally decisions about Jordan and the nature of Jordanian national identity; about Islam, piety, morality, and its gendered manifestations; and about the nature of progress. Their schooling experience is also shaped by the range of actors and institutions—global development organizations, the monarchy, state bureaucracies, religious leaders, educational officials, teachers, parents, and other adolescent girls—that have a hand in defining education and its worth and in delineating what counts as progress and who should benefit from it.

Global and national narratives about contemporary mass schooling and its effects construct particular expectations for young people in Jordan, most prominently for increased social and economic status. Yet these expectations are complicated by other desires, expectations, and socioeconomic realities that shape and limit the options available to them. For young women, the dynamics are particularly complex because the pathways available to them once they complete their schooling are unclear and because competing visions of desirable womanhood circulate among them. Throughout this book, I point to the multiplicity of these visions in the curriculum, in school talk among peers and teachers, in the media, and in the wider discourse about Arab Muslim women. Girls at al-Khatwa struggled to make sense of the meaning of their education—"education for what?"—and to reconcile conflicting messages about what might constitute a successful future.

Gender, Schooling, and Development: The Significance of the al-Khatwa Experience

These young women and their families are not meant to be representative of the Arab world, the Middle East, or even Jordan. They are particular and historically situated lives that provide a view of the range of ideas, beliefs, and practices linked to education for girls in one community. At the same time, the profiles of young women here enable us to transcend the specter of "Arab Muslim youth" and see the possibilities embedded in the lives of particular young people—particular girls. On a similar note, the experiences of al-Khatwa students complicate reified images of oppressed Arab and Muslim women and provide new insight into the ways in which we understand the making of gender through education. The literature on schooling in the Middle East has been quite thin in this respect; a lack of ethnographic research means that schools in the region have been treated as opaque state institutions (Mazawi 1999, 2002); meanwhile, textbooks have been treated as the sources par excellence of educational discourse and its effects. Developments in anthropology and education have been largely absent in the literature on schooling in the region. In recent decades, anthropologists and sociologists of education have worked to complicate social reproduction theories of schooling. While acknowledging the tendency of schools to reproduce particular power relations—class, gender, race, etc.—this scholarship has sought to identify ways in which young people resist the forces of reproduction and create new, potentially transformative cultural forms (e.g., Holland and Eisenhart 1990; Levinson and Holland 1996). Despite these scholarly developments, reproduction/resistance/production questions have been framed in such a way that assumptions about what should be opposed and what forms resistance can predictably take are often built into them.[2] The result of such bias is the failure to fully appreciate the significance of social action that is not outright oppositional and to give greater weight to cultural forms that are more familiar to outside observers.

Responding to this literature on schooling and student resistance to authoritative structures, Dorothy C. Holland and Margaret A. Eisenhart (1990) argue that girls tend to engage in more pragmatic strategies in their responses to a range of structures that seek to constrain their activities and particularly their romantic activities. The authors contend that too much emphasis on resistance has led to an oversimplified analysis of schools and not enough engagement with theories of production and practice:

> Instead of trying immediately to answer the ultimate questions—whether particular responses constitute resistance and the possible birth of a social movement that will ultimately challenge the status quo—we must instead tack back and forth between our recognition that students are creative and our growing understanding of the shape and content of the gender hierarchies to which girls and women respond. (59)

This conceptualization of resistance by Holland and Eisenhart resonates with my own experiences in Jordan. At al-Khatwa I observed a good deal of "strategic compliance" (Holland and Eisenhart 1990: 222). Most young women worked within the existing sociocultural limits, at times even embracing them. Nevertheless, they were not passive objects. Rather, they worked within these parameters to navigate among the possibilities available to them and to create their own paths, given the limits they encountered. In addition, as I have shown in preceding chapters, these constraints and possibilities varied significantly. Some young women sought or imagined different possibilities—whether to transform gender relations (as in the ideas conveyed by Indira or Rita); to live in a more "Islamic" society (as exemplified in Amina, Dunya, and Miss Suheil); or to overcome major economic barriers through a good education, good marriage, and/or good job (among many, we have read about Rand and Yasmine). Although all desired change in their lives, they imagined that such change would be enabled by significantly different projects.

This analysis also has important implications for the study of youth in the Middle East. As discussed in chapter 1, the large number of "youth" in the region has captured the concern of a range of actors in the region and beyond. Much of the scholarly research and the journalistic coverage focus on youth oppositional cultures, particularly in areas like music and dance.[3] The tendency to focus on the most obvious signs of youth resisting dominant cultural norms and creating their own "subcultures" overlooks the ways in which young people are engaged in everyday practices to define desirable and acceptable pathways to adulthood, family, security, and happiness. Schools and educational institutions more broadly are a central arena in which to explore such everyday practices (Adely 2009b). In order to do so we must examine schools as multilayered institutions. Schools are formal institutions of the state, but although the state requires citizens to send their children to school, it does not completely control the form and nature of interactions within this space. The practice of going to school it-self leads to the construction of particular expectations and enables a set of everyday practices—patriotic performances, religious debates, gendered discipline, and talk about love, marriage, and careers—that both reflects and produces contemporary cultural conflicts. Schools, and the ideology of education, produce contradictions that have a hand in shaping images of what is possible.

The young women at al-Khatwa were engaged in a process of negotiat-ing norms and competing visions of what it means to be Jordanian, a good Muslim, and a respectable woman in Jordan. The transformations brought on by globalization, development, state building, and consolidation are al-most everywhere apparent in Jordan today.[4] The constellation of projects young women face in Jordan today present a particular historical moment in which the terms of national, cultural, and religious identity have been significantly clouded or made ambiguous. Although they pose a challenge for young people, this ambiguity and its attendant contradictions are pro-ductive (Booth 1997; Giddens 1979; Ortner 1989, 1996). They motivate particular forms of action and reflection that require the reinscription and at times reconceptualization of dominant norms. Schooling and the spread of education represent one project that has had a hand in creating such am-biguities; schools are also a space in which such ambiguities are negotiated. As the experiences of students at al-Khatwa reveal, this does not necessarily result in outright resistance to dominant norms; but to say this does not minimize the myriad ways in which young women are engaged in making sense and constructing meaning in the face of such ambiguity.

Young women in Jordan face many challenges as they move through their education and navigate a path to womanhood. Some imagined and even worked toward possibilities that went against the current, but many accepted the terms that they had learned to accept as preferable and even natural (Bourdieu 1977). The adults in their lives tell them that they need to be good students, but being a successful secondary school student is no longer sufficient. They should receive high marks on *tawjihi*, go on to the university, and preferably enter one of the more prestigious or lucrative fields in the sciences or mathematics. All of this will enable them to marry well, their many advisors tell them. At times they hear from their moth-ers, sisters, or others in their lives that a woman should work so that she may depend on herself should a marriage fall apart or should she fail to marry. Increasingly, they are also told that economic circumstances require a woman to work and that potential suitors desire young women with jobs. However, the working women the al-Khatwa students know often complain about the double burden of work in and outside the home. Many of the girls find the idea of work to be appealing but consider motherhood to be an equally important job. They typically view these as two different phases in one's life—a phase in which one works outside the home and a phase in which one focuses on the important work of raising children in the home. What preoccupies them most in high school is getting the grades that might actually enable them to have such choices. For those who do not excel academically or whose families have few resources to fund higher education, the challenges are more immediate.

School-to-Life Transitions

This book has focused on a particular phase in the lives of young women in Bawadi al-Naseem—their time in high school. The plans and desires articulated by these young women at al-Khatwa "represented only one moment in a process of coming of age" (Hurtig 2008: 59). Since then, I have continued to visit and speak with many of the girls and their families, and I have come to learn about how their lives unfolded and how education figured into their trajectories. The practical realities of grades, finances, appealing suitors, marriage, family crises, and parental authority have all come to be more immediate factors in the projects of fashioning their futures—projects not entirely of their own making. Despite this, these young women are not mere objects of such forces but rather are actively engaged in shaping their own life path. In the face of a range of constraints and opportunities, Yasmine, Rand, Amina, Dunya, Jamileh, and Indira have each pursued different paths; however, education has figured strongly and distinctly in their trajectories.

Yasmine

In chapter 2, I described my first meeting with Yasmine, the avid soccer fan who invited me to her home in 2002. In 2007, I received word from Yasmine's brother via Facebook that she had married. I was a bit surprised. After the tremendous efforts her mother had put forth—working night and day at multiple jobs—to ensure that Yasmine could go to the university, I had assumed that she would finish college before marrying. When I heard she had married, I thought she would likely drop out. My own assumptions got the better of me, as I could not help feeling troubled by the timing of her marriage. I visited Yasmine in the summer of 2008; we looked at her wedding photos and I met her husband. Later when she and I were alone, I asked, "Yasmine, what about your studies?" She assured me that she would continue and that she had only taken a semester off. She said, "My husband will pay for my studies, and he said he will even pay for my master's degree."

When I returned to Jordan in 2009, Yasmine informed me that she was eight months pregnant.[5] Again I wondered if this signaled the end of her education. Yasmine gave birth soon after I left, and about six months later I received an e-mail from her brother informing me that she had graduated from the university and was about to start a master's degree. When I saw Yasmine in early 2011, she had two children. She informed me that she was nearly done with the master's degree and that her husband was encouraging her to pursue a Ph.D. She went on, "My husband never finished his schooling. He left school in fifth grade to help with his family herds and farming. He never studied but he wants to make sure I do." Yasmine herself is not so sure that she would like to pursue a doctoral degree. She says the kids and home are a big responsibility, and although her mother and her sisters have been very supportive of her, she could use a break from studying. But her husband took pride in the status that came from his wife's educational achievements, even if he had never had these opportunities himself.

Rand

Rand was only a tenth grader when I met her in 2005. She struck me at the time as a confident and bright young woman. I lost touch with her for some time, but she held onto my e-mail address and after a couple of years contacted me to say that all was well.[6] When I saw her in 2008, I was surprised to hear that she was struggling. She had passed her *tawjihi* exams, although her scores were much lower than expected. She broke into tears when she explained to me that her father had died just before the exams and as a result she had performed poorly.

Despite the death of her father and her low grades, which meant she had to pay a higher tuition rate for certain majors as a *mawazi* student, her family managed to enroll her in the university. Since her father was deceased, she was eligible for some financial aid from the state. She also had an older sister and two older brothers who were employed, the former in a relatively well-paid profession. However, her siblings were also paying for the family's day-to-day household expenses, and her oldest bother was trying to save enough money to get married. Somehow the family managed to piece together the funds for Rand's first-year tuition. When I saw Rand that summer, she had completed her first year as a chemistry major but was not doing particularly well. She had not wanted to study chemistry but was persuaded to do so by her relatives, who argued that she would have better job prospects with chemistry than with foreign languages as she preferred. Thus, her family viewed the investment in her education as linked to economic possibilities.

When we spoke in 2008, Rand was considering switching to an English major. She had done very well in her English electives, and one of her professors was encouraging her. He also promised that he would help her secure a scholarship from the department if she did well in her second year. Rand was anxious as we sat and talked; she owed the university money and was not sure how she would even manage to complete her semester. Yet she was excited about the prospects of studying English. Rand's family managed to borrow money for the next year and through personal connections lobbied for more financial aid from the university. Rand excelled in her new major and received a scholarship from the English department. When I saw her again in 2009, she was doing extremely well and was volunteering to tutor her peers who were struggling with English. In 2010, her major advisor told her he might be able to arrange for a U.S.-funded grant for her to study abroad after graduating. Rand said her family agreed to allow her to do this should the opportunity arise. When I saw her in 2011, the prospects of a scholarship had not materialized; however, Rand had graduated at the top of her class and was looking for work that would enable her to pay for a master's degree. She seemed anxious about being unemployed, and I tried to suggest different job-search strategies. Her brother had recently moved to Amman, and so she was considering jobs in the capital as she could live with him there.

Amina and Dunya

Amina was a strong figure at the al-Khatwa School in 2005, as evinced in chapter 4 of this book. She had clarity of purpose based on her religious convictions and very consciously rejected certain life trajectories as undesirable and un-Islamic. When I asked about Amina, some of her peers told me that she had married a well-known religious man who was a professor of Islamic studies and that she had moved to Amman. Amal, one of her former classmates, said that Amina was proud to have gotten married on the day that all her peers were rushing to find out their *tawjihi* scores; Amina took pride in her disregard for the exam and its results. Although she paid little attention to the results of the exam, she had passed. For Amina, her marriage to this educated religious man represented a much greater success than passing *tawjihi*. Indeed, as I described in chapter 4, Amina was one of the very few girls whom I met who had no interest in going to the university. When I asked after her again in 2009, her friends told me she was very content with her new life in Amman.

Amina's closest friend in high school, Dunya, who was also religious and very active in the prayer room committee, had chosen a different path. She took her exams quite seriously and scored among the highest in the humanities track in her year. In 2008, her teachers told me she was doing well and enrolled in one of the more prestigious public universities. Dunya's older sisters had all been excellent students, among the top students in their high school and at the university. Perhaps they presented a model for her that was more desirable than that offered by Amina. Dunya's success as a student was also a significant determinant, as it enabled her to have more choices beyond high school.

Jamileh

Jamileh was in tenth grade in 2005. She was a very attractive girl who paid careful attention to her clothes. She always wore matching headscarves, *jelbabs,* and shoes in a range of colors. As I mention briefly in chapter 5, during tenth grade, Jamileh announced to her classmates and teachers that she was getting engaged and that she would leave school. Although several students at al-Khatwa were engaged, Jamileh's father did not want her to stay in school once engaged, and so Jamileh was preparing herself to leave. At the time most of the teachers disapproved of her engagement; they felt she was too young to get married. Her homeroom teacher, however, deviated from this perspective, telling me that Jamileh was a "problem student" who distracted other students and was not really engaged in schoolwork. She thought it would not be such a bad thing if Jamileh left school. Interestingly, Jamileh's peers were generally more supportive of her engagement. Her friends told me that Jamileh was not a very good student and that they saw no problem with her leaving school. "Besides," one added, "she is in love." Her prospective fiancé was a young soldier stationed near her home. Rumor had it that the young couple had been exchanging glances and small talk for some time. Given the absence of other acceptable means through which to have a relationship with a male, it was not surprising that some of her peers found love to be a sufficient motivation to drop out, particularly since she was not a good student.

However, Jamileh's plans to become engaged were abruptly canceled. Jamileh was quite upset about this turn of events; she told me that her father had had second thoughts and refused to give his approval. He decided that his daughter and the potential groom were too young, and he reenrolled Jamileh in school. In 2008, I heard from Rand, one of her good friends, that she had gotten engaged in eleventh grade to a different man and dropped out of school. Initially, according to Rand, Jamileh was quite excited; the period of engagement and marriage can be one of the most exciting times in a young woman's life. As a high school student, Jamileh never liked school and did not do well academically. Thus leaving and marrying seemed a very good option. However, she soon had two young children, and the excitement of it all seemed to wear off for her. Rand told me that Jamileh had recently been regretful, wishing she had waited a bit longer before marrying.

Indira

I saw Indira in March of 2011. I had not seen her since she was an eleventh grader at al-Khatwa in 2005, when she complained to me that education was a false promise for girls as it would never make them equal to boys. She had changed quite a bit over the intervening years. She was taller, thinner, and shyer than I remembered her. She had just graduated from the university with a bachelor's degree in lab sciences, and I brought her some chocolates to celebrate her graduation. I sat with Indira, her mother, and older sister who had also just graduated with a degree in science. Indira said she was hoping to get a job at the public hospital in Bawadi al-Naseem. I knew these jobs were hard to come by so asked her if she was looking elsewhere. She said this was the only suitable job. She said that she could work only in Bawadi al-Naseem and that the public sector was a better option for her than anything that might be open in the private sector. Although she initially presented these decisions as her own, she eventually made it clear that these were her father's preferences.

Her sister Jehan was vibrant and very excited to meet me. She asked me what I thought about a girl going to study abroad, but before I could answer, Indira said it was a bad idea. She said that no family could accept their daughter's going abroad. It turned out that Jehan had received a scholarship offer to complete her studies in Europe but her father would not allow her to go abroad. "He won't even let me go to Amman!" she told me. Her mother said that her husband was quite overprotective and had tried to get her to quit her job but she refused. She said unfortunately all his energy was devoted to the girls now.

It is hard to say how Indira was feeling at this stage of her life. She seemed resigned to sitting at home for the time being and was also surprisingly ignorant of other possibilities. When I told her that a significant number of Jordanian women went abroad to study, she insisted that this was not possible and that no Jordanian family would send their daughter abroad. When I told her that children in elite schools in Amman all went abroad—males and females alike—she looked at me in disbelief and said, "They must be foreigners." Jehan appeared less acquiescent to her current situation, although she was trying to make good use of her time by teaching herself Chinese online. Despite Indira's remarks in eleventh grade when she had chafed at society's limits on her as a girl and complained about the false promises of education, it appeared as if she was now resigned to these limits, if not wholly accepting of them.

In these updated narratives, Yasmine, Rand, Amina, Dunya, Jamileh, and Indira are not meant to be representative of their peers. Rather, the narratives give a sense of the constellation of factors that can shape the future of a young woman in Jordan. Amina's family shared her religious convictions but did not necessarily agree with her educational choices. Her parents had urged her to at least consider a community college degree before ceasing her education, but she was not interested. Amina wanted to focus on raising a family and studying and teaching Islam independently. Her friend Dunya, who had shared many of the same convictions as she in high school, went on to the university, as had her older sisters. She saw no conflict between her commitment to Islam and higher education in a coeducational institution. Rand, with equal conviction, cultivated relationships with her professors, studied hard, and created opportunities for herself despite formidable financial obstacles. Her older sister's economic success both supported her with financial resources and led the family to view the educational and subsequent economic success of their daughters as critical to the family's maintenance. However, some Jordanians with whom I spoke did not see such a scenario in a positive light. They viewed the dependence on the income of unmarried daughters for too long as exploitative because it delayed their daughters' marriages unnecessarily, risking the possibility that daughters might not be able to have families of their own. Conversely, others argued that in this day and age, daughters were indispensable as supporters of their parents.

Rand's uncles believed she would have more options with a degree in science, and science was a higher-status field in Jordan and in the global narratives that equate math and science with empowerment for women. However, her family supported her change in major despite the financial losses they incurred. In this way, Rand pursued both what she desired and what she believed would work better for her in the end. The support of her professor had proved indispensable, but now that she had graduated, the path forward was more uncertain.

Following the news about Yasmine and her family has been a source of great learning for me; many of my assumptions have come undone as a result of watching the path that Yasmine's life has taken. I assumed she would not continue her education if she married, although I have learned that many young women do. Most illuminating in my reaction, however, was that I overlooked how marriage itself was part of Yasmine's success and her mother's efforts to secure a future for her, one that would be better than her own. Also, the degree to which her spouse supported her education—both financially and emotionally—also seemed to go against expectations, although I have since encountered many examples of young women marrying and completing their education after marriage at their husband's expense. In part, it is a testament to the status that comes with being educated and having an educated marriage partner. Although many Jordanians tell me that a man should marry a woman of equal or less education, many couples do not fit this mold, and not all men are intimidated by women with higher degrees. Yasmine, her family, and her education provide a powerful testament to the immense faith that many people, especially those struggling economically, place in education. However, hers is also a story of how education works with and through other equally important life choices and experiences, namely, marriage and family. Um Waleed, her mother, has been a central actor in all these developments.

Jamileh opted out of education. Academics did not suit her well, and she really wanted to get married. Her parents initially tried to dissuade her from leaving school, encouraging her to at least finish high school first. But they relented because Jamileh was intent on getting married and exerted little effort at school. Although I have not had that much opportunity to speak directly with her since that time, from what I have heard Jamileh is not entirely satisfied with this choice. She is still young, and her situation could change for better or for worse. In some respects, the biggest barriers to the expansion of choices for young people like Jamileh, male and female, is the rigidity of an educational system that leads young people to make major life decisions after exams in tenth grade. Others of Jamileh's peers also dropped out, but most persisted until *tawjihi*. For those who failed *tawjihi* there were few options. One classmate became a hairdresser, and others sat at home hoping to get married.

Given the long lapse in my relationship with Indira, and my limited interaction with her parents, I find it difficult to make sense of our meeting in

2011. I know that even in 2005, Indira felt as if coming back to Jordan from the Gulf had negatively influenced her opportunities. She felt that her father had become stricter and that she was constantly under the gaze of relatives. In 2011, I also found out that Indira's family's relationship with their paternal extended family in Bawadi al-Naseem was strained. Strained relations could lead to competition and jealousy among families—and both Indira and Jehan spoke about the jealousy of their cousins—which in turn could lead to greater pressures on one's children to "succeed" and behave in certain ways. This explained some of the pressures and limits that these two young women were facing.

The young women from al-Khatwa are today in their early twenties. I have remained in close contact with a handful of these young women and their families, while also keeping abreast of the major life developments—marriages, graduations, and children—of many of their peers. Some have married, some have recently completed college, and others are still studying. Some like Yasmine continued their studies after marrying and having children. Others, who are just completing college, will marry soon, although some will opt to finish their master's degree first. It is still early to tell whether these university graduates will go on to work outside the home. However, having finished college and married, they have already achieved great success, for both their education and their marriages accord them status. Given their youth, it's still unclear where their lives might go from here, but many of their opportunities and sense of what is desirable have been shaped by their education and the meaning attached to it by themselves, their families, and their broader communities.

Conclusion

When I try to represent the richness and complexity of the lives of young women from al-Khatwa to American audiences, I am often surprised by some reactions. Many have concluded that my work is more evidence of the persistence of female oppression. I have been told by a colleague, "I am glad I am not a woman in that country!" A co-panelist at a conference questioned, "Where is the agency of these young women?" A student wrote, "This is an example of bad culture." While a scholar cannot completely control how his or her work is received and read, many with whom I have spoken already assume that they know what the lives of these women must be like. Given the persistent reification and villainization of Arab Muslim cultures by much of mainstream U.S. media, such assumptions should not be surprising.

Despite the significant contributions of scholars studying women in the region for decades, the popular image of Muslim women continues to be one of oppressed, weak, and passive victims. Political events of the past decade have served only to solidify if not deepen such images, as the narrative about saving Muslim women has figured strongly into U.S. foreign policy in the region (Abu-Lughod 2002; Hirschkind and Mahmood 2002), although the revolutions of 2011 may turn the tide of simplistic and Orientalist depictions of Arabs and Muslims since so many women have been directly involved in the demonstrations and the labor strikes. Such stereotypes make it difficult for U.S. observers to see what Jordanian women share with many American women. In many respects, learning about these young women in Jordan, staying in touch with them as they mature into adulthood, and sharing the stories of their mothers and teachers have reinforced for me how similar are the desires of men and women everywhere. We want to be respected and loved. We want to feel as if our lives are meaningful and even successful, even if where we find this meaning can be tremendously varied.

The spread of mass education has led to great transformations in the Arab world as it has elsewhere. Education has facilitated the spread of knowledge through literacy; it has produced skilled young men and women who have contributed to Jordan's economic development; it has led to a significant increase in the age of first marriage among men and women, in the process transforming notions of youth and adulthood; and, in some respects, it has given young women a resource or tool through which they contribute to their own future security. Yet education is no panacea—neither for women nor for men. As I write in summer 2011 from Amman, the Arab Spring has been under way for several months.[7] Education has not been directly responsible for these historical events in any simple sense. However, educational transformations are part of the picture of what is unfolding. Education may not teach young people to demand their rights, but it does stimulate expectations and desires—not solely economic in nature—that move people to demand more from their governments and societies.

The lives of the young women from al-Khatwa may not be revolutionary, but they are no less significant. These young women struggle to make a good life, to be happy, and to be respected. This good life can draw on many accomplishments—receiving a high score on *tawjihi*; finding a good husband who is kind and responsible; having children; pursuing an enjoyable course of study; being selected to give a lecture to peers about aspects of faith; graduating at the top of the class; earning an opportunity to complete a postgraduate degree or study abroad; or finding a job that enables them to help support their parents or their own new family. One of the very first days in which I spoke with Jordanian high school girls about their education, in May of 2002, I asked a group of eleventh graders about their dreams and aspirations. Most responded that they wanted to go to college, marry, and have a family. One young woman told me she wanted to be a soccer player, another a university professor, and a third said she wanted to join the army. However, the response from one student that day resonates with me as I near the end of this book with fond memories of these young women. She told me, "We want to be inventors. We don't want to just consume what others invent for us." This young woman was specifically referencing scientific and technological inventions, but I cannot help but end with the thought that the girls at al-Khatwa—Yasmine, Jenine, Rand, Selma, Amal, Amina, Jamileh and their families—are in many respects engaged in the struggle to invent their own progress, their own development, inventions that are shaped by the realities that they have been given and that they make.

NOTES

1. This introduction does not provide a depiction of any one student's experiences. Rather, it is a composite story that draws on observations, interviews, and informal discussions with many students at the al-Khatwa Secondary School for Girls, as well as with their teachers and parents. Details about the extent and nature of this research are provided in the next chapter. All of the names of people and places are pseudonyms.
2. "Jordan First" is a campaign launched by the Jordanian regime in 2004. I discuss it more extensively in chapter 3.

CHAPTER ONE
1. Specifically, in the World Bank report (2005), the authors describe low labor rates and high fertility as a "significant paradox" (4). Alternatively there are references to "Jordan's paradox" (23) and "gender paradoxes in Jordan" (61).
2. Despite references to high fertility rates in the World Bank Gender Assessment of Jordan (World Bank 2005), fertility rates have decreased significantly over the past three decades. In 1983, the total fertility rate for women in Jordan was 6.6; in 1997 it was 4.4; and in 2009 it had decreased to 3.9 (Department of Statistics). Data referenced as "Department of Statistics" have been accessed from the website of the Department of Statistics of the Hashemite Kingdom of Jordan, unless otherwise noted, http://www.dos.gov.jo/home_e.htm. The World Bank measured fertility at 3.6 in its country profile for Jordan on its website dated July 2011, http://go.worldbank.or/KQ035DBYA0.
3. See also UNDP 2006; World Bank 2004. For a broader discussion on the representation of development problems as technical ones both in need of Western expertise and existing outside the political and economic policies of foreign funding agencies, see Timothy Mitchell's (2002) *Rule of Experts*. See also James Ferguson (1994) and Arturo Escobar (1995).
4. For a recent contribution to such Orientalist narratives, see Nicholas Kristoff and Sheryl WuDunn (2009), who characterize Muslim women as largely "passive and silent" (158). In 2011, Kristoff changed his tune somewhat, when he reported on political developments in Egypt and Bahrain and began to blog and twitter about women participating in protests in each of these countries.

5. The very public involvement of women in the "Arab Spring," particularly in Tunisia and Egypt, did garner attention in the mainstream Western media. It remains to be seen whether this will significantly change the dominant narrative about oppressed and weak Arab and Muslim women.

6. Another persistent trope has been that of the veil and female clothing more generally as a marker of oppression or progress. The vast literature on this topic is too numerous to fully enumerate here. Leila Ahmed (1992) traces the discourse about the veil back to colonial Egypt, arguing that these earlier polemics surrounding woman and the veil cemented the links between an article of clothing and "matters of far broader political and cultural import," a link that persists till this day (129). Many scholars have analyzed the phenomenon of "new veiling" in the region (Gole 1997; el-Guindi 1999; MacLeod 1991). More recently, the veil as a political and cultural marker of difference and female oppression has emerged with full force. See Abu-Lughod (2002) on the politics of the burqa at the advent of the U.S. invasion of Afghanistan and Bowen (2008) and Scott (2007) on the politicization of the veil in France.

7. Similarly, Lara Deeb (2006) states that her interlocutors, pious Shia women, often engage with the assumptions that others—Lebanese and Westerners—have about them.

8. Francis Vavrus and Lesley Bartlett (2009) use the term "inter/national" to "draw attention to the difficulty in separating 'national' policy and practice in many countries from the 'international' institutions that fund or provide other support to federal institutions" (12).

9. Lesley Bartlett (2007) defines "educational projects" as "durable (but not permanent) constellations of institutions, financial resources, social actors, ideologies, discourses, pedagogies and theories of knowledge and learning that shape the way people think about schooling and its purpose" (152).

10. Throughout, I refer to "schools" or schooling to label the formal institution of schooling—its structures, the official actors within this institution, and its intended curriculum. Education refers to the multitude of ways in which people are engaged in processes of teaching each other in their daily interactions. Education incorporates schooling but also refers to the array of broader educational processes and exchanges that school enables by bringing certain actors into contact with each other and by providing the "material" with which people engage (Cremin 1978; Varenne 2007).

11. I previously lived in Bawadi al-Naseem for several months in 1995 and in Amman for two years in 1993–95. All public high schools in Jordan are single-sex.

12. This is not to say that no other spaces exist. Anne Meneley (1996) argues for a reconsideration of the public/private divide that has often been used to point to female isolation. She argues that rather than labeling the social space of women's hosting and visiting "private," it is more appropriate to consider it "a public sphere that is separate from the public that men face" (40). Ironically, with transformations brought about by urbanization, new forms of media, and related uses of leisure time, such public "female" spaces may be less accessible to a generation of young women in the region. Farha Ghannam (2002) argues that the assumption of a fixed dichotomy between male (public) and female (private) spaces "fails to account for the continuous struggle to define the boundaries between the private and the public and how their definitions are central to the reproduction of power relationships and the reinforcement of gender inequalities" (91–92). For the young women in Bawadi al-Naseem, school was largely the main space outside of the home available to them.

However, extended family gatherings could be particularly significant socializing opportunities if a girl had extended family nearby (which many did) and if they were on good terms with this family.

13. As I discuss in chapter 2, however, a growing percentage of Jordanians, particularly in the capital, are opting out of public education. Nevertheless, with the exception of the most elite of these schools, children still use the same curriculum, particularly for social studies and history.

14. In 2006 about 4 percent of Jordan's gross national income came from foreign aid, the large majority from the United States and the European Union (this figure excludes military aid). See OECD Development Co-operation Directorate, "Aid Statistics: Data and Databases," accessed June 29, 2010, http://www.oecd.org/dac/stats/data. In 2011, the *Jordan Times* reported that aid to Jordan from the United States would exceed $700 million (July 13, 2011). In addition, in June 2011, the Jordanian finance minister announced a $400 million gift from Saudi Arabia in a move that was widely accepted to be an effort to buttress the regime and ensure "stability" amidst instability in the region and increasing vocalization of political grievances in Jordan.

15. In Jordan, "youth" can refer to a much broader age group, and it is not necessarily fixed to age but depends on life transitions like marriage and parenthood, as I have already mentioned.

16. See the Middle East Youth Initiative website, http://www.shababinclusion.org/ for more information.

17. We Are All Jordan Youth Commission, http://www.allyouth.jo/about.aspx (accessed June 14, 2010).

18. For example, on May 29, 2009, the *Jordan Times* reported the launching of an effort on the part of USAID and its Jordan Tourism Development Project to teach students about "tourism ethics" by training their teachers in the Global Code of Ethics for Tourism.

19. Males too are subject to the advice and control of family and kin, although they are typically given greater autonomy in decisionmaking than their sisters, and the consequences of going against their families is less severe.

20. At times I was asked to carry out tasks I was not comfortable with, so I declined, such as monitoring an exam. However, I did take up offers to accompany girls on trips or to special events and once helped administer an English exam by reading the oral comprehension section.

21. With the exception of two teachers, all teacher interviews were conducted on a one-on-one basis. Student interviews were conducted individually, in pairs, or in groups of three or four. Most students preferred speaking with me accompanied by a friend. I also found that the dynamic of speaking with a group of friends made for interesting discussion and allowed me to observe peer-to-peer dynamics.

22. I also attended the Tel Yahya Secondary School for Girls for two months in 2002. This meant that I went to school daily, observed classes, attended special events, and had informal discussion with students during recess and with teachers in their lounge. Although the data in this book draw almost entirely from my observations at the al-Khatwa School, my experiences at Tel Yahya very much informed this later research, and the members of the Tel Yahya community with whom I maintain a relationship do appear in parts of this book.

23. Frequently, I reviewed the textbook lesson I had observed the teacher present after the fact.

24. One mother, whose son was excelling academically, discussed how concerned she was about her son because of the poor conditions in boys' schools and the negative influence of other boys. The overwhelming majority of the parents I spoke with shared the perception that boys were undisciplined and that the boys' schools were chaotic and academically inferior to the girls' schools. In 2011, the parents and grandparents of two teenage boys in Bawadi al-Naseem again made this assertion to me. In addition, a Jordanian woman working with schools throughout Jordan on an educational reform effort complained that the boys' schools were chaotic and difficult to work with, which indicates that these differences go beyond Bawadi al-Naseem.

25. As of 2011, I continue to maintain a relationship with several of these families and teachers from al-Khatwa.

CHAPTER TWO

1. The Hashemite family came from the Hijaz in what is today Saudi Arabia.

2. Linda Layne (1994) asserts that three themes have been key to "Jordanian nationalist rhetoric" and Hashemite rule: "The Great Arab Revolt . . . genealogical links to the Prophet Muhammad and their traditional role as protectors of Islam's holy places, and Jordan's 'tribal' character" (26). Laurie Brand (1995) presents a similar list, adding to them a commitment to Palestine (51). See Kimberly Katz (2005) for an analysis of Jordan's relationship with Jerusalem and the role of the Hashemites as keepers of the holy place in the construction of Hashemite legitimacy and Jordanian identity.

3. I use the term "kin-based" allegiances rather than "tribal" ones, as I find the use of the term "tribe" in the current historical context does more to cloud than clarify (Conte and Walentowitz 2009). The term is typically used to describe particular groups in Jordan and functions to create distinctions between Jordanian citizens that are arbitrary and built on dichotomies (tribal/Palestinian; Bedouin/peasant; Jordanian Jordanian/Palestinian Jordanian) that simplify the nature of social and political relations in Jordan. The term "Bedouin" or nomad is at times conflated with tribal. In part, the construction of an ideal Bedouin identity as central to a distinctly Jordanian national history and character has fueled this confusion (Layne 1994; Massad 2001; Shryock 1997). This is misleading in that almost all of the peoples who populated Transjordan when it was first created were organized along kin-based lines. According to Mary Wilson (1987), "Virtually everyone in Transjordan was identified by family, clan, and tribal affiliation. This social organization reflected the territory's low level of urbanization and marginal relationship to the center of power. . . . Hence, tribalism in Transjordan was not limited to nomads; rather, the tribes of Transjordan filled every economic niche from nomadic camel breeders to settled farmers" (57). Richard Antoun's (1972) work among peasants or *fallah* in Jordan in 1959 and 1960 is further evidence of this, as the rural folk in the village where he conducted research aligned themselves along clan and tribal lines. As Antoun argues, however, what tribal and clan loyalties meant in practical terms depended much on the specific contexts, events, and persons involved. This is even more true today than it was then.

4. For example, see media coverage of such conflicts in *Al-Ghad* and *Ad-Dustour* (August 16, 2009). Many more examples exist.

5. Exact numbers are hard to come by as Jordanian officials have deliberately refrained from undertaking a survey of the population using such categories (i.e., national ori-

gin). Estimates on the number of citizens of Palestinian origin range from 60 to 75 percent of the population. Amongst the Palestinian Jordanians there are also distinctions, with some segments of this population viewing themselves as more Jordanian than others and some having more established roots in Jordan. As many as 30 percent of Jordanian citizens are Palestinian refugees (Human Rights Watch 2006).

6. See Brand (1995), R. Farah (2005), and Massad (2001) for further discussion about Palestinian Jordanians and issues of national identity. As each points out, how Palestinian Jordanians perceive their citizenship status has much to do with when they came to Jordan, the circumstances of their migration, and their economic status.

7. In Arabic, these groups are referred to as the *fida'iyyun*.

8. The Jordanian regime reported much lower numbers of dead.

9. For full text of this speech see "King Abdullah II Official Website," http://www .kingabdullah.jo/ (accessed October 17, 2011).

10. The Ministry of Education reported that about 22 percent of Jordanian students were in private schools (*Jordan Times*, August 25, 2009). The percentage of students in private schools in the capital is reported to be over 30 percent (Ministry of Education). In addition, in 2005–6 about 8 percent of students were enrolled in UNRWA schools for Palestinian refugees (Ministry of Education).

11. The correlation between education and employment is different for males and females. Employed males are likely to have less education than employed females. Fifty-five percent of employed men have less than high school education, while more than two-thirds of women who are employed have some years of higher education (European Training Foundation 2005: 23–24).

12. According to the Department of Statistics, in 2005, 37.3 percent of the population was under fifteen. In Bawadi al-Naseem this percentage was slightly higher at 40.9 percent. "Kingdom Indicators," http://www.dos.gov.jo/sdb_pop/sdb_pop_e/indec_ e.pdf (accessed June 8, 2010).

13. There is an industrial zone relatively close to Bawadi al-Naseem as well as lone factories. To date these employ more foreign nationals than local residents. For information on working conditions in such factories, see National Labor Committee (2006). The International Labor Organization and the Jordanian Ministry of Labor (2002) also produced a report focused specifically on the experience of Jordanian women working in textile and garment industries.

14. The emergence of these schools in the late nineteenth century was a product of both Christian missions and the policies of the late Ottoman Empire, particularly under Sultan Abdulhamid II (Fortna 2002; Rogan 1999). Local *kutab* or Qur'anic schools also provided basic literacy and numeracy prior to this period. Evidence from this period, as well as from the early years of the mandate, shows significant unmet demand for educational access (Amadouny 1994; Rogan 1999).

15. Pupil-teacher ratios were quite high in government schools, explaining the discrepancy in enrollment (Matthews and Akrawi 1949).

16. Data cited as "UNESCO Institute for Statistics" in this book is from the UNESCO online Institute for Statistics "Data Centre" unless otherwise noted. http://stats.uis .unesco.org/unesco/TableViewer/document.aspx?ReportId=143&IF_Language=eng (accessed on June 30, 2010).

17. Although no private high schools are found in Bawadi al-Naseem, in 2005 four private elementary schools did exist.

18. Information management is a relatively new academic track whose establishment was promoted by foreign-funded educational reform efforts focused on technology.

19. In addition to the *mawazi* system, which gives an advantage to those who can pay higher rates of tuition, admissions policies give other students advantages as well. A form of affirmative action has been in place for students from rural areas and from underrepresented regions more generally. In addition, children of educators (teachers and university professors) as well as children of members of the military are given advantages, such as a lower admission requirement, and in the case of children of military personnel, generous scholarships as well. These scholarships are referred to as *makramat al-jaysh* (noble gift for the military). Since Palestinian Jordanians are underrepresented in the civil service and the military, such policies disadvantage them.

20. The 3 percent ratio at al-Khatwa was representative of the larger population of Christians in Jordan, which is typically estimated to be 3–5 percent.

21. The term used by the girls was *'ashira*, which translates as clan, kinsfolk, or tribe. Typically in Jordan *qabileh* is used to refer to tribe, so the reference here is to clan or kin group.

22. For example, the frequency with which conflicts among university students have spilled over into larger kin and/or geographically based fights on university campuses has become such a problem that government officials have made violence on university campuses a subject of public discussion and an issue to be tackled through workshops, youth groups, and security cameras, among other things. The National Campaign for Defending Students' Rights, also known as "Thabahtoona," has argued that the government is partly responsible for the persistence of this violence, as it has banned any political activities on university campuses that would enable students to organize along nonkin affiliations.

23. Some kin groups have formalized this support role by forming formally registered organizations that provide services such as small loans, scholarships, and a place to hold weddings and engagement ceremonies (Baylouny 2006).

24. Typically the distinction is thought of as the disparity between the socially liberal west Amman and the poorer and more socially conservative east Amman, but this distinction can be overly simplistic and both east and west Amman overly homogenized. When people said to me, "You should see Amman," they were usually referring to a few upscale neighborhoods like Abdoun and Sweifiyye with high-end shops and restaurants and noticeably more liberal social norms apparent in dress and in the interaction between males and females.

25. By 2011, Mecca Mall was surpassed by other more luxurious malls and was considered by some of Amman's wealthy to be beneath them.

26. For the region in which Bawadi al-Naseem is located, average annual household income was 4,433.90 JD in 2003 (Department of Statistics).

27. By law (the Nationality Law) in Jordan, a woman cannot pass on her Jordan citizenship to her children and can pass it on to a spouse only under certain limited circumstances. Thus, if she marries a noncitizen, her children cannot become Jordanian citizens, even if they are born in Jordan and/or reside there (Amawi 2000). Ongoing efforts by activists to change this law have not succeeded to date.

28. A major cost incurred by noncitizens in schools is the purchase of school textbooks. According to the school principal at al-Khatwa, the schools helped such students by giving them used books free of charge.

29. She was getting licensed to teach at government-sponsored Islamic education centers and not in schools that require a bachelor's degree.

30. Although the World Bank reported a significant decline in poverty between 1997

and 2003 in Jordan (World Bank 2004), a number of other analysts have contested this conclusion, arguing that the poverty measure used by the Bank grossly underestimated the extent of poverty in Jordan (Alyssa 2007). Although Jordan has recorded growth in GDP each year since 1992, after a precipitous decline during the economic crisis of 1989, research has shown that this growth has not resulted in decreased inequality (Saif and Tabbaa 2008).

31. United Nations Relief and Works Agency for Palestine Refugees website, http://www .unrwa.org/etemplate.php?id=66 (accessed on June 18, 2010).

32. Joseph Sassoon (2009) estimates that the number is 500,000–750,000 (60). However, he also indicates that some of these Iraqis were in Jordan prior to 2003. In 1996, he reports that about 100,000 Iraqis were in Jordan, and in 2003, before the U.S. invasion of Iraq, 250,000–300,000 Iraqis were in Jordan. Of this number, only 30,000 were legal residents (34).

33. Among the most vulnerable families in Jordan were those headed by divorced or separated women (World Bank 2004).

34. Apprehension was also fueled by the perception held by many Jordanians of skyrocketing divorce rates.

35. In her discussion of piety movements in Egypt, Saba Mahmood (2005) describes piety activists as those who "seek to imbue each of the various spheres of contemporary life with a regulative sensibility that takes its cue from the Islamic theological corpus rather than from modern secular ethics" (47).

36. I knew of one family quite active in da'wa activities in Bawadi al-Naseem whose members traveled abroad to preach to Muslims and non-Muslims in Asia; thus, such preaching could also be a part of the da'wa.

37. Some exceptions are the work of Linda Herrera (1992, 2000, and 2006) on private Islamic Schools in Egypt and Natasha Ridge's (2009) comparative study of boys' and girls' high schools in the United Arab Emirates and the problem of boys' underperformance. In addition, see Willy Jansen (2006) on the meaning of being an educated university woman in Jordan.

38. During the period in which the parliament was suspended (2001–3), the regime passed over two hundred temporary laws (Clark 2006).

39. After signing the peace treaty with Israel, for example, Jordan removed a course titled "The Issue of Palestine" from its curriculum.

CHAPTER THREE

1. Earlier versions of this chapter have appeared previously as "Is Music Haram? Jordanian Girls Educating Each Other about Nation, Faith and Gender in School." *Teachers College Record* 109, no. 7 (2007): 1663–81, and "Performing Patriotism: Rituals and Moral Authority in a Jordanian High School," in *Education and the Arab "World": Political Projects, Struggles, and Geometries of Power* [World Yearbook of Education 2010], ed. A. E. Mazawi and R. G. Sultana, 132–44 (New York: Routledge, 2010). Reprinted by permission.

2. See, for example, news stories about the participation of Queen Rania, government officials, and various other entities in a massive parade expressing disapproval of terrorism and loyalty to the nation (*Ad-Dustour*, April 30, 2004).

3. It's easy to overlook the nationalistic rituals and school-based socialization in one's own community when our lens and analysis have been turned toward another. My comments about the limits of patriotism in the United States here seem less than genuine in retrospect. My daughter's entry into kindergarten in 2009 was a vivid

reminder of our own projects to socialize loyal citizens in schools. Among the primary bits of knowledge that kindergartners must acquire in the first weeks of school are the words to the Pledge of Allegiance, the symbols and symbolism of the flag, and soon thereafter a patriotic song or two. My daughter was so enamored with these symbols of the nation that she invented a game in which she marched around the house waving her homemade flag and we, her family, were instructed to follow her around proclaiming "It's the flag. It's the flag."

4. In 2009, when Abdullah II's teenage son Hussein was officially designated crown prince, his picture began to appear alongside those of his father and grandfather.

5. A vast literature exists on the central place that women have occupied in ideas about the nation, national identity, modernization, and national development in the Middle East and North Africa. For example, see Abu-Lughod 1998; Ahmed 1992; Kandiyoti 1991; Lazreg 1994; Najmabadi 1998a.

6. Although the discourse about women's development has taken on a new form in a relatively recent era of development, a focus on "modernizing" women has existed since at least the mid-nineteenth century in the region (Abu-Lughod 1998).

7. Shryock (2004) also describes the ways in which tribes and tribal ideals such as hospitality have been packaged for tourists. In a neoliberal era, the work of making national tradition has also become the work of promoting tourism and attracting foreign capital.

8. BBC News, "Japan's Schools to Teach Patriotism," May 18, 2007. http://news.bbc.co .uk/2/hi/asia-pacific/6669061.stm.

9. The unit on the Hashemites encompassed the lessons on the Hashemite genealogy, their history, their role in the Arab Revolution and their role in the "modern Arab awakening" (Abdullah et al. 2004).

10. Scott Greenwood (2003a: 90) argues that the regime calculated that its survival was linked to continued U.S. aid and attracting foreign investment.

11. In recent years, teachers have been required to attend workshops co-sponsored by the Ministry for Political Development that address the state's political development goals for schools. The Ministry for Political Development was established in October 2003.

12. They are often referred to as "Jordanian Jordanians" by many non-Jordanian observers.

13. Although the rumors related to such sales could be significantly exaggerated, the government had indeed begun a program of privatization in the early 1990s, and in 2008 a number of major development projects, particularly in real estate, were being undertaken by foreign Arab investors. Furthermore, a number of government industries and institutions had been sold to private investors. In 2011, criticisms of the regime and its management of public resources emerged again. *Ammon News*, February 6, 2011, "Statement by National Figures Warns of Dangers to Jordan If Reform Is Not Implemented Fast," http://en.ammonnews.net/article.aspx?articleNO=11523.

14. See *Al-Rai*, July 2, 2008.

15. See Massad's (2001) discussion of different accents and they way in which they represent Palestinianness and Jordanianness, as well as femininity and masculinity. In practice, these have also become rural/urban distinctions as well as classed distinctions, as they are among Palestinians themselves.

16. Although as Brand (1995, 1998) has argued, the regime has not hesitated to exploit communal tensions when it has perceived them to be in its interest. Still, this was beyond the pale.

17. This is not to say that nationalistic rhetoric does not ever come to the surface. Insults exchanged at soccer matches between the teams associated with Palestinians (Wihdat) and the team associated with Jordanians (Faysali) regularly devolve into political taunts and xenophobia. In the summer of 2009, taunts against a Jordanian-Palestinian soccer club during a match were deemed so offensive as to warrant public censure and a fine (*Al-Rai*, July 20, 2009). However, Nadine's speech took place at an official event commemorating a national holiday.

18. In the spring of 2011, the Jordanian regime was again blamed by its critics for fueling the Palestinian/Jordanian divide when a protest demanding an end to corruption and genuine political reforms resulted in security force and citizen violence against protestors. Some government officials worked to paint the protestors as Islamists and Palestinians so as to elicit popular support against protestors. However, the regime seemed to sense that this had gone too far—and that increased violence was possible—and within weeks worked to publicly remind Jordanians of their shared interest in stability and security.

19. I was informed by several people in Jordan at the time of the campaign's launch that the "Jordan First" campaign was developed by a Western advertising agency hired by the royal court.

20. "Mawtini" was originally a poem composed by the Palestinian poet Ibrahim Tuqan in the late 1930s, which was put to music by Muhammad Fuliefil. "Mawtini" is also the Palestinian national anthem, and it was decreed the Iraqi national anthem in 2004.

21. Even today the regime's legitimacy narrative still draws on this pillar of the "Arab Nation." For example, the Ministry of Education's 2006 "National Education Strategy" lists the Great Arab Revolt as a key principle upon which the "philosophy of the Jordanian education system is based."

22. The only exception I encountered was when a student or teacher was asked to give some sort of presentation during the *tabur*, which happened from time to time. In those instances, the presenter put much effort into delivering a good presentation.

23. Anderson (2005: 10) has argued that local actors and institutions were as influential as the political elite in the construction of national identities in Jordan . The activities and performances of school children, boy scouts, and various clubs figure strongly in her analysis of this influence.

24. Wideen (1999), in her analysis of the cult of Hafiz al-Asad, Syria's late leader, argues that the need to enforce national rituals has contradictory effects. She argues that by forcing citizens to publically avow the terms that constitute the cult (however outlandish), the regime conveys its power; however, the need to deploy this force is also evidence of the state's weakness.

25. The belief that women's voices should be concealed stems from a particular interpretation of a *hadith*, a saying of the Prophet, regarding the response of worshipers in the mosque when an imam or prayer leader has made a mistake. According to the *hadith*, women worshipers should clap (as opposed to the men who should praise God loudly) to bring the imam's attention to the mistake. Thus, some have interpreted this *hadith* to mean that a woman's voice is 'awrah. Those who oppose this interpretation interpret the *hadith* to be specific to the mosque only. They cite the fact that women addressed the prophet Muhammad in public settings where other men were in attendance. See Sahih al-Bukhari, vol.1, book 11, 652 (Khan 1971).

26. I had seen obscenities carved into desks before, as well as drawings of male sexual organs on classroom walls. However, the majority of the graffiti I saw were about love, boys, pop stars, and friends.

27. Extracurricular activities in Jordanian schools differ from the activities that typically fall within this category in the United States, for example. First, the activities to be undertaken are typically directives of the Ministry of Education—usually passed on through the regional or district education office and then to the schools. Once the principal receives the directive for certain activities to happen or for a certain number of students to participate in an event, he or she selects a teacher to manage the activity, and the teacher in turn selects a few "good" students to be involved. At times, teachers and administrators complained about the burdens involved in participating in such events, such as having to bring students to a particular event, having to attend meetings and workshops, or having to use limited resources.

28. The one exception I observed was a coed chorus from a Jordanian university that performed on the king's birthday in 2002.

29. I attended the same event—a celebration in honor of Independence and Armed Services Day—at the municipal hall in 2002, along with a similar event in a soccer field in the neighboring town. In 2005, I attended four additional celebrations and performances on national holidays, two of which were held at the al-Khatwa School. I also talked with some of the girls about events I was not able to attend, in particular two events that were held in honor of the king's birthday.

30. Layne (1994) discusses the importance of "traditional" dress in the repertoire of national symbols in Jordan. See also Massad (2001).

31. Moderation in religion has been a key theme of King Abdullah's regime, and it is a central tenet in Islam. In November 2004, the king delivered a speech entitled "The Amman Message," which emphasized that Islam is a religion of moderation, peace, tolerance, and progress. I discuss this further in chapter 4.

32. Two of the songs sung on this occasion were patriotic songs: "Rayeti takhfiqu bal majd, Rayeti anti howai" (My flag fluttering with glory, My flag you are my love) and "Itha shtadu al laylu, ughaniki 'amman" (If the night gets darker, I sing for you, Amman). In addition three folk songs were sung: "Wayli mahlaha bint al rifiyye" (Oh, how beautiful she is, the rural girl), "Balla ya ghali salim 'ala walifi" (Please, my dear, give my greetings to my love), and "Yuma andahalu, shogi marag kheal" (Oh, mother, call him to stop in, my love is passing by on his horse).

33. In contrast to my observations in Jordan, Luykx's (1999) study of the Normal School in Bolivia found that females typically "took a back seat in the ceremonial life of the school" (164), except in specifically feminized events such as Mother's Day and during an annual beauty pageant of sorts in which one female student was crowned queen on Students' Day. However, Levinson's (2001) research in a Mexican secondary school describes a similar pattern of boys taking a back seat at such events. When Levinson asked teachers and staff why they thought boys participated in such events less than girls (or in some instances why the adults themselves preferred girls), they said girls were more responsible, mature, and disciplined.

34. At times parents also criticized boys' schools, claiming that male teachers were apathetic and the schools chaotic.

35. Earlier research on decisions to veil or cover one's hair focused on university women in urban areas of Egypt and examined their decision to veil as a form of religious protest and a means to legitimize their presence in public spaces like the university (e.g., el-Guindi 1999; MacLeod 1991). Mahmood (2005) has argued for the need to give greater credence to religious motivations and the desire on the part of some women to be more pious. In this community and region, given the reality that the large number of females did cover their hair, particularly once they reached the university, donning

the veil was a very common occurrence and did not necessarily signal greater religiosity or protest as it may have a decade ago and may still in other parts of the country.

36. See Herrera's (2000: 138-42) discussion of down-veiling and the expectations that girls at an Islamic school had that once their teachers took on a more conservative form of *hijab*, they should not "down-veil" to more "revealing" forms of head covering. Herrera notes that teachers were more reluctant to "up-veil" because of the expectations that this would create.

37. At the al-Khatwa School only one of the Muslim teachers did not cover her hair. Another teacher, originally from Amman, had begun to cover her hair only in her mid-forties.

38. As in many parts of the world, there has been a mushrooming of satellite TV access in Jordan. In the early 1990s when I lived in Jordan, the only television programming was provided by two state channels that broadcast for only part of the day. Today many Jordanians have access to programming from around the Arab world and beyond. Among the most popular channels for young people were music video channels. These channels, as well as other programs, were frequent targets of criticism by some teachers, who argued that satellite TV was a corrupting influence.

39. *Haram* literally means forbidden, prohibited, or sin. In religious terms, then, it means that which has been prohibited by religion. In colloquial form it is also used to convey pity, as in "too bad" or "what a shame." *Halal* is that which is allowed in Islam. In between *haram* and *halal* are a number of other categories of actions including those disliked but not expressly forbidden, those toward which Islam is neutral, and those actions considered favorable.

40. Indeed, young Muslims who viewed this video on YouTube engaged in a debate about this same issue, with some sharing the opinion that the video was unacceptable, while others argued that this was a legitimate way for the young woman in the video to remain religiously committed while participating in this artistic medium.

41. Sami Yusuf has links to some of his videos and songs at http://www.samiyusuf.com/home/ (accessed December 10, 2009).

42. The debates about permissibility of music, or some types of music, stem from competing interpretations of several *hadith* having to do with music directly or indirectly. These debates are not new but emerge in new forms as a result of contemporary developments in music and religious sentiments. Scholars range in their interpretations on music from those who argue that all singing and music are forbidden, to those who argue that musical instruments (with the exception of the *daff*) are forbidden, to those who argue that all music is permissible, as long as the content is moral. In Arabic, one finds an extensive literature related to music and Islam and related debates (e.g., 'Imarah 1999; al-Mahdi 2002; Qaradawi 2001).

43. Herrera (2000), in her study of private Islamic Schools in Egypt, relates very similar comments from a group of seventh- and eighth-grade girls about the permissibility of music in Islam. The girls she speaks with struggle with the terms of the music prohibition in their school and debate which if any music is *haram* in Islam. As Herrera surmises through her observations and discussion with students, "No one is certain what is forbidden or what is accepted which is why the students are in a constant state of discussion and interpretation of these issues" (160). See also Marc Schade-Poulsen (1999) on young Algerian men negotiating when, where, and with whom it is appropriate to listen to ra'i music.

44. As discussed in footnote 42, some religious scholars interpret Islamic teachings on music to call for the prohibition of all musical instruments save for the *daff*.

45. I am grateful to Abdellatif Cristillo for pointing to these potential implications.
46. Here Farial uses the Arabic word *hub* which can be used for many forms of love—platonic and romantic. Here she uses the general term to reference romantic love.
47. Abu-Lughod (2000), in her analysis of poetry among the Awlad al Ali Bedouin in Egypt, argues that sentiments about love and longing are often given a space to flourish as an alternative or contradictory discourse even in a context where a dominant discourse characterizes the expression of such sentiments as weak and immoral.
48. In some songs the mother or a romantic love acts as a metaphor for city or country in the Arab world. For example, Najat al-Saghira sang a song about Amman that likened Amman to a woman whose braids have been loosened, her hair flowing over her shoulder, who is kissed between the eyes. The song, written by the Jordanian poet Haydar Mahmud, was entitled "Arkhat 'Amman jada'ilaha fauq al-katifayn. Fahtaza al-majd wa qabbalaha bayn al-'ainayn."
49. See also Comaroff (1985: 125).

CHAPTER FOUR

1. As discussed in chapter 2, *da'wa* literally means calling, and in the context of Islam it refers to the "call to Islam." In its more specific sense, today in Jordan it refers to a range of activities in mosques, study circles, Islamic centers, the press, and media aimed at calling fellow Muslims to be more pious (Mahmood 2005; Wiktorowicz 2001).
2. Asad's (1993) conceptualization of orthodoxy is similar to Raymond Williams's (1977) concept of hegemony in that orthodoxy must recreate or redefine itself in response to challenges and changing material realities.
3. Other government responses have included closer monitoring of preaching, the training of preachers, and the issuance of *fatwas*.
4. In the fall of 2006, the regime put forth several pieces of legislation aimed at tighter controls over the religious realm, and the government took control over the largest Islamic charity, the Islamic Center Society (*Al-Rai*, July 6, 2006, July 7, 2006, July 11, 2006). As of February 2011, it still held the charity in receivership.
5. Research about state efforts to control or shape Islamic discourse in the region has typically focused on the sphere of the mosque and the media, Islamic law, and preachers or imams. The degree to which schooling has been included in such research has been limited. One approach has been the historical analysis of "traditional" Islamic schooling, *kuttab* and *madrasas*, and the transformation of such institutions as a result of colonization, nation building, and modernizing reforms (e.g., Berkey 2006; Eickelman 1985; Gesink 2006; Messick 1996; Mitchell 1988; Wagner 1993). More recently a body of work has emerged about contemporary forms of Islamic schooling and private Islamic schools (Hefner and Zaman 2006; Herrera 2000, 2004, 2006). In addition, one finds a rich and growing literature concerned with educational spaces that have emerged alongside new Islamic movements, particularly among the female participants in these movements (Deeb 2006; Limbert 2005; Mahmood 2005; Shively 2008). The literature that addresses state schooling and religion has focused largely on school textbooks and/or curriculum (e.g., Doumato and Starrett 2007). One exception is Gregory Starrett's (1998) *Putting Islam to Work*.
6. As discussed in footnote 4, since 2006 the Jordanian government has put forth new efforts to bring these centers under their control.

7. Most often students attended religion classes, specifically with a focus on Qur'an, in the summer, and local religious centers held summer camps for this purpose. However, as students approached their final year in high school, they typically ceased these supplemental religious classes so that they could focus on studying for *tawjihi*.

8. For the majority of the private schools, religious education consists of the state curriculum and state-produced textbooks. The only exceptions to my knowledge are "foreign" schools such as the American School that are not subject to Ministry of Education mandates.

9. Shari'a, or Islamic law/jurisprudence, is also one of the academic streams, although it was not offered at al-Khatwa or in Bawadi al-Naseem. Presumably, students in this track take much more religion.

10. In communities where a significant Christian population exists, the local Christian community may lobby to have a teacher come in and teach Christian students about Christianity. Outside of these instances, Christian students can attend the regular religion class (the Islamic one) if they choose to do so. A private school my children attended in Amman offered classes for Christian students. The Jordanian government had adopted textbooks developed by the Roman Catholic Patriarchate of Jerusalem for this purpose. Thus, regardless of Christian denomination, all Christian students used Roman Catholic textbooks.

11. A Christian acquaintance of mine in his forties told me that as a youth he was curious about Islam and attended religion classes. However, some of his Christian peers resented this and one even picked a fight with him as a result.

12. The same curriculum is used in boys' and girls' schools. Note that textbook and curriculum are essentially synonymous in this context in that the textbook acts as the curricular guide and is commissioned and published by the Ministry of Education. Teachers' versions of some texts are available.

13. In 2005, all tenth graders took a course titled "Islamic Education," or Al-Tarbiyya al-Islamiyya, which consisted of seven units: the [Islamic] creed; the study of the Holy Qur'an; the study of the prophetic *hadith*; the life of the prophet; ethics and moral cultivation; jurisprudence; Islamic systems and thought (al-Dughmi et al. 1996). All eleventh graders took "Islamic Culture" or Al-Thaqafa al-Islamiyya, which consisted of the following units: the Islamic view on human beings; the family in Islam; the Islamic society and system; the life of the Prophet and Islamic civilization; *da'wa* (or calling to the faith) and *jihad* (or struggle); and the Holy Qur'an (Jabr et al. 2004). Twelfth graders similarly took a course titled "Islamic Culture" which consisted of the same topics as those for eleventh grade, with the addition of "The Holy Qur'an: Recitation, Interpretation, and Memorization" and "The Contemporary Islamic World." In addition to the general curriculum for all students, students in the humanities track at the secondary level (eleventh and twelfth grades) also took one additional Islamic studies course: for the eleventh graders it was "Islamic Education," and for the twelfth graders it was "Islamic Studies." The topics covered for eleventh graders in this track were family, work, and knowledge in Islam, as well as topics related to worship and the Islamic creed (al-Dughmi et al.1996). For twelfth graders, the focus was primarily on jurisprudence, *ahadith*, and Qur'anic studies, as well as monotheism and the Islamic creed (al-Sawa et al. 2001).

14. Devout Muslims believe that Islam has an "answer" for any and all issues that may arise. The distinction I am trying to make here is between those aspects of life ex-

plicitly addressed in the texts and teachings of Islam and those that require greater degrees of interpretation.

15. A representative at the Department of Curriculum in the Ministry of Education informed me that teachers did participate on curriculum development committees, and I know of at least one retired teacher who was hired as a consultant to work on curricular revisions. Also, many of the staff in the Ministry of Education had previously been teachers themselves. My point here is that as in most U.S. school systems with which I have worked, decisions about curricular goals, content, and even pedagogical methods are typically top-down decisions.

16. Teachers are, however, subject to supervision and inspections from regional ministry staff.

17. The "progressive education" movement grew out of the work of John Dewey around the turn of the twentieth century and was concerned with the broader mission of schools to encourage the development of democratic societies. Dewey stressed the social nature of learning and argued that education should help young people address the practical concerns of their societies. Hence, his educational philosophy emphasized problem solving, critical-thinking skills, and knowledge that would connect young people to their communities and would encourage them to be active citizens and help to construct a democratic society (Dewey 1916; Phillips and Soltis 2004).

18. Miss Suheil wrote about topics of personal interest such as emotional intelligence and developing the creative self, as well as a range of other topics her publisher commissioned her to write about. When I met her she was pursuing a Ph.D. in education (she was one of three al-Khatwa teachers seeking doctoral degrees in 2005), regularly contributed to a number of websites, and had written several books.

19. A number of scholars writing about women's movements in the region discuss the importance of Islamist reformers or Islamic feminists. See Barlas (2002), Baron (1994, 2005), and Mahmood (2005).

20. "Islamic Culture," or *Al-Thaqafa al-Islamiyya*, was the title of the textbook and the class that all eleventh graders regardless of track had to take. Twelfth graders in both tracks also took "Islamic Culture."

21. Missionary work here refers specifically to work among other Muslims who were perceived to have strayed from Islam or who were not sufficiently committed to practicing the faith. Some Jordanians involved in such activities traveled abroad to pursue *da'wa* among Muslims and non-Muslims in other countries, although in my experience their numbers were few.

22. Here, Miss Suheil is referring to Amina, the president of the prayer room committee. See my discussion about Amina and the prayer room later in this chapter.

23. As I discuss in chapter 3, the overwhelming majority of adult women (over 90 percent) in Bawadi al-Naseem covered their hair, and in the high school the majority of girls already covered their hair.

24. As high school students, many of whom still had little experience outside of their hometowns, the students may not yet have been attuned to these different perspectives within Jordan.

25. Thanks to Lou (Abdellatif) Cristillo for pointing this out.

26. Islamic teaching is specific about whom one is allowed to marry and who is forbidden to a Muslim in marriage. Close relatives who are forbidden in marriage are called *mahram* (*maharim* is the plural), and according to some interpretations of Islam only

men and women who are *maharim* should be left alone unchaperoned. Each of the units on marriage at the secondary level has lessons on this topic (Jabr et al. 2004).

27. This is specifically referenced in the textbook as evidence of the moderate nature of the Islamic faith ('Oweidhah et al. 2001: 211).

28. The third lesson in the tenth-grade religion textbook, *Al-Tarbiyya al-Islamiyya*, deals with death and its significance in Islam. The students covered this lesson before my arrival. The lesson addresses the afterlife, the relationship between life on earth and the afterlife, and the need for Muslims to lead moral lives and to remember that they will meet God after death and will have to account for their deeds on earth ('Oweidhah et al. 2001: 23–26).

29. Even the requirement to cover one's hair, neck, and chest is open to interpretation and some debate within Islam. In particular, some feminist Islamic scholars have taken up this question, arguing that the references to veiling or covering are too general to indicate that covering one's hair is mandated (e.g., Barlas 2002).

30. As Starrett points out, local regimes have pursued a policy of coopting and controlling "traditional" religious authorities and their institutions throughout the region as a means of consolidating state power. For a discussion of this phenomenon in Jordan, see Wiktorowicz (2001). See also Zeghal's (2010) analysis of Egypt and Tunis.

31. Observant Muslims pray five times a day at prescribed times. However, based on Islamic teachings students do not have to pray during the schooldays but can make up for their "missed" prayer once they go home. Students were not allowed to miss class to pray but had the opportunity to do their midday prayer during the midday break or after their last period. Teachers who prayed at school did not do so in the prayer room but chose to use other spaces in the main building.

32. In a subsequent discussion with Miss Suheil four years after the initial research was conducted, she discussed efforts earlier in her career to supplement her classroom teaching with lessons in the prayer room. Specifically she focused on Qur'anic recitation.

33. As discussed in chapter 3, all other extracurricular activities were very much top-down affairs, originating in directives from government ministries to local officials and eventually to principals. Principals would in turn recruit a teacher to oversee select students in a particular project. Furthermore, most of these activities were undertaken during the course of the day and required that students miss class.

34. However, I have talked with some Jordanians (both Muslims and Christians), whom I would loosely categorize as secular in orientation, who are troubled by the increasing influence of religion in public life.

35. The Muslim Brotherhood is also known to be influential in the Ministry of Education and previously held this portfolio as well (Anderson 2007; Brand 1998).

36. One form of punishment or discipline in schools in Jordan is a disciplinary transfer whereby a student can be transferred to a distant village or another city for serious disciplinary infractions.

37. For a different opinion about the significance of Sufism in Al-Ahbash, see Hamzeh and Dekmejian (1996).

CHAPTER FIVE

1. Janice Hurtig (2008: 28, 67–68) describes secondary schools in a Venezuelan town as between the street (public) and the home (private). In some respects, this was the

case with al-Khatwa as well; the space of school was neither entirely public nor really private.

2. No such girl materialized that day. However, the principal's inquiries ran the risk of generating rumors about any unfortunate girls who happened to wear pink that day.

3. In some respects my own initial assumptions about the clarity surrounding gendered expectations had to do more with my status as a Jordanian living in the United States than with my status as an American. My parents were born and raised in Jordan and their marriage was arranged. My parents tried to impart to their American children what they referred to as "our customs and traditions." Having spent very little time in Jordan until adulthood, I had an image of Jordan and rules in Jordan as more rigid than they might be in practice. Furthermore, since my parents were raised in rural areas and left the country in 1970, their own perceptions of life in Jordan had not undergone the same shifts that they have for most Jordanians living in Jordan over the last few decades.

4. I deliberately leave "relations" (*'alaqat*) vague, as the way the term was used in such contexts was vague. The most serious concern was to prevent sexual relations between males and females who were not married to each other; however, in the interest of preventing sexual relations, any type of relationship between a male and a female was suspect (except for close relatives who were not potential marriage partners). Talk of relationships among the students could refer to something as limited as brief passing conversations in person or on the phone.

5. The concern about marriage in crisis is in fact widespread in the region. In Egypt, for example, a significant body of research now exists about the economic barriers to setting up a household and marrying (e.g., Assaad and Ramadan 2008; Ghannam 1998; Singerman 2007). Similar concerns have been voiced in the media in countries throughout the region. Hanan Kholoussy's (2010) research, pointing to concerns about marriage in early twentieth-century Egypt, reminds us that the discourse of "marriage crisis" is not entirely new.

6. As discussed in chapter 4, in Islam and in local practice, the relatives whom one cannot marry are considered *mahram* (*maharim* in the plural) or "those who are forbidden." In theory, then, these are the only members of the opposite sex with whom Muslim men and women should be alone. In practice this varied from family to family.

7. By way of example, wedding parties, one of the most central events for socializing to this day, were historically mixed-sex events. Today the majority of such parties are split, with one space reserved for men and the other for women. See Linda Layne (1994) for a description of these parties in the late 1970s and early 1980s. One family I spoke with that lived in a village about half an hour from Bawadi al-Naseem said that they had always had mixed weddings but that in the past few years people have begun to prefer separate parties.

8. According to the Economic and Social Council, the female labor force participation rate in Jordan is 14.9 percent as compared with 28 percent for the Middle East and North Africa (Tabbaa 2010).

9. In some instances, the media have reported such rumors to be real. See "Criminals Hiding behind Islamic Face Veil Trigger Controversy" in the *Jordan Times*, July 29, 2009.

10. Portia Sabin (2007), in her study of college freshman at a university in the United States, points to the centrality of "sentimental education," lessons about romance and love, to the enactment of friendship.

11. One of the oldest and most famed of these love tales, one that has been sung in verse as well, is the story of "Majnun Layla" (Madman of Layla), a story of star-crossed love that is dated back as early as the seventh century.

12. This distinction existed in most societies until very recently. On Europe and the Western world more broadly, see Eva Illouz's (1997) analysis of the transformation of romantic love and of conceptualizations of marriage and courtship with the onset of capitalism.

13. In 2001 the personal status law was revised, extending the legal age of marriage for boys and girls to 18. In practice, some girls are still married before the age of 18, and people are still able to circumvent this law. In 2005, 60 percent of the females who married were between the ages of 20 and 29, and 29 percent were between the ages of 15 and 19. These ratios had not changed significantly as of 2009 (Department of Statistics).

14. Same-sex attractions were never discussed openly, although on one occasion a very religious student talked about the problem of girls who loved each other too much. Otherwise, relationships were always assumed to be heterosexual. But homosexual relationships and/or sexual practices did exist, even if they were not openly discussed.

15. Crude divorce rates have increased from 1.7 in 2000 to 2.2 in 2008 (Department of Statistics); however, this is a measure of divorce per thousand members of the population, which is a poor measure of how many marriages end in divorce. Calculating the "current divorce rate" (number of divorces registered as a proportion of the number of marriages registered in the same period of time), I found that the "current divorce rate" increased from 18 percent to 24 percent between 2005 and 2009. However, the *Jordan Times* reported that almost 80 percent of registered divorces are among couples who never consummated their marriage (June 22, 2011). According to the Supreme Judge Department of Jordan, in 2003, 77 percent of divorces were registered before the marriage was consummated. In 2008, 79 percent were registered before the marriage was consummated. (http://www.sjd.gov.jo/, accessed July 14, 2011). Consummation here entails both a public celebration to announce the marriage and the initiation of sexual relations between the couple. These high percentages reflect the practice among many families of signing the marriage contract at the onset of a couple's engagement, at times several months and even years before a marriage is consummated. For these families, the signing of the marriage contract is considered a necessary condition for the couple to be together unchaperoned during their engagement.

16. I spent much of my time in casual conversation with the girls in the schoolyard and between classes. However, I also made "appointments" with girls so that I could speak with them one on one or in small groups. I structured these conversations with general questions about school, future plans, friends, and leisure time. I also used this time to follow up on issues or questions I had about things I had heard in casual conversation and the like.

17. When I first began my research on education in Jordan, one of my relatives in Jordan told me of an aunt who had not been allowed to continue school after fourth grade, for fear that knowledge of the English language, which was taught in the fifth grade and beyond, would enable her to write love letters without the knowledge of her family. For illiterate parents, literacy may have initially caused similar fears. In some respects, cell phones fit into this category of skills or tools that enable young women to communicate outside the monitoring of adults.

18. Now that phones are ubiquitous in almost all sectors of Jordanian society, these fears may have diminished.

19. The primary responsibility of men—husbands and fathers—as providers for the family is explicitly articulated in Islamic teachings, and this is also clearly conveyed in the religion textbooks for the eleventh and twelfth grades (Jabr et al. 2004). However, as I discuss in chapter 6, the *National and Civic Education* textbook discusses the need for women to contribute economically to the household, in keeping with a broader public discourse that I encountered about the need for two-wage-earning families in the current economic climate.

20. Other explanations were also given for this, such as the earlier maturity of girls.

21. The religion textbooks emphasize the importance of the financial status of the potential groom and also explicitly talk about the marriage problems that may emerge if a man is of lesser financial means than a woman and her family. The authors, drawing on religious teachings, argue that it is preferable for a man to marry a woman of equal status; however, this recommendation is tempered with the qualification that a potential marriage partner's morals are the most important characteristic, that marriage is an imperative for all Muslims, and that a poor man should have the opportunity to marry, for in the end "one's livelihood is in God's hands" (Jabr et al. 2004: 56).

22. These classmates were her homeroom group; at al-Khatwa students remained with the same group of students throughout the day. At least one other girl in this class was suspended, and one was transferred to another school. Two girls' parents were brought in at the end of the year and the students threatened with transfer. All of this was viewed as part of an effort by the administration to break up a class that had gotten out of control.

23. Tradition held that as her cousin he had a right to ask for her hand in marriage first. Indeed some families in Jordan still go through the pro forma process of asking cousins—usually the available and age-appropriate paternal cousin and/or his father—for their permission to consummate a marriage to someone else. In addition, the number of Jordanians who marry their cousins today is between 20 and 30 percent (Hamamy et al. 2005; Khoury and Massad 2005).

24. In her piece titled "The Marriage of Feminism and Islamism in Egypt," Abu-Lughod (1998) argues that today's Islamists in Egypt have appropriated much of the same discourse about modern marriages, taking the position that a marriage based on love or at least compatibility is preferable to an arranged marriage. Abu-Lughod locates the roots of this emphasis on the conjugal unit and love marriage in the turn-of-the-century discourse about modernizing women and specifically in the writings of reformers such as Qasim Amin. See Amin ([1899] 1992, [1900] 1995).

25. Some of the parents of potential brides made an independent household a condition for accepting a marriage proposal. Yet because of difficult economic circumstances, the reality is that many young men still live in the same home or at least building as their parents, and so young women today can still find themselves living with their in-laws.

26. "Arranged" here refers to a set of practices that are more varied then this term implies in English; indeed in Arabic no such term exists to categorize marriage. When I was conducting research on marriage in Jordan in 2011, most of my interviewees used the term "traditional way" to characterize marriages that were initiated when a potential suitor (and sometimes only his mother to start with) went to have a cup of coffee at a prospective bride's house. However, even the traditional way encompassed a range

of possibilities. For example, if it is determined that mutual interest exists on the part of both prospective partners and their families, the young couple could get engaged and/or married almost immediately; or they might get to know each other for several months through chaperoned visits in the bride's home or, in the case of more socially liberal families, go out on unchaperoned dates to get to know each other better. In some cases, relationships that seem to be "traditional" actually involve a period in which the couple gets to know each other without the knowledge of their families until they have determined that they want to get their families involved. In such cases, they sometimes confide in siblings and/or their mothers.

27. Religiously speaking, engagement can be informal, in other words, without signing a marriage contract. However, as discussed above (note 15), in practice many families sign a marriage contract at the onset of the initial agreement on marriage so as to allow the couple more leeway to get to know each other without family supervision. Thus, the couple is legally married during the engagement period but has not yet consummated the marriage. Couples who are "engaged" by signing a marriage contract and then decide to break the engagement before the marriage is consummated are considered divorced. Breaking the contract is often met with resistance by family members because of potential repercussions for a girl's reputation. Among Christian families, although no contract is signed for one's engagement, breaking off an engagement is met with equal social resistance. In both cases, the girl risks slights to her reputation, as she has been in a serious relationship for all to see and then has broken it off.

28. The religion curriculum for secondary students cites a verse from the Qur'an acknowledging that the marriage of cousins is permitted in Islam (Jabr et al. 2004: 58). However, just a few pages earlier the authors explain that in Islam it is preferred that one not marry close relatives. They argue that "it is better for the married partners to be distant in their relationship" for both physical and social reasons (49).

29. In the capital, particularly among the upper classes, young men and women have much more opportunity to interact, and some date. Also, students at universities, all of which are coeducational, have much more opportunity to initiate relationships. Interestingly, as I have discussed in the case of Ghaliye, cell phones have opened up a whole new arena for "relationships" between boys and girls, and increasingly the internet has begun to do this as well.

30. See articles 19 and 37 in the 1976 personal status law, which remains unchanged. "Jordanian Legislation" (official website) http://www.lob.gov.jo/ui/laws/search_ no.jsp?no=61&year=1976 (accessed June 17, 2010).

31. In colloquial Jordanian, a woman who does not marry is referred to as *bint* or girl for her whole life, as *bint* also denotes virginity. Males, however, are referred to as men, *rijal*, regardless of their marital status.

32. Of course despite being forbidden by religion, law, and custom, premarital sexual relations occur. In the course of my research in Bawadi al-Naseem, I learned of one case in which a young woman married because she was pregnant. In addition, in the course of my research on marriage in Amman in 2011, many whom I interviewed claimed that premarital sex was commonplace among certain segments of the elite.

33. This is a reference to the waiting period for public sector jobs.

34. In Arabic *nasib* means literally fate or fortune. A typical phrase for girls about to get married is *aja nasibha*, her fate has arrived, or in other words "the time to marry and the person to marry had arrived." One might say in reference to a girl who never married, *ma jaha nasib*" or "fortune never came to her."

35. Both Lynn Welchman (2007) and Sami Zubaida (2003) note recent controversy over the practice, particularly in Egypt, where a 2000 law allowed *'urfi* marriage disputes to be heard in court, whereas prior to that a 1931 law had decreed that marriages not registered with state authorities could not be disputed in court. Critics alleged that this change essentially legitimized the practice of *'urfi* marriage. Both authors note the sociological context of these critiques: increasingly young people are using this form of marriage as a means of remaining in line with Islamic law while also subverting traditional channels of power such as the state and parents. See also Frances Hasso 2011).

36. The concept of learning disabilities or literally "learning difficulties," as it is referred to in Jordan, has only recently entered the Jordanian educational lexicon, although resources and policies to address such issues among students and in teacher training are limited if not absent, particularly outside the capital. Some students had learning disabilities that were so severe as to be obvious to all. For example, there were at least three students at al-Khatwa who teachers claimed could do little more than write their names on exams and possibly copy some of the exam questions. Owing to a policy of social promotion, they were able to get to the secondary level but could barely function in the classroom. Beyond such extreme cases, there was little awareness and/or resources available to identify or address other learning difficulties that students might face.

37. After 2005, a new academic track called "Information Management" was added to the options for high school students in some schools in Jordan, including al-Khatwa.

38. To be fair to the adults in the school, one of the *adabi* classes was frequently out of control and a source of behavioral problems for teachers and staff alike, to the point where some teachers seemed unable to control the class sufficiently to be able to teach. However, some teachers seemed better able to manage the situation than others, and one could argue that the girls were at least in part acting out in fulfillment of the low expectations they were convinced others had for them.

39. Despite the government's efforts for several years now to promote vocational training as useful and critical to Jordan's development, in reality those in the vocational track still have a difficult time competing with their peers for places at the university or community colleges, and for jobs.

40. Siba had scored an average in the low 80s on the midyear high school completion exams (a good indication of what her overall score would be), which left her with no hope to be accepted into the medical colleges in Jordan, and so she was seeking some other route to this career. For wealthy students, of course, there were always other alternatives. Siba had neither the finances nor the grades to access such alternatives.

41. In my experience in Jordan, negative assumptions are made about the upbringing of a girl who is raised in a house without a father. People assumed that without a male guardian, a young woman was more prone to immoral activity. In fact, this was often used to convince women who wanted to leave their husbands to stay with them— "for the sake of the children." Since Siba's father was deceased, she ascertained that the best way to protect her precarious reputation—made precarious by the conflict within her family—was to live with her older brother.

42. A study on the middle class in Jordan and rising income inequality found that the wealthiest Jordanians spent significantly more resources on education than the poorest and even the middle class (Saif and Tabbaa 2008). These quantitative data point to the fact that increasingly the masses and the elite are educated separately (with the growth of a private sector) and that the educations are of disparate quality.

43. Jeffrey et al. (2008) document the limits of education for lower-caste and/or lower-class men in India.

44. The scholarship in this vein is too numerous to enumerate here. Some of the most well known are Bourdieu and Passeron (1977); Bowels and Gintis (1976); and Willis (1977).

45. To get into a college of medicine in Jordan, a high school student must score amongst the highest on the high school completion exam (in the high 90s). Alternatively, students who have the financial resources can enter with a lower score if they pay significantly higher tuition. As discussed in chapter 2, this system is called the *mawazi* or "parallel" system. In addition, those with resources and greater mobility (typically male students) can also study medicine abroad.

46. Thanks to Sam Dolbee for this important insight.

CHAPTER SIX

1. *Ustadh* means teacher, but it is also an honorific used for civil servants and other professionals. Yahya was still called *Ustadh* by all of his former students and most of the community despite having been retired for several years.

2. Another measure of empowerment that is typically incorporated into measures of progress for women is their representation in political office (Abu-Lughod 2009; N. Farah 2006).

3. For a review of this research, see Kevin Watkins (2000) and Robert LeVine et al. (2001).

4. For a critique of this perspective, see Vavrus's (2003) discussion about the presumed links between schools and safe health practices in the absence of curriculum related to sex education and family planning.

5. In 2008, net enrollment of girls in primary school was 90 percent, while boys were enrolled at 89 percent. At the secondary level, net enrollment for girls was 84 percent and for boys 80 percent. At the tertiary level, gross enrollment for females was 43 percent, while it was 39 percent for males (UNESCO Institute for Statistics).

6. As discussed in chapter 1 (see specifically note 2), fertility rates have actually significantly decreased.

7. The World Bank (2005) estimates that women's labor force participation is somewhere between 12 and 26 percent, depending on the measure used. The unemployment rate among women, particularly young women, is higher than that of males. In 2008, the Department of Statistics reported that the overall female unemployment rate was 24.4 percent as compared with 10.1 percent for males (Department of Statistics). Many economic observers of Jordan believe these numbers to be significantly underestimating actual unemployment. Over 50 percent of unemployed women in 2003 were ages 20–24; the overwhelming majority of unemployed women (94 percent) were between the ages of 20 and 39 (European Training Foundation 2005).

8. N. Farah (2006) also raises concerns about the use of literacy rates as a proxy for educational development.

9. Mary Kawar (2000) grounds her analysis of reasons for women's work patterns in qualitative research that gives a clear sense of the variety of factors that influence a women's work and education life in Jordan. See also Rebecca Miles on Jordanian women and work (2002). Homa Hoodfar's (1997) examination of the economic contributions of Egyptian women and the economic dimensions of marriage is an important contribution in this vein. See also Jenny White (1994) for ethnography of working women in Turkey.

10. The impact of the oil industry has also been felt beyond the wealthy oil nations, as men from other countries such as Jordan have migrated to the wealthier states for lucrative work.

11. Some local governments have pursued a policy of promoting employment for lower-income women in low-wage manufacturing jobs in newly constructed "free trade zones." The low wages and the exploitative nature of many of these jobs leave them less than desirable and not always economically viable. For an argument about the importance of such low-wage jobs for female entry into the labor force, see Moghadam (2005) and Ross (2008). For perspectives on why such jobs may not be desirable, see Hoodfar (1997). For an example from Latin America, see Preito (1997) on the lives of women working in Mexican *maquiladoras*.

12. The government did provide subsidized childcare for preschool-aged children at al-Khatwa, but the quality of this care was quite low, and some teachers were reluctant to leave their children there.

13. In the course of my research on marriage in 2011, several women expressed a concern that men might marry them for their salaries. In the marriage negotiation process, some of these women insisted that they did not want to work after they married as a test to see what potential suitors would do if the prospective bride no longer came with her salary. Most of the single men I interviewed said they needed to marry a woman who worked as they could not support a family on their own.

14. *New York Times*, April 27. 2007, "Change the World and That Diaper," http://www .nytimes.com/2007/04/27/opinion/127work.html?_r=1&oref=slogin.

15. As discussed in chapter 5, this perspective on the education of women has its roots in a modernizing discourse that is over a century old, one that also has had distinct implications for the conceptualization of marriage (Abu-Lughod 1998; Amin [1899] 1992; Najmabadi 1998a; Shakry 1998).

16. In Janise Hurtig's (2008) study of a Venezuelan high school, female students conveyed similar sentiments, namely, the need to take care of oneself in the future should things go bad. In this context, going bad referred to abandonment by a spouse or boyfriend, or the failure of the male head of household to provide for his family. Hurtig terms this phenomenon "negligent patriarchy" (14).

17. Again, the belief that men bear the primary responsibility for providing for the family is grounded in Islamic teaching and referenced in the Qur'an.

18. References to financial independence were more frequent among parents, although even some of the girls spoke in these terms.

19. Of course these were parents whose daughters were still in high school, so they do not represent the perspective of those whose daughters had dropped out already. However, as mentioned earlier, some of the older siblings of al-Khatwa students (for example, Reem, Yasmine, Selma, and Jenine) had dropped out for a variety of reasons.

20. Even for the poorest families, a father's army service opened up the possibility for educating his children at the university. As mentioned in chapter 2, those under-represented in the army, namely, Jordanians of Palestinian descent (especially after 1970s), were disproportionately deprived of such scholarships.

21. I am not sure if any of the boys had gone to the university.

22. As discussed in chapter 2, in the twelfth grade, Jordanian students, male and female, take the *tawjihi*, or high school completion exam. Their score on this exam determines if they can study in a public university and what major they can choose.

23. As discussed earlier in this chapter, comparatively speaking, many more females go

into the sciences and engineering than in countries like the United States. In my experience math and science are not gendered in the way they are in the United States. High-achieving students are expected to study in fields related to math and science regardless of their gender.

24. Some researchers have argued that women's work in the informal labor sector has increased significantly, especially among the poorest families. However, the scope of this is hard to measure. It is estimated that as a percentage of overall economic activity, informal activities range anywhere from 12 to 40 percent (World Bank 2005).

25. The other problems listed were "culture shock" from sudden changes such as those brought on by migration from rural to urban areas; "identity crisis"; the "cultural gap or lag" that occurs when material changes outpace cultural changes; "generational conflict" or the conflict brought on by the generation gap; "new behavior patterns especially among youth"; and unemployment (al-Masad et al. 2004: 62–63).

26. For a discussion about similar issues in a U.S. context, see Arlie Hochschild's *The Second Shift: Working Parents and the Revolution at Home* (1990). In 2009, women were still spending significantly more time than men on housework and childcare, although the amount of time men put into such tasks has increased. See "American Time Use Survey," U.S. Department of Labor, http://www.bls.gov/news.release/atus .nr0.htm (accessed June 25, 2010).

27. For example, there has been much attention given to training women for participation in the ICT sector (World Bank 2005) and regular coverage of technology training for women in the press (e.g., *Jordan Times*, March 13, 2003).

28. In the past few years several stories have appeared in the press about the establishment of garment factories in the south of the country in free trade and qualifying industrial zones. This has been presented as a groundbreaking opportunity for poor rural women to join the labor force. For example the Arabic daily *Al-Quds al-'Arabi* (December 5, 2002) ran a story entitled "Girls from Tafileh Go Out to Work for the First Time." In November of that same year the *Jordan Times* (November 29, November 30, 2002) ran stories about the new textile factory in Tafileh that was said to be planning to hire 150 local women. On April 3, 2005, almost three years later, the *Jordan Times* again ran a story about a new garment factory in Tafileh. This time it was reported that the new factory would hire 180 women as well as 100 men.

29. Periodically, stories appear in the press about women taking on traditionally male jobs such as plumbers and taxi drivers. I have also seen several stories about women police officers. Many of the tenth graders at al-Khatwa told me that they wanted to be police officers, and some of them were convinced it was a real possibility, while others thought it unlikely that their families would permit it. I often saw female police officers, so this is a career path that some women are pursuing. Mary Kawar (2000: 58) describes how members of the community in which she conducted research spoke proudly about a woman trained as a mechanic, as did the woman's family, even if most believed she should not actually work as a mechanic.

30. Indeed, the personal status laws in Jordan actually imply the same, namely, that a woman should have her husband's permission to work; otherwise she forfeits her legal right to financial support from her spouse. Also, if she works against his will, this could be grounds for divorce unless she has written stipulations into her marriage contract allowing her to work (Amawi 2000).

31. For example, the Muslim Brotherhood has a strong presence in the Ministry of Education owing to previous periods of controlling this portfolio as well as the widespread presence of the party's members in the field of education (Anderson 2007).

32. Women entering the labor force, particularly in fields dominated by men, have faced the accusation of being or acting like men in many different contexts. For example, see Melissa Fisher's (2004) research on Wall Street women.
33. *Jahil* literally means ignorance. *Jahiliyya* refers to the period of time before the arrival of Islam and its prophet Muhammad—the time of ignorance.
34. See Homa Hoodfar (1997) on women and their social networking as important non-income-generating economic activity.

CHAPTER SEVEN

1. This report was the fourth in a series of Arab Human Development Reports that had received much acclaim from the media around the globe and from politicians in the West. The reports were considered to be groundbreaking self-critiques produced by Arab intellectuals for an Arab audience. However, the reports may have received less attention in the Arab world than in the West (Abu-Lughod et al. 2009; Bayet 2005).
2. A significant body of scholarship has emerged that problematizes the resistance concept in education and beyond (e.g., Abu-Lughod 1990; Holland and Eisenhart 1990; Mahmood 2005; Ortner 1995).
3. See for example the research and expansive media coverage of rap and hip-hop in the region, as well as heavy metal bands (e.g., Kahf 2007; Levine 2008).
4. This is not meant to imply that such transformations are unprecedented; the flow of culture and ideas, as well as commerce and trade, is centuries old. However, owing to technological innovations and the spread of capitalism in the contemporary era, the scale and reach of globalization are dramatic.
5. Her brother's wife, a classmate of Yasmine's from high school who had not gone on to the university, was also pregnant, and Um Waleed was anxiously awaiting the arrival of her first two grandchildren.
6. I gave my e-mail address to several of the girls, but most of them did not have access to e-mail when we first met in 2002 or 2005. Over time, more and more of them have obtained access, especially if they are at the university. The cost of maintaining a connection is prohibitive for most families, so even for those with a computer at home, many did not have internet access.
7. Although no "revolutionary" change has been underfoot in Jordan, much is happening on the ground. Jordanians have demanded and won a wider space for criticisms of the regime—its economic policies, rampant corruption, and the lack of political freedoms. In the summer of 2011, political demonstrations, which had been mostly limited to Amman and Madaba, spread to several regions in the country, including Bawadi al-Naseem, where such demonstrations are rare.

REFERENCES

Abdalla, A. 2000. Employees or beneficiaries? *Middle East Studies Association Bulletin* 34 (2): 184–86.

Abdullah, Ghazi M., et al. 2004. *Al-thaqafa al- amma* [General culture]. Comprehensive secondary-level civic education and social studies textbook (eleventh and twelfth grades). Ministry of Education, Department of Curriculum and Textbooks.

Abimourched, R. 2008. Handpicked and carefully selected: An exploration of the lives of migrant domestic workers in Jordan. M.A. thesis, Georgetown University.

Abu-Lughod, L. 1989. Zones of theory in the anthropology of the Arab world. *Annual Review of Anthropology* 18: 267–306.

———. 1990. The romance of resistance: Tracing transformations of power through Bedouin women. *American Ethnologist* 17 (1): 41–55.

———. 1991. Writing against culture. In *Recapturing anthropology: Working in the present,* ed. R. Fox, 137–62. Santa Fe, NM: School of American Research Press.

———. 1993. *Writing women's worlds: Bedouin stories.* Berkeley: University of California Press.

———. 2000. *Veiled sentiments: Honor and poetry in Bedouin society.* Berkeley: University of California Press.

———, ed. 1998. *Remaking women: Feminism and modernity in the Middle East.* Princeton, NJ: Princeton University Press.

———. 2002. Do Muslim women really need saving? Anthropological reflections on cultural relativism and its others. *American Anthropologist* 104 (3): 783–90.

———. 2005. *Dramas of nationhood: The politics of television in Egypt.* Chicago: University of Chicago Press.

———. 2009. Dialects of women's empowerment: The international circuitry of the Arab Human Development Report 2005. *International Journal of Middle East Studies* 41 (1): 83–103.

Abu-Lughod, L., F. Adely, and F. Hasso. 2009. Overview: Engaging the Arab Human Development Report 2005 on women. *International Journal of Middle East Studies* 41 (1): 59–60.

Adely, F. 2004. The mixed effects of schooling for high school girls in Jordan: The case of Tel Yahya. *Comparative Education Review* 48 (4): 353–73.

———. 2007. "Is music haram?" Jordanian girls educating each other about nation, faith and gender in school. *Teachers College Record* 109 (7): 1663–81.

———. 2009a. Educating women for development: The Arab Human Development Report 2005 and the problem with women's choices. *International Journal of Middle East Studies* 41 (1): 105–22.

———. 2009b. Everyday youth places: Youth in educational spaces. *International Journal of Middle East Studies* 41 (3): 372–73.

———. 2010. Performing patriotism: Rituals and moral authority in a Jordanian high school. In *Education and the Arab "world": Political projects, struggles, and geometries of power* [World Yearbook of Education 2010], ed. A. E. Mazawi and R. G. Sultana, 132–44. New York: Routledge.

Ahearn, L. 2001. *Invitations to love: Literacy, love letters, and social change in Nepal.* Ann Arbor: University of Michigan Press.

Ahmed, L. 1992. *Women and gender in Islam: Historical roots of a modern debate.* New Haven, CT: Yale University Press.

Ali, K. A. 1997. Modernization and family planning programs in Egypt. Middle East Report 205, 40–44.

———. 2002. *Planning the family in Egypt: New bodies, new selves.* Austin: University of Texas Press.

Alon, Y. 2005. The tribal system in the face of the state-formation process: Mandatory Transjordan, 1921–46. *International Journal of Middle East Studies* 37 (2): 213–40.

Alyssa, S. 2007. Rethinking economic reform in Jordan: Confronting socioeconomic realities. Washington, DC: Carnegie Middle East Center. http://www.carnegieendowment .org/files/cmec4_alissa_jordan_final.pdf

Amadouny, V. M. 1994. Infrastructure development under the British mandate. In *Village, steppe and state*, ed. E. Rogan and T. Tell, 128–61. London: I. B. Tauris.

Amawi, A. 2000. Gender and citizenship in Jordan. In *Gender and citizenship in the Middle East*, ed. S. Joseph, 158–84. Syracuse, NY: Syracuse University Press.

Amin, Q. (1899) 1992. *The liberation of women.* Trans. S. Peterson. Cairo: American University in Cairo Press.

———. (1900) 1995. *The new woman.* Trans. S. Peterson. Cairo: American University in Cairo Press.

"Amman Message." The Official Website of the Amman Message. http://ammanmessage .com/ (accessed October 17, 2011).

Anderson, B. 1997. The status of "democracy" in Jordan. *Critique: Critical Middle Eastern Studies* 6 (10): 55–76.

———. 2001. Writing the nation: Textbooks of the Hashemite Kingdom of Jordan. *Comparative Studies of South Asia, Africa and the Middle East* 12 (1): 5–11.

———. 2005. *Nationalist voices in Jordan: The street and the state.* Austin: University of Texas Press.

———. 2007. Sources of authority: Islamic textbooks of the Hashemite Kingdom of Jordan. In *Teaching Islam: Textbooks and religion in the Middle East*, ed. E. Doumato and G. Starrett, 71–88. Boulder, CO: Lynne Rienner.

Antoun, R. T. 1972. *Arab village: A social structural study of a Trans-Jordanian peasant community.* Bloomington: Indiana University Press.

———. 1989. *Muslim preacher in the modern world: A Jordanian case study in comparative perspective.* Princeton, NJ: Princeton University Press.

———. 2006. Fundamentalism, bureaucratization, and the state's co-optation of religion: A Jordanian case study. *International Journal of Middle East Studies* 38 (3): 369–93.

Appadurai, A. 1996. *Modernity at large: Cultural dimensions of globalization.* Minneapolis: University of Minnesota Press.

Arab Fund for Economic and Social Development. 2003. Modernizing Islam: Religion in the public sphere in the Middle East and Europe. In *Arab women and economic development*, ed. H. Handoussa, 134–67. Cairo: American University in Cairo Press.

Armbrust, W. 2005. What would Sayyid Qutb say? Some reflections on video clips. *Transnational Broadcasting Studies* 14: 18–29.

Asad, T. 1986. The idea of an anthropology of Islam. Occasional Papers Series. Washington, DC: Georgetown University, Center for Contemporary Arab Studies.

———. 1993. *Genealogies of religion: Discipline and reasons of power in Christianity and Islam*. Baltimore: Johns Hopkins University Press.

Assaad, R., and M. Ramadan. 2008. Did housing policy reforms curb the delay in marriage among young men in Egypt? Middle East Youth Initiative Working Paper. Washington, DC: Wolfensohn Center for Development at Brookings and the Dubai School of Government.

Badran, M. 1995. *Feminists, Islam, and nation: Gender in the making of modern Egypt*. Princeton, NJ: Princeton University Press.

Barlas, A. 2002. *Believing women in Islam: Unreading patriarchal interpretations of the Qur'an*. Austin: University of Texas Press.

Baron, B. 1991. The making and breaking of marital bonds in modern Egypt. In *Women in Middle Eastern history: Shifting boundaries in sex and gender*, ed. N. Keddie and B. Baron, 275–91. New Haven, CT: Yale University Press.

———. 1994. *The women's awakening in Egypt*. New Haven, CT: Yale University Press.

———. 2005. *Egypt as a woman: Nationalism, gender, and politics*. Berkeley: University of California Press.

Bartlett, L. 2003. World culture or transnational project? Competing educational projects in Brazil. In *Local meanings, global schooling: Anthropology and world culture theory*, ed. K. Anderson-Levitt, 183–200. New York: Palgrave Global.

———. 2007. To seem and to feel: Situated identities and literacy practices. *Teachers College Record* 109 (1): 51–69.

Bayet, A. 2005. Transforming the Arab world: The *Arab Human Development Report* and the politics of change. *Development and Change* 36 (6): 1225–37.

Baylouny, A. 2006. Creating kin: New family associations as welfare providers in liberalizing Jordan. *International Journal of Middle East Studies* 38 (3): 349–68.

Berkey, J. 1992. *The transmission of knowledge in medieval Cairo: A social history of Islamic education*. Princeton, NJ: Princeton University Press.

———. 2006. Madrasas medieval and modern: Politics, education, and the problem of Muslim identity. In *Schooling Islam: The culture and politics of modern Muslim education*, ed. R. Hefner and M. Q. Zaman, 40–60. Princeton, NJ: Princeton University Press.

Bernal, V. 1994. Gender, culture and capitalism: Women and the remaking of Islamic 'tradition' in a Sudanese village. *Comparative Studies in Society and History* 36 (1): 36–67.

Bettie, J. 2000. Women without class: Chicas, cholas, trash, and the presence/absence of class identity. *Signs: Journal of Women in Culture and Society* 26 (1): 1–36.

———. 2002. *Women without class: Girls, race, and identity*. Berkeley: University of California Press.

Booth, M. 1997. "May her likes be multiplied": "Famous women" biography and gendered prescription in Egypt, 1892–1935. *Signs: Journal of Women in Culture and Society* 22 (4): 827–90.

———. 1998. The Egyptian lives of Jeanne d'Arc. In *Remaking women: Feminism and modernity in the Middle East*, ed. L. Abu-Lughod, 171–211. Princeton, NJ: Princeton University Press.

Bourdieu, P. 1977. *Outline of a theory of practice*. Cambridge: Cambridge University Press.

Bourdieu, P., and J. Passeron. 1977. *Reproduction in education, society, and culture*. Trans. R. Nice. London: Sage.

Bourdieu, P., and L. H. Wacquant. 1992. *An invitation to reflexive sociology*. Chicago: University of Chicago Press.

Bowels, S., and H. Gintis. 1976. *Schooling in capitalist America: Educational reform and the conditions of economic life*. New York: Basic Books.

Bowen, J. R. 2008. *Why the French don't like headscarves: Islam, the state, and public space*. Princeton: Princeton University Press.

Boyle, H. 2006. Memorization and learning in Islamic schools. *Comparative Education Review* 50 (3): 478–95.

Brand, L. 1995. Palestinians and Jordanians: A crisis of identity. *Journal of Palestine Studies* 24 (4): 46–61.

———. 1998. *Women, the state and political liberalization: Middle Eastern and North African experiences*. New York: Columbia University Press.

Bucholtz, M. 2002. Youth and cultural practice. *Annual Review of Anthropology* 31: 525–52.

Butler, J. 1988. Performative acts and gender constitution: An essay in phenomenology and feminist theory. *Theatre Journal* 40: 519–31.

———.1993. *Bodies that matter: On the discursive limits of sex."* New York: Routledge.

Chatterjee, P. 1993. *The nation and its fragments: Colonial and postcolonial histories*. Princeton, NJ: Princeton University Press.

Clancy-Smith, J. 1999. A woman without her distaff: Gender, work and handicraft production in colonial North Africa. In *Social history of women and gender in the modern Middle East*, ed. M. Meriwether and J. Tucker, 25–62. Boulder, CO: Westview Press.

Clark, J. A. 2004. *Islam, charity, and activism: Middle-class networks and social welfare in Egypt, Jordan, and Yemen*. Bloomington: Indiana University Press.

———. 2006. The conditions of Islamist moderation: Unpacking cross-ideological cooperation in Jordan. *International Journal of Middle East Studies* 38 (4): 539–60.

Clifford, J., and G. Marcus, eds. 1986. *Writing culture: The poetics and politics of ethnography*. Berkeley: University of California Press.

Coe, C. 2005. *Dilemmas of culture in African schools: Youth, nationalism, and the transformation of knowledge*. Chicago: University of Chicago Press.

Comaroff, J. 1985. *Body of power, spirit of resistance: The culture and history of a South African people*. Chicago: University of Chicago Press.

Comaroff, J., and J. L. Comaroff. 1991. *Of revelation and revolution: Christianity, colonialism, and consciousness in South Africa*. Chicago: University of Chicago Press.

Combs-Schilling, M. E. 1989. *Sacred performances: Islam, sexuality and sacrifice*. New York: Columbia University Press.

Conte, E., and S. Walentowitz. 2009. Kinship matters: Tribals, cousins, and citizens in Southwest Asia and beyond. *Etudes Rurales* 184: 217–48.

Crehan, K. 2000. *Gramsci, culture and anthropology*. Berkeley: University of California Press.

Cremin, L. 1978. The education of the educating professions. Research Bulletin, vol. 18. New York: Horace Mann–Lincoln Institute, Teachers College, Columbia University.

Daragahi, B. 2006. Jordan's king risks shah's fate, critics warn. *Los Angeles Times*, October 1. http://articles.latimes.com/2006/oct/01/world/fg-jordan1.

Deeb, L. 2006. *An enchanted modern: Gender and public piety in Shi'i Lebanon*. Princeton, NJ: Princeton University Press.

Dewey, J. 1916. *Democracy and education: An introduction to the philosophy of education*. New York: Free Press.

Dolbee, S. 2008. Re-writing Jordan: National identity and political challenge in 1950s Jordan. M.A. thesis, University of North Carolina at Chapel Hill.

Doumato, E. 2003. Manning the barricades: Islam according to Saudi Arabia's school texts. *Middle East Journal* 57 (2): 230–47.

Doumato, E., and G. Starrett. 2007. *Teaching Islam: Textbooks and religion in the Middle East*. Boulder, CO: Lynne Rienner.

Dughmi, Mohammad R. al-, et al. 1996. *Al-tarbiyya al- islamiyya* [Islamic education]. Eleventh-grade humanities track religious studies textbook. Amman: Ministry of Education, Department of Curriculum and Textbooks.

Durkheim, E. 1956. *Education and sociology*. Glencoe, IL: Free Press.

———. 1961. *Moral education: A study in the theory and application of the sociology of education*. New York: Free Press of Glencoe.

Eickelman, D. 1985. *Knowledge and power in Morocco: The education of a twentieth-century notable*. Princeton, NJ: Princeton University Press.

———. 1992. Mass higher education and the religious imagination in contemporary Arab societies. *American Ethnologist* 19 (4): 643–55.

Engineering Workforce Commission. 2006. Engineering and technology enrollments: Fall 2005. Washington, DC.

Escobar, A. 1995. *Encountering development: The making and the unmaking of the third world*. Princeton, NJ: Princeton University Press.

Esposito, J. 1998. *Islam and politics*. Syracuse, NY: Syracuse University Press.

———. 2003. Islam and civil society. In *Modernizing Islam: Religion in the public sphere in the Middle East and Europe*, ed. J. Esposito and F. Burgat, 69–100. New Brunswick, NJ: Rutgers University Press.

Esposito, J., and F. Burgat, eds. 2003. *Modernizing Islam: Religion in the public sphere in the Middle East and Europe*. New Brunswick, NJ: Rutgers University Press.

European Training Foundation. 2005. Unemployment in Jordan. http://www.etf.europa.eu/pubmgmt.nsf/(getAttachment)/4E4904B283AC4CAAC12570E0003D00E7/$File/NOTE6KCEZX.pdf .

Fafo Institute and the Jordanian Department of Statistics. 2007. Iraqis in Jordan: Their number and characteristics. http://www.fafo.no/ais/middeast/jordan/IJ.pdf.

Fagerlind, I., and L. Saha. 1989. *Education and national development*. 2nd ed. New York: Pergamon.

Farah, N. 2006. Arab women's development: How relevant are UNDP measurements? *Middle East Policy* 13 (2): 38–47.

Farah, R. 2005. Palestinian refugee children and caregivers in Jordan. In *Children of Palestine: Experiencing forced migration in the Middle East*, ed. D. Chatty and G. L. Hundt, 87–121. New York: Berghahn Books.

Feinberg, W., and J. Soltis. 2004. *School and society*. New York: Teachers College.

Ferguson, J. 1994. *The anti-politics machine: "Development," depoliticization, and bureaucratic power in Lesotho*. Minneapolis: University of Minnesota Press.

Fernea, E. 2000. Islamic feminism finds a different voice. *Foreign Service Journal* 77 (5). http://www.afsa.org/fsj/may00/fernea.cfm.

Fisher, M. 2004. Wall Street women's herstories. In *Constructing corporate America: History, politics, culture*, ed. K. Lipartito and D. Sicilia, 294–320. Oxford: Oxford University Press.

Fleischmann, E. 2002. The impact of American Protestant missions in Lebanon on the construction of female identity, c. 1860–1950. *Islam and Christian-Muslim Relations* 13 (4): 412–26.

Fortna, B. C. 2002. *Imperial classroom: Islam, the state, and education in the late Ottoman Empire*. New York: Oxford University Press.

Foucault, M. 1977. *Discipline and punish: The birth of the prison*. New York: Vintage Books.

———. 1990. *The History of sexuality: An introduction*. Trans. R. Hurley. Vol. 1. New York: Vintage Books.

Geertz, C. 1973. Thick description: Toward an interpretive theory of culture. In *The interpretation of cultures: Selected essays*. 3–30. New York: Basic Books.

Gertner, J. 2010. The rise and fall of the GDP. *New York Times Magazine*, May 10. http://www.nytimes.com/2010/05/16/magazine/16GDP-t.html?scp=2&sq=GDP&st=cse.

Gesink, I. F. 2006. Islamic reformation: A history of *madrassa* reform and legal change in Egypt. *Comparative Education Review* 50 (3): 325–45.

Ghannam, F. 1998. Keeping him connected: Labor migration and the production of locality in Cairo. *City and Society* 10 (1): 65–82.

———. 2002. *Remaking the modern: Space, relocation, and the politics of identity in a global Cairo*. Berkeley: University of California Press.

Giddens, A. 1979. *Central problems in social theory: Action, structure and contradiction in social analysis*. Berkeley: University of California Press.

Goffman, C. 2002. Masking the mission: Cultural conversion at the American College for Girls. In *Altruism and imperialism: Western cultural and religious missions in the Middle East*, ed. E. H. Tejirian and R. S. Simon, 88–119. Occasional Papers 4. New York: Middle East Institute, Columbia University.

Gole, N. 1997. Secularism and Islamism in Turkey: The making of elites and counterelites. *Middle East Journal* 51 (1): 56–58.

Greenwood, S. 2003a. Jordan, the Al-Aqsa Intifada and America's war on terror. *Middle East Policy* 10 (3): 90–111.

———. 2003b. Jordan's "new bargain": The political economy of regime security. *Middle East Journal* 57 (2): 248–68.

Guindi, F. el-. 1999. *Veil: Modesty, privacy and resistance*. Oxford: Berg.

Haddad, Y., and J. Esposito, eds. 1998. *Islam, gender and social change*. New York: Oxford University Press.

Hall, K. D. 2002. *Lives in translation: Sikh youth as British citizens*. Philadelphia: University of Pennsylvania Press.

Hamamy, H., L. Jamhawi, J. al-Darawsheh, and K. Ajlouni. 2005. Consanguineous marriages in Jordan: Why is the rate changing with time? *Clinical Genetics* 67: 511–16.

Hamzeh, A. N., and R. H. Dekmejian. 1996. A Sufi response to political Islamism: Al-Ahbash of Lebanon. *International Journal of Middle East Studies* 28 (2): 217–29.

Hanssen-Bauer, J., J. Pedersen, and A. Tiltnes. 1998. *Jordanian society: Living conditions in the Hashemite Kingdom of Jordan*. Oslo: Fafo Institute for Applied Social Science.

Haq, M. ul-. 1995. *Reflections on human development*. New York: Oxford University Press.

Hasso, F. 2007. Comparing Emirati and Egyptian narratives on marriage, sexuality, and the body. In *Global migration, social changes, and cultural transformation*, ed. E. Elliott, J. Payne, and P. Ploesch, 59–74. New York: Palgrave.

———. 2009. Empowering governmentalities rather than women: The *Arab Human Development Report 2005* and Western development logics. *International Journal of Middle East Studies* 41 (1): 63–82.

———. 2010. *Consuming desires: Family, crisis and the state in the Middle East*. Stanford, CA: Stanford University Press.

Hatem, M. 2005. In the shadow of the state: Changing definitions of Arab women's developmental citizenship rights. *Journal of Middle East Women's Studies* 1 (3): 20–45.

Hefner, R., and M. Q. Zaman, eds. 2006. *Schooling Islam: The culture and politics of modern Muslim education*. Princeton, NJ: Princeton University Press.

Herrera, L. A. 1992. *Scenes of schooling: Inside a girls' school in Cairo*. Cairo Papers in Social Science 15, Monograph 1. Cairo: American University in Cairo Press.

———. 2000. The sanctity of the school: New Islamic education and modern Egypt. Ph.D. diss., Columbia University.

———. 2003. Islamization and education in Egypt: Between politics, culture and the market. In *Modernizing Islam: Religion in the public sphere in the Middle East and Europe*, ed. J. Esposito and F. Burgat, 167–89. New Brunswick, NJ: Rutgers University Press.

———. 2004. Education, Islam and modernity: Beyond Westernization and centralization. *Comparative Education Review* 48 (3): 318–26.

———. 2006. In *Cultures of Arab schooling: Critical ethnographies from Egypt*, ed. L. A. Herrera and A. Torres, 25–52. Albany: State University of New York Press.

Heward, C., and S. Bunwaree. 1999. *Gender, education and development: Beyond access to empowerment*. London: Zed Books.

Hirschkind, C. 2001. Civic virtue and religious reason: An Islamic counterpublic. *Cultural Anthropology* 16 (1): 3–34.

Hirschkind, C., and S. Mahmood. 2002. Feminism, the Taliban, and politics of counterinsurgency. *Anthropological Quarterly* 75 (2): 339–54.

Hirshman, L. 2007. Off to work she should go. *New York Times*, April 25. http://www.nytimes.com/2007/04/25/opinion/25hirshman.html?_r=1&oref=slogi.

Hobsbawm, E. 1983. Inventing traditions. In *The invention of tradition*, ed. E. Hobsbawm and T. Ranger, 16–40. Cambridge: Cambridge University Press.

Hochschild, A. 1990. *The second shift: Working parents and the revolution at home*. New York: Avon.

Holland, D., and M. A. Eisenhart. 1990. *Educated in romance: Women, achievement and college culture*. Chicago: University of Chicago Press.

Hoodfar, H. 1997. *Between marriage and the market: Intimate politics and survival in Cairo*. Berkeley: University of California Press.

hooks, b. 1984. *Feminist theory: From margin to center*. Cambridge, MA: South End Press.

Human Rights Watch. 2006. The silent treatment: Fleeing Iraq, surviving in Jordan. HRW Index No. E1810.

Hurtig, J. 1998. Gender lessons: Schooling and the reproduction of patriarchy in a Venezuelan town. PhD diss., University of Michigan.

———. 2008. *Coming of age in times of crisis: Youth, schooling, and patriarchy in a Venezuelan town*. New York: Palgrave McMillan.

Illouz, E. 1997. *Consuming the romantic Utopia: Love and the cultural contradictions of capitalism*. Berkeley: University of California Press.

'Imarah, M. 1999. *Al-Ghina wa-al-musiqa: halal am haram* [Singing and music: lawful or forbidden]. Cairo: Dar Nahdat Misr.

International Crisis Group. 2003. Red alert in Jordan: Recurrent unrest in Maan. http://www.unhcr.org/refworld/docid/3efdebab4.html.

———. 2005. Jordan's 9/11: Dealing with *jihadi* Islamism. Middle East Report 47.

International Labour Organization with the Ministry of Labour (Jordan). 2002. *Women workers in the textiles and garments industries in Jordan: Research on the impact of globalization*. ILO Publication written by Kholoud Al-Khaldi.

Ismail, S. 2003. *Rethinking Islamist politics: Culture, the state and Islamism*. London: I. B. Tauris.

Jabr, Sa di Hussein, et al. 2004. *Al-thaqafa al-islamiyya* [Islamic culture]. Comprehensive secondary-level religious studies textbook (eleventh and twelfth grades). Amman: Ministry of Education, Department of Curriculum and Textbooks.

Jad, I. 2009. Comments from an author: Engaging the Arab Human Development Report 2005 on women. *International Journal of Middle East Studies* 41 (1): 61–62.

Jansen, W. 2006. Gender and the expansion of the university system in Jordan. *Gender and Education* 18 (5): 473–90.

Jaworski, A., and N. Coupland. 1999. Introduction: Perspectives on discourse analysis. In *The discourse reader*, ed. A. Jaworski and N. Coupland, 1–44. London: Routledge.

Jeffrey, C., P. Jeffrey, and R. Jeffrey. 2008. *Degrees without freedom? Education, masculinities and unemployment in Northern India*. Stanford, CA: Stanford University Press.

Jordan First National Commission. 2002. "Jordan First" Document. King Abdullah II Official Website, December 22. http://www.kingabdullah.jo/main.php?main_page=0&lang_hmka1=1.

Joseph, S. 1993. Gender and relationality among Arab families in Lebanon. *Feminist Studies* 19 (3): 465–86.

———. 1994. Brother/sister relationships: Connectivity, love, and power in the reproduction of Arab patriarchy. *American Ethnologist* 21 (1): 50–73.

Joseph, S., and S. Slyomovics, eds. 2001. *Women and power in the Middle East*. Philadelphia: University of Pennsylvania Press.

Kabeer, N. 1994. *Reversed realities: Gender hierarchies in development thought*. London: Verso.

Kabha, M., and H. Erlich. 2006. Al-Ahbash and Wahabiyya: Interpretations of Islam. *International Journal of Middle East Studies* 38 (4): 519–38.

Kahf, U. 2007. Arabic Hip Hop: Claims of authenticity and identity of a new genre. *Journal of Popular Music Studies* 19 (4): 359–85.

Kandiyoti, D. 1988. Bargaining with patriarchy. *Gender and Society* 2 (3): 274–90.

———. 1991. *Women, Islam and the state*. Philadelphia: Temple University Press.

———. 1998. Some awkward questions on women and modernity in Turkey. In *Remaking women: Feminism and modernity in the Middle East*, ed. L. Abu-Lughod, 270–87. Princeton, NJ: Princeton University Press.

———. 2001. The politics of gender and conundrums of citizenship. In *Women and power in the Middle East*, ed. S. Joseph and S. Slyomovics, 52–58. Philadelphia: University of Pennsylvania Press.

Kaplan, S. 2006. *The pedagogical state: Education and the politics of national culture in post-1980 Turkey*. Stanford, CA: Stanford University.

Katz, K. 2005. *Jordanian Jerusalem: Holy places and national spaces*. Gainesville: University of Florida Press.

Kawar, M. 2000. Transitions and boundaries: Research into the impact of paid work on young women's lives in Jordan. *Gender and Development* 8 (2): 56–65.

Keddie, N. R., and B. Baron, eds. 1991. *Women in Middle Eastern History: Shifting boundaries in sex and gender*. New Haven, CT: Yale University Press.

Khan, M. M. 1971. The translation of the meanings of Sahih al-Bukhari. Al-Medina al-Munauwara: Islamic University.

Kharinu, S. 2000. *Al-Harakah al-tullabiyah al-urduniyah, 1948–1998: tarikhuha wa tatawwuruha fi al-urdun wa al-kharij* [The Jordanian student movement, 1948–1998: Its history and its development in Jordan and abroad]. Amman: Markaz al-Urdun al-Jadid lil-Dirasat.

Kholoussy, H. 2010. *For better, for worse: The marriage crisis that made modern Egypt.* Stanford, CA: Stanford University Press.

Khoury, S. A., and D. Massad. 2005. Consanguineous marriage in Jordan. *American Journal of Medical Genetics* 43 (5): 769–75.

King, E. M., and M. A. Hill. 1993. *Women's education in developing countries: Barriers, benefits and policies.* Baltimore: John Hopkins University Press (published for the World Bank).

Kristof, N., and S. WuDunn. 2009. *Half the sky: Turning oppression into opportunity for women worldwide.* New York: Random House.

Kubala, P. 2005. The other face of the video clip: Sami Yusuf and the call for al-fann al-hafi. *Transnational Broadcasting Studies* 13: 38–47.

Landis, J. 2007. Islamic education in Syria: Undoing secularism. In *Teaching Islam: Textbooks and religion in the Middle East,* ed. E. Doumato and G. Starrett, 177–96. Boulder, CO: Lynne Rienner.

Lave, J., P. Duguid, and N. Fernandez. 1992. Coming of age in Birmingham: Cultural studies and conceptions of subjectivity. *Annual Review of Anthropology* 21: 257–82.

Layne, L. 1994. *Home and homeland: The dialogics of tribal and national identities in Jordan.* Princeton, NJ: Princeton University Press.

Lazreg, M. 1994. *The eloquence of silence: Algerian women in question.* London: Routledge.

Lesko, N. 1988. The curriculum of the body: Lessons from a Catholic high school. In *Becoming feminine: The politics of popular culture,* ed. L. Roman, L. Christian-Smith, and E. Ellsworth, 123–42. London: Falmer Press.

———. 1996a. Denaturalizing adolescence: The politics of contemporary representations. *Youth and Society* 28 (2): 139–61.

———. 1996b. Past, present, and future conceptions of adolescence. *Educational Theory* 46 (4): 453–72.

———. 2001. *Act your age! A cultural construction of adolescence.* New York: Routledge Falmer.

Levine, M. 2008. *Heavy metal Islam: Rock, resistance, and the struggle for the soul of Islam.* New York: Three Rivers Press.

LeVine, R., S. LeVine, and B. Schnell. 2001. "Improve the woman": Mass schooling, female literacy, and worldwide social change. *Harvard Educational Review* 71 (1): 1–50.

Levinson, B. 1999. Resituating the place of an educational discourse in anthropology. *American Anthropologist* 101 (3): 594–604.

———. 2001. *We are all equal: Student culture and identity in a Mexican secondary school.* Durham, NC: Duke University Press.

———. 2005. Citizenship, identity, democracy: Engaging the political in the anthropology of education. *Anthropology and Education Quarterly* 36 (4): 329–40.

Levinson, B., D. Foley, and D. Holland, eds. 1996. *The cultural production of an educated person: Critical ethnographies of schooling and local practice.* Albany: State University of New York Press.

Levinson, B., and D. Holland. 1996. The cultural production of the educated person. In *The cultural production of an educated person: Critical ethnographies of schooling and local practice,* ed. B. Levinson, D. Foley, and D. Holland, 1–54. Albany: State University of New York Press.

Levy, R. 1984. Mead, Freeman, and Samoa: The problem of seeing things as they are. *Ethos* 1: 85–92.

Limbert, M. 2005. Gender, religious knowledge and education in an Omani town. In *Monarchies and nations: Globalization and identity in the Arab states of the Gulf*, ed. P. Dresch and J. Piscatori, 182–202. London: I. B. Tauris.

———. 2007. Oman: Cultivating good citizens and religious virtue. In *Teaching Islam: Textbooks and religion in the Middle East*, ed. E. Doumato and G. Starrett, 103–24. Boulder, CO: Lynne Rienner.

Long, N. 2004. Actors, interfaces and development intervention: Meanings, purposes and powers. In *Development intervention: Actor and activity perspectives*, ed. T. Kontinen. University of Helsinki: Center for Activity Theory and Developmental Work Research and Institute for Development Studies.

Luykx, A. 1999. *The citizen factory: Schooling and cultural production in Bolivia*. Albany: State University of New York Press.

Lynch, M. 2002. Jordan's King Abdallah in Washington. *Middle East Report Online*, May 8. http://www.merip.org/mero/mero050802.html.

———. 2004. No Jordan option. *Middle East Report Online*, June 21. http://www.merip.org/mero/mero062104.html.

MacLeod, A. 1991. *Accommodating protest: Working women, the new veiling and change in Cairo*. New York: Columbia University.

Mahdi, Muhammad Salih, al-. 2002. *Makanat al-musiqa fi al-hadara al-islamiyya* [The place of music in Islamic civilization]. London: Mu'assasat al-Furqan Lil-Turath al-Islami.

Mahmood, S. 2005. *The politics of piety: The Islamic revival and the feminist subject*. Princeton, NJ: Princeton University Press.

Mamdani, M. 2002. Good Muslim, bad Muslim: A political perspective on culture and terrorism. *American Anthropologist* 104 (3): 766–75.

Marcus, G. 1995. Ethnography in/of the world system: The emergence of multi-sited ethnography. *Annual Review of Anthropology* 24: 95–117.

Masad, M. al-, et al. 2004. *Al-tarbiyya al-wataniyya wa al-medaniyya* [National and civic education]. Tenth grade civic education and social studies textbook. Amman: Ministry of Education, Department of Curriculum and Textbooks.

Massad, J. 2001. *Colonial effects: The making of national identity in Jordan*. New York: Columbia University Press.

Massialas, B., and S. A. Jarrar. 1991. *Arab education in transition: A source book*. New York: Garland.

Matthews, R. D., and M. Akrawi. 1949. *Education in the Arab countries of the Near East: Egypt, Iraq, Palestine, Transjordan, Syria, Lebanon*. Washington, DC: American Council on Education.

Mazawi, A. 1999. The contested terrains of education in the Arab states. *Comparative Education Review* 43 (3): 332–52.

———. 2002. Educational expansion and the mediation of discontent: The cultural politics of schooling in the Arab states. *Discourse: Studies in the Cultural Politics of Education* 23 (1): 59–74.

———. 2010. Naming the imaginary: Building an Arab knowledge society and the contested terrain of educational reforms for development. In *Trajectories of education in the Arab world: Legacies and challenges*, ed. O. Abi-Mershed, 201–25. London: Routledge.

McLaren, P. 1999. *Schooling as a ritual performance: Toward a political economy of educational symbols and gestures*. 3rd ed. Lanham, MD: Rowman & Littlefield.

Mead, M. 2001. *Coming of age in Samoa*. New York: Harper Collins.

Meneley, A. 1996. *Tournaments of value: Sociability and hierarchy in a Yemeni town*. Toronto: University of Toronto Press.

Messick, B. 1996. *The calligraphic state: Textual domination and history in a Muslim society*. Berkeley: University of California Press.

Miles, R. 2002. Employment and unemployment in Jordan: The importance of the gender system. *World Development* 30 (3): 413–27.

Ministry of Education. 2006. *National education strategy*. Amman, Jordan: Directorate of Educational Research and Development.

Mitchell, T. 1988. *Colonising Egypt*. Cambridge: Cambridge University Press.

————. 2002. *Rule of experts: Egypt, techno-politics, modernity*. Berkeley: University of California Press.

Moghadam, V. 2005. Women's economic participation in the Middle East: What difference has the neoliberal policy turn made? *Journal of Middle East Women's Studies* 1 (1): 110–46.

Mohanty, C. 1984. Under Western eyes: Feminist scholarship and colonial discourses. *Boundary* 2 (12): 333–58.

Mustafa, M., and C. Cullingford. 2008. Teacher autonomy and centralised control: The case of textbooks. *International Journal of Educational Development* 28 (1): 81–88.

Najar, A. 2008. *Banat 'Amman ayyam zaman: Dhakirat al-madrasah wa-al-tariq* [The girls of Amman long ago: The memory of the school and the road]. Amman: al-Salwa lil darasat wa-al-nashar.

Najmabadi, A. 1993. Veiled discourse—unveiled bodies. *Feminist Studies* 19 (3): 487–518.

————.1998a. Crafting an educated housewife in Iran. In *Remaking women: Feminism and modernity in the Middle East*, ed. L. Abu-Lughod, 91–125. Princeton, NJ: Princeton University Press.

————. 1998b. Feminism in the Islamic Republic: Years of hardship, years of growth. In *Islam, gender and social change*, ed. Y. Haddad and J. Esposito, 59–84. New York: Oxford University Press.

————. 2000. (Un)veiling feminism. *Social Text* 18 (3): 29–45.

————. 2005. *Women with mustaches and men without beards: Gender and sexual anxieties of Iranian modernity*. Berkeley: University of California Press.

National Labor Committee. 2006. US-Jordan Free Trade Agreement descends into human trafficking and involuntary servitude. New York. http://www.nlcnet.org/admin/reports/files/Jordan_Report_2006.pdf

Nussbaum, M. 2000. *Women and human development: The capabilities approach*. Cambridge: Cambridge University Press.

————. 2003. Capabilities as fundamental entitlements: Sen and social justice. *Feminist Economics* 9 (2/3): 33–59.

Olmsted, J. 2005a. Gender, aging and the evolving Arab patriarchal contract. *Feminist Economics* 11 (2): 53–78.

————. 2005b. Is paid work the (only) answer? Women's well-being, neoliberalism, and the social contract in Southwest Asia and North Africa. *Journal of Middle East Women's Studies* 1 (2): 112–39.

Ortner, S. 1984. Theory in anthropology since the sixties. *Comparative Studies in Society and History* 26 (1): 126–66.

————. 1989. *High religion: A cultural and political history of Sherpa Buddhism*. Princeton, NJ: Princeton University Press.

————. 1995. Resistance and the problem of ethnographic refusal. *Comparative Studies in Society and History* 37 (1): 173–93.

————. 1996. *Making gender: The politics and erotics of culture*. Boston: Beacon Press.

Oweidhah, Mohammad Abdullah, et al. 2001. *Al-tarbiyya al-islamiyya* [Islamic education]. Tenth-grade religious studies textbook. Amman: Ministry of Education, Department of Curriculum and Textbooks.

Peet, R., and E. Hartwick. 1999. *Theories of development*. New York: Guilford Press.

Phillips, D. C., and J. F. Soltis. 2004. *Perspectives on learning*. New York: Teachers College Press.

Pollard, L. 2005. *Nurturing the nation: The family politics of modernizing, colonizing and liberating Egypt, 1805–1923*. Berkeley: University of California Press.

Popkewitz, T. S., and L. Fendler. 1999. Critical theories in education: Changing terrains of knowledge and politics. London: Routledge.

Prieto, N. I. 1997. *Beautiful flowers of the maquiladora: Life histories of women workers in Tijuana*. Austin: University of Texas Press.

Programme on Governance in the Arab Region. Country theme: Gender: Jordan. http://www.pogar.org/countries/theme.aspx?t=4&cid=7 (accessed September 28, 2011).

Qaradawi, Y. 2001. *Fiqh al-ghina' wa al-musiqa fi daw' al-Qur'an wa-al-sunnah* [Jurisprudence of singing and music in light of the Qur'an and the Sunnah]. Cairo: Maktabat Wahbah.

Racy, A. J. 2003. *Making music in the Arab world: The culture and artistry of tarab*. Cambridge: Cambridge University Press.

Reimer, M. 2005. Becoming urban: Town administrations in Transjordan. *International Journal of Middle East Studies* 37 (2): 189–211.

Ridge, N. 2009. Privileged and penalized: The education of boys in the United Arab Emirates. Ph.D. diss., Columbia University.

Rivard , J., and M. Amadio. 2003. Teaching time allocated to religious education in official timetables. *Prospects* 33 (2): 211–17.

Rogan, E. 1999. *Frontiers of the state in the late Ottoman Empire: Transjordan, 1850–1921*. Cambridge: Cambridge University Press.

Ross, M. (2008). Oil, Islam, and women. *American Political Science Review* 102 (1): 107–23.

Royal Hashemite Court. 2008. Jordan First. King Abdullah II Official Website. http://www.kingabdullah.jo/main.php?main_page=0&lang_hmka1=1 (accessed February 3, 2006).

Ryan, C. 2004. "Jordan First": Jordan's inter-Arab relations and foreign policy under King Abdullah II. *Arab Studies Quarterly* 26 (3): 43–62.

———. 2005. Reform retreats amid Jordan's political storms. *Middle East Report Online*, June 10. http://www.merip.org/mero/mero061005.html.

Sabin, P. 2007. On sentimental education among college students. *Teachers College Record* 109 (7): 1682–1704.

Sahlins, M. 1981. *Historical metaphors and mythical realities: Structure in the early history of the Sandwich Islands Kingdom*. Ann Arbor: University of Michigan Press.

Said, E. 1978. *Orientalism*. New York: Vintage Books.

Saif, I., and Y. Tabbaa. 2008. Economic growth, income distribution and the middle class in Jordan (2002–2006). Center for Strategic Studies, University of Jordan. http://www.jcss.org/UploadEvents/166.pdf.

Sassoon, J. 2009. *Iraqi refugees: The new crisis in the Middle East*. London: I. B. Tauris.

Sawa, Ali M. al-, et al. 2001. *Al- ulumm al-islamiyya* [Islamic studies]. Twelfth-grade literary track religious studies textbook. Amman: Ministry of Education, Department of Curriculum and Textbooks.

Schade-Poulsen, M. 1999. *Men and popular music in Algeria: The social significance of Raï.* Austin: University of Texas Press.

Schlegal, A., and H. Barry. 1991. *Adolescence: An anthropological inquiry.* New York: Free Press.

Schwedler, J. 2002. Occupied Maan: Jordan's closed military zone. *Middle East Report Online,* July 3. http://www.merip.org/mero/mero120302html.

———. 2006. *Faith in moderation: Islamist parties in Jordan and Yemen.* Cambridge: Cambridge University Press.

Scott, J. W. 2007. *Politics of the veil.* Princeton: Princeton University Press.

Sen, A. 1999. *Development as freedom.* New York: Random House.

Shakhatreh, H. 1995. Determinants of female labour-force participation in Jordan. In *Gender and development in the Arab world: Economic participation, patterns and policies,* ed. N. Khoury and V. Moghadam, 125–47. Helsinki: United Nations University.

Shakry, O. 1998. Schooled mothers and structured play: Child rearing in turn-of-the-century Egypt. In *Remaking women: Feminism and modernity in the Middle East,* ed. L. Abu-Lughod, 126–70. Princeton, NJ: Princeton University Press.

Shami, S. 1996. Gender, domestic space, and urban upgrading: A case study from Amman. *Gender and Development* 4 (1): 17–23.

Shankman, P. 1996. The history of Samoan sexual conduct and the Mead-Freeman controversy. *American Anthropologist* 98 (3): 555–67.

Shannon, J. 2003. Emotion, performance, and temporality in Arab music: Reflections on tarab. *Cultural Anthropology* 18 (1): 72–98.

Shively, K. 2008. Taming Islam: Studying religion in secular Turkey. *Anthropological Quarterly* 81 (3): 683–711.

Shryock, A. 1997. *Nationalism and the genealogical imagination: Oral history and textual authority in tribal Jordan.* Berkeley: University of California Press.

———. 2004. The new Jordanian hospitality: House, host, and guest in the culture of public display. *Comparative Studies in Society and History* 46 (1): 35–62.

Shtwei, M. 1999. *Gender roles in school textbooks in basic schooling in Jordan.* Amman: Jordanian Center for Social Research.

Singerman, D. 2007. The economic imperatives of marriage: Emerging practices and identities among youth in the Middle East. Middle East Youth Initiative working paper.

Skinner, D., and D. Holland. 1996. Schools and the cultural production of the educated person in a Nepalese hill community. In *The cultural production of an educated person: Critical ethnographies of schooling and local practice,* ed. B. Levinson, D. Foley, and D. Holland, 273–99. Albany: State University of New York Press.

Smith, C., and M. Denton. 2005. *Soul searching: The religious and spiritual lives of American teenagers.* New York: Oxford University Press.

Sonbol, A. 2003. *Women of Jordan: Islam, labor and the law.* Syracuse, NY: Syracuse University Press.

Stambach, A. 2000. *Lessons from Mount Kilimanjaro: Schooling, community, and gender in East Africa.* London: Routledge.

Starrett, G. 1998. *Putting Islam to work: Education, politics, and the transformation of faith.* Berkeley: University of California Press.

———. 2006. The American interest in Islamic schooling: A misplaced emphasis? *Middle East Policy* 8 (1): 120–31.

Swedenburg, T. 2007. Imagined youths. Middle East Report 245. http://www.merip.org/mer/mer245/swedenburg.html

Tabbaa, Y. 2010. Female labour force participation in Jordan. Amman: Economic and Social Council Policy Paper. http://esc.jo/sites/default/files/Female_Labour_Force_ Participation_-_Policy_Paper.pdf

Tal, L. 1995. Dealing with radical Islam: The case of Jordan. *Survival* 37 (3): 139–56.

Tall, A. Y. al-. 1978. Education in Jordan. Ph.D. diss., Sind University, Pakistan.

Tall, S. al-. 1985. *Muqaddimat hawla qadiyat al-mar ah wa-al-harakah al-nisa iyyah fi al-Urdunn* [Introduction on the issues of women and the women's movement in Jordan]. Beirut: al Mu'assasah al Arabiyyah l-il-Dirasat w-al-Nashr.

Taraki, L. 1995. Islam is the solution: Jordanian Islamists and the dilemma of the "modern woman." *British Journal of Sociology* 46 (4): 643–61.

Tilly, C., ed. 1996. *Citizenship, identity and social history.* Cambridge: Cambridge University Press.

Torres, C. A. 1999. Critical theory and political sociology of education: Arguments. In *Critical theories in education: Changing terrains of knowledge and politics,* ed. T. S. Popkewitz and L. Fendler, 87–115. London: Routledge.

Tucker, J. 1985. *Women in nineteenth-century Egypt.* Cambridge: Cambridge University Press.

UNDP. 2004. Jordan human development report 2004: Building sustainable livelihoods. Amman: Jordanian Ministry of Planning and International Cooperation and UNDP.

———. 2006. Arab human development report 2005: Towards the rise of women in the Arab world. New York: UNDP and Regional Bureau for Arab States.

UNICEF. 1997. The situation of Jordanian children and women: A rights-based analysis. Amman: UNICEF Country Office.

———. 2004. At a glance: Jordan. www.unicef.org/infobycountry/Jordan_statistics (accessed August 12, 2006).

UNIFEM. 2004. Progress of Arab women: One paradigm, four arenas, and more than 140 million women. Amman, Jordan: United Nations Development Fund for Women, Arab States Regional Office.

Van Hear, N. 1995. The impact of involuntary mass "return" to Jordan in the wake of the Gulf crisis. *International Migration Review* 29 (2): 352–74.

Varenne, H. 1995. The social facting of education: Durkheim's legacy. *Journal of Curriculum Studies* 27: 373–89.

———. 2007. Difficult collective deliberations: Anthropological notes toward a theory of education. *Teachers College Record* 109 (7): 1559–88.

Varenne, H., and R. McDermott. 1998. *Successful failure: The school America builds.* Boulder, CO: Westview Press.

Vavrus, F. 2003. *Desire and decline: Schooling amid crisis in Tanzania.* New York: Peter Lang.

Vavrus, F., and L. Bartlett. 2009. *Critical approaches to comparative education.* New York: Palgrave Macmillan.

Villaverde, L. 2003. *Secondary schools: A reference handbook.* Santa Barbara, CA: ABC-CLIO.

Wagner, D. 1993. *Literacy, culture and development: Becoming literate in Morocco.* Cambridge: Cambridge University Press.

Wahlin, L. 1987. Diffusion and acceptance of modern schooling in rural Jordan. In *The Middle Eastern village,* ed. R. Lawless, 145–74. London: Croom Helm.

Watkins, K. 2000. *The Oxfam education report.* Oxford, Eng.: Oxfam Publishing.

Welchman, L. 2007. *Women and Muslim family laws in Arab states: A comparative overview of textual development and advocacy.* Amsterdam: Amsterdam University Press.

White, J. 1994. *Money makes us relatives: Women's labor in urban Turkey.* Austin: University of Texas Press.

Wideen, L. 1999. *Ambiguities of domination: Politics, rhetoric, and symbols in contemporary Syria.* Chicago: University of Chicago Press.

Wiktorowicz, Q. 2000. Civil society as social control: State power in Jordan. *Comparative Politics* 33 (1): 43–61.

———. 2001. *The management of Islamic activism: Salafis, the Muslim Brotherhood, and state power in Jordan.* Albany: State University of New York Press.

Wilkins, A. 2008. *Wannabes, Goths, and Christians: The boundaries of sex, style, and status.* Chicago: University of Chicago Press.

Williams, R. 1977. *Marxism and literature.* New York: Oxford University Press.

Willis, P. *1977.* Learning to labor: How working class kids get working class jobs. New York: Columbia University Press.

Wilson, M. 1987. *King Abdullah, Britain and the making of Jordan.* Cambridge: Cambridge University Press.

World Bank. 2004. Gender and development in the Middle East and North Africa: Women in the public sphere. Washington, DC: World Bank.

———. 2005. The economic advancement of women in Jordan: A country gender assessment. Social and Economic Development Group Middle East and North Africa Region.

———. 2008. The road not traveled: Education reform in the Middle East and North Africa. Washington, DC: World Bank.

Zeghal, M. 2007. The "recentering" of religious knowledge and discourse: The case of al-Azhar in twentieth-century Egypt. In *Schooling Islam: The culture and politics of modern Muslim education,* ed. R. Hefner and M. Q. Zaman, 107–30. Princeton, NJ: Princeton University Press.

———. 2010. Public institutions of religious education in Egypt and Tunisia: Contrasting the post-colonial reforms of al-Azhar and Zaytuna. In *Trajectories of Education in the Arab World: Legacies and challenges,* ed. O. Abi-Mershed, 111–24. London: Routledge.

Zubaida, S. 2003. *Law and power in the Islamic world.* London: I. B. Tauris.

Zuhur, S. 2005. Singing a new song: Bonding and breaking with the past. In *On shifting ground: Muslim women in the global era,* ed. F. Nouraie-Simone, 36–60. New York: Feminist Press at the City University of New York.

INDEX